THE AMERICAN REVOLUTION

BY

JOHN FISKE

IN TWO VOLUMES

VOL. II.

BOSTON AND NEW YORK
HOUGHTON, MIFFLIN AND COMPANY
The Riverside Press, Cambridge
1897

FOURTEENTH THOUSAND.

•

The Riverside Press, Cambridge, Mass., U. S. A.
Electrotyped and Printed by H. O. Houghton & Co.

CONTENTS.

CHAPTER VIII.

THE FRENCH ALLIANCE.

CHAPTER IX.

VALLEY FORGE.

CHAPTER X.

MONMOUTH AND NEWPORT.

CHAPTER XI.

WAR ON THE FRONTIER.

CHAPTER XII.

WAR ON THE OCEAN.

CHAPTER XIII.

A YEAR OF DISASTERS.

CHAPTER XIV.

BENEDICT ARNOLD.

CHAPTER XV.

YORKTOWN.

MAPS.

THE AMERICAN REVOLUTION.

CHAPTER VIII.

THE FRENCH ALLIANCE.

THE history of the Revolutionary War may be divided into four well-marked periods. The first period begins in 1761 with the resistance of James Otis to the general search-warrants, and it may be regarded as ending in June, 1774, when the acts for changing the government of Massachusetts were intended to take effect. This period of constitutional discussion culminated in the defiance of Great Britain by the people of Boston when they threw the tea into the harbour; and the acts of April, 1774, by which Parliament replied to the challenge, were virtually a declaration of war against the American colonies, though yet another year elapsed before the first bloodshed at Lexington.

The second period opens with June, 1774, when Massachusetts began to nullify the acts of Parliament, and it closes with the Declaration of Independence. During this period warfare was carried on only for the purpose of obtaining a redress of grievances, and without any design of bringing

about a political separation of the English people
in America from the English people in Britain.
The theatre of war was mainly confined to New
England and Canada; and while the Americans
failed in the attempt to conquer Canada, their de-
fensive warfare was crowned with success. The
fighting of this period began with the victory of
Lexington; it ended with the victory of Fort
Moultrie. New England, except the island of
Newport, was finally freed from the presence of the
British, and no further attack was made upon the
southern states for more than two years.

The essential feature of the third period, comprising the years 1776 and 1777, was the struggle
for the state of New York and the great natural
strategic line of the Mohawk and Hudson rivers.
Independence having been declared, the United
States and Great Britain were now fighting each
other single-handed, like two separate and foreign
powers. It was the object of Great Britain to
conquer the United States, and accordingly she
struck at the commercial and military centre of
the confederation. If she could have thoroughly
conquered the state of New York and secured the
line of the Hudson, she would have broken the confederation in two, and might perhaps have proceeded to overcome its different parts in detail.
Hence in this period of the war everything centres
about New York, such an outlying expedition as
that of Howe against Philadelphia having no decisive military value except in its bearings upon the
issue of the great central conflict. The strategy of
the Americans was mainly defensive, though with

regard to certain operations they assumed the offensive with brilliant success. The period began with the disasters of Long Island and Fort Washington; it ended with the triumph of Saratoga. As the net result of the two years' work, the British had taken and held the cities of New York and Philadelphia and the town of Newport. The fortress of Ticonderoga, which they had likewise taken, they abandoned after the overthrow of Burgoyne; and in like manner they retired from the highlands of the Hudson, which the Americans now proceeded to occupy with a stronger force than before. In short, while the British had lost an army, they had conquered nothing but the ground on which they were actually encamped. Their attempt to break through the centre of the American position had ended in a total defeat, and it now began to seem clear to discerning minds that there was small chance of their being able to conquer the United States.

The fourth period, upon which we are now entering, begins with the immediate consequences of the victory of Saratoga, and extends to the treaty of 1783, whereby Great Britain acknowledged the independence of the United States. The military history of this period ends with the surrender of Cornwallis at Yorktown, in October, 1781, just four years after the surrender of Burgoyne. Except as regards the ultimate triumph of the American arms, the history of these four years presents striking contrasts to the history of the two years we have just passed in review. The struggle is no longer confined to the arms of Great Britain and the United States, but it extends in some measure over the whole civilized world, though it is only France, with its army and more especially its navy, that comes into direct relation with the final result in America. Moreover, instead of a well-aimed and concentrated blow at the centre of the American position, the last period of the war consisted partly of a straggling and disorderly series of movements, designed simply to harass the Americans and wear out their patience, and partly of an attempt to conquer the southern states and detach them from the Union. There is, accordingly, less dramatic unity in this last stage of the war than in the period which ended at Saratoga, and it is less susceptible of close and consecutive treatment; but, on the other hand, in richness of incidents and in variety of human interest it is in no wise inferior to the earlier periods.

The first consequence of Saratoga was the retreat of the British government from every one of the positions for the sake of which it had begun the war. The news of Burgoyne's surrender reached England just before Parliament adjourned for Christmas, and Lord North immediately gave notice that as soon as the holidays were over he should bring in measures for conciliating the Americans. The general feeling in England was Consternation one of amazement and consternation. in England. In these days, when we are accustomed to contemplate military phenomena of enormous magnitude, when we have lately carried on a war in which more than two million men were under arms, and more than two million dollars were expended every day, we must not forget how different was the historic background upon which events were projected a century ago. Those were not the days of submarine telegraphs and Cunard steamships, and in trying to carry on warfare across three thousand miles of ocean the problem before George III. was far more arduous than that which the great Frederick had solved, when, acting on interior lines and supported by British gold, he overcame the combined assaults of France and Austria and Russia. The loss which Great Britain had now suffered could not easily be made good. At the same time it was generally believed, both in England and on the continent of Europe, that the loss of the American colonies would entail the ruin of the British Empire. Only a few wise political economists, "literary men," like Adam Smith and Josiah Tucker, were far-seeing enough to escape this prodigious fallacy; even Chatham was misled by it. It was not understood that English America and English Britain were bound together by commercial and social ties so strong that no question of political union or severance could permanently affect them. It was not foreseen that within a century the dealings of Great Britain with the independent United States would far exceed her dealings with the rest of the world. On the contrary, it was believed that if political independence were conceded to the Americans, the whole stream of transatlantic commerce would somehow be diverted to other parts of Europe, that the British naval power would forthwith decay, and that England would sink from her imperial position into such a mere insular nation as that over which Henry VIII. had ruled. So greatly did men overrate political conditions; so far were they from appreciating those economic conditions which are so much more deep-seated and essential.

Under these circumstances, the only people in England who were willing to concede the independence of the United States were the Rockingham Whigs, and these were now in a small minority. Lord Rockingham and his friends, with Burke as their leader, had always condemned the harsh and stupid policy of the government toward America, and they were now ready to concede independence because they were convinced that conciliation was no longer practicable. Lord Chatham, on the other hand, with his section of the Whig party, while even more emphatically condemning the policy of the government, still clung to the hope of conciliation, and could not bear to think of the disruption of the empire. But with the Tory party, which had all along supported the government, the war was still popular, and no calamity seemed so great as the loss of the American colonies. Most of the country squires believed in crushing out rebellion, no matter where it occurred or for what reason, and this view was almost unanimously taken by the clergy. In the House of Lords none were so bloodthirsty as the bishops, and country parsons preached from all the texts of the Old Testament which refer to smiting Jehovah's enemies hip and thigh. The trading classes in the large towns,

Views of the different parties.

and the few manufacturers who had come upon the scene, were so afraid of losing the American market that they were ready to vote men and money without stint. The town of Manchester even raised and equipped two regiments at its own expense. Thus while the great majority of the British nation believed that America must be retained at whatever cost, a majority of this majority believed that it must be conquered before it could be conciliated or reasoned with; and this was the opinion which had thus far found favour with Lord North and controlled the policy of the government.

We may imagine, then, the unspeakable amazement of the House of Commons, on the 17th of February, 1778, when Lord North arose in his place and moved that every one of the points for which Samuel Adams

Lord North's political somersault.

and his friends had zealously contended, from the passage of the Stamp Act to the breaking out of war, should at once be conceded forever and without further parley. By the bill which he now proceeded to read, the famous Tea Act and the act for changing the constitution of Massachusetts were unconditionally repealed. It was furthermore declared that Parliament would renounce forever the right of raising a revenue in America; and it was provided that commissioners should be sent over to treat with Congress, armed with full powers for negotiating a peace. Pending the negotiations the commissioners might proclaim a truce, and might suspend the operation of any act of Parliament relating to America which had been passed since 1763. They might also proclaim complete amnesty for all political offences.

So complete a political somersault has seldom been turned by an English minister, and the speech in which Lord North defended himself was worthy of the occasion. Instead of resigning when he saw that his policy had proved a failure, as an English minister would naturally do; he suddenly shifted his ground, and adopted the policy which the opposition had urged in vain against him three years before, and which, if then adopted, would unquestionably have prevented bloodshed. Not only did he thus shift his ground, but he declared that this policy of conciliation was really the one which he had favoured from the beginning. There was more truth in this than appeared at the moment, for in more than one instance Lord North had, with culpable weakness, carried out the king's policy in defiance of his own convictions. It was in vain, however, that he sought to clear himself of responsibility for the Tea Act, the oppressive edicts of 1774, and the recent events in America generally. The House received his bill

Strange scene in the House of Commons. and his speech in profound silence. Disgust and dejection filled every bosom, yet no one could very well help voting for the measures. The Tories, already chagrined by the bitter news from Saratoga, were enraged at being thus required to abandon all the ground for which they had been fighting, yet no way seemed open for them but to follow their leader. The Whigs were vexed at seeing the wind taken out of their sails, but they could not in honour oppose a policy which they had always earnestly supported. All sat for some moments in grim, melancholy silence, till Charles Fox, arising, sarcastically began his speech by congratulating his Whig friends on having gained such a powerful and unexpected ally in the prime minister. Taunts and innuendoes flew back and forth across the House. From the Tory side came sullen cries that the country was betrayed, while from among the Whigs the premier was asked if he supposed himself armed with the spear of Achilles, which could heal the wounds that itself had made. It was very pointedly hinted that the proposed measures would not be likely to produce much effect upon the Americans unless accompanied by Lord North's resignation, since, coming from him, they would come as from a tainted spring. But in spite of all this ill-feeling the bill was passed, and the same reasons which had operated here carried it also through the House of Lords. On the 11th of March it received the royal signature, and three commissioners were immediately appointed to convey information of this action to Congress, and make arrangements for a treaty of peace.

The conciliatory policy of Lord North had come at least two years too late. The American leaders were now unwilling to consider the question of reunion with the mother-country upon any terms; and even before the extraordinary scene in Parliament which we have just witnessed, a treaty had been made with France, by which the Americans solemnly agreed, in consideration of armed support

Treaty between France and the United States, Feb. 6, 1778.

to be furnished by that power, never to entertain
proposals of peace from Great Britain until their
independence should be acknowledged, and never
to conclude a treaty of peace except with the con-
currence of their new ally. The French government had secretly assisted the Americans as early
as the summer of 1776 by occasional loans of
money, and by receiving American privateers in
French ports. The longer Great Britain and her
colonies could be kept weakening each other by
warfare, the greater the hope that France might
at some time be enabled to step in and regain
her lost maritime empire. But it was no part
of French policy to take an active share in the
struggle until the proper moment should come for
reaping some decisive material advantage. At
the beginning of the year 1778 that moment
seemed to have arrived. The capture of Burgoyne and the masterly strategy which Washington had shown, in spite of his ill-success on the
field, had furnished convincing proof that the
American alliance was worth having. At the
same time, the announcement that Lord North
was about to bring in conciliatory measures indi-
cated that the British government was weakening
in its purpose. Should such measures succeed in
conciliating the Americans and in bringing about
a firm reunion with the mother - country, the
schemes of France would be irretrievably ruined.
Now, therefore, was the golden opportunity, and
France was not slow to seize it. On the 6th of
February the treaty with the United States was
signed at Paris. By a special article it was stipu-

lated that Spain might enter into the alliance at her earliest convenience. Just now, too, Frederick the Great publicly opened the port of Dantzic to American cruisers and prohibited Hessian soldiers from passing through his dominions to the seaboard, while he wrote to Franklin at Paris that he should probably soon follow the king of France in recognizing the independence of the United States.

Rumours of all these things kept coming to England while the conciliatory measures were passing through Parliament, and on the 13th of March, two days after those measures had become law, the action of France was formally communicated to the British government, and war was instantly declared.

Great Britain declares war against France, March 13.

The situation of England seemed desperate. With one army lost in America, with the recruiting ground in Germany barred against her, with a debt piling up at the rate of a million dollars a week, and with a very inadequate force of troops at home in case of sudden invasion, she was now called upon to contend with the whole maritime power of France, to which that of Spain was certain soon to be added, and to crown all, the government had just written its own condemnation by confessing before the world that its policy toward America, which had been the cause of all this mischief, was impracticable as well as unrighteous.

At this terrible moment the eyes of all England were turned upon one great man, old now and wasted by disease, but the fire of whose genius still burned bright and clear. The government

must be changed, and in the Earl of Chatham
The Earl of Chatham. the country had still a leader whose
very name was synonymous with vic-
tory. Not thus had matters gone in the glorious days of Quiberon and Minden and Quebec,
when his skilful hand was at the helm, and every
heart in England and America beat high with the
consciousness of worthy ends achieved by well-
directed valour. To whom but Chatham should
appeal be made to repair the drooping fortunes of
the empire? It was in his hands alone that a
conciliatory policy could have any chance of success. From the first he had been the consistent
advocate of the constitutional rights of the Americans ; and throughout America he was the object
of veneration no less hearty and enthusiastic than
that which was accorded to Washington himself.
Overtures that would be laughed at as coming
from North would at least find respectful hearing
if urged by Chatham. On the other hand, should
the day for conciliation have irrevocably passed
by, the magic of his name was of itself sufficient
to create a panic in France, while in England it
would kindle that popular enthusiasm which is of
itself the best guarantee of success. In Germany,
too, the remembrance of the priceless services he
had rendered could not but dispel the hostile feeling with which Frederick had regardèd England
since the accession of George III. Moved by such
thoughts as these, statesmen of all parties, beginning with Lord North himself, implored the king to
form a new ministry under Chatham. Lord Mansfield, his bitterest enemy, for once declared that

without Chatham at the helm the ship of state
must founder, and his words were echoed by Bute
and the young George Grenville. At the opposite extreme of politics, the Duke of Richmond,
who had long since made up his mind that the
colonies must be allowed to go, declared, nevertheless, that if it were to be Chatham who should
see fit to make another attempt to retain them,
he would aid him in every possible way. The
press teemed with expressions of the popular faith
in Chatham, and every one impatiently wondered
that the king should lose a day in calling to the
head of affairs the only man who could save the
country.

But all this unanimity of public opinion went
for nothing with the selfish and obdurate king.
All the old reasons for keeping Chatham out of
office had now vanished, so far as the American
question was concerned; for by consenting to
North's conciliatory measures the king had virtually come over to Chatham's position, and as
regarded the separation of the colonies from the
mother - country, Chatham was no less unwilling
than the king to admit the necessity of The king's
such a step. Indeed, the policy upon rage.
which the king had now been obliged to enter absolutely demanded Chatham as its exponent instead
of North. Everybody saw this, and no doubt the
king saw it himself, but it had no weight with him
in the presence of personal considerations. He
hated Chatham with all the ferocity of hatred that
a mean and rancorous spirit can feel toward one
that is generous and noble; and he well knew

besides that, with that statesman at the head of affairs, his own share in the government would be reduced to nullity. To see the government administered in accordance with the policy of a responsible minister, and in disregard of his own irresponsible whims, was a humiliation to which he was not yet ready to submit. For eight years now, by coaxing and bullying the frivolous North, he had contrived to keep the reins in his own hands; and having so long tasted the sweets of power, he was resolved in future to have none but milksops for his ministers. In face of these personal considerations the welfare of the nation was of little account to him.[1] He flew into a rage. No power in heaven or earth, he said, should ever make him stoop to treat with "Lord Chatham and his crew;" he refused to be "shackled by those desperate men" and "made a slave for the remainder of his days." Rather than yield to the wishes of his people at this solemn crisis, he would submit to lose his crown. Better thus, he added, than to wear it in bondage and disgrace.

In spite of the royal wrath, however, the popular demand for a change of government was too strong to be resisted. But for Lord Chatham's sudden death, a few weeks later, he would doubtless have been called upon to fill the position which North was so anxious to relinquish. The king would have had to swallow his resentment, as he was af-

[1] "This episode appears to me the most criminal in the whole reign of George III., and in my own judgment it is as criminal as any of those acts which led Charles I. to the scaffold." (Lecky, *History of England in the Eighteenth Century*, vol. iv. p. 83.)

terwards obliged to do in 1782. Had Chatham
now become prime minister, it was his What Chatham would have tried to do.
design to follow up the repeal of all ob-
noxious legislation concerning America
by withdrawing every British soldier from our soil,
and attacking France with might and main, as in
the Seven Years' War, on the ocean and through
Germany, where the invincible Ferdinand of
Brunswick was again to lead the armies of Great
Britain. In America such a policy could hardly
have failed to strengthen not only the loyalists and
waverers, but also the patriots of conciliatory
mould, such as Dickinson and Robert Morris. Nor
was the moment an inopportune one. Many Americans, who were earnest in withstanding the legisla-
tive encroachments of Parliament, had formerly
been alienated from the popular cause by what
they deemed the needlessly radical step of the Declaration of Independence. Many others were now
alienated by the French alliance. In New England, the chief stronghold of the revolutionary
party, many people were disgusted at an alliance
with the Catholic and despotic power which in
days gone by had so often let loose the Indian
hell-hounds upon their frontier. The treaty with
France was indeed a marriage of convenience
rather than of affection. The American leaders,
even while arranging it, dreaded the revulsion of
feeling that might ensue in the country at large;
and their dread was the legitimate hope of Chatham. To return to the state of things which had
existed previous to 1765 would no doubt be impossible. Independence of some sort must be con-

ceded, and in this Lord Rockingham and the Duke
of Richmond were unquestionably right. But
Chatham was in no wise foolish in hoping that
some sort of federal bond might be established
which should maintain Americans and British in
perpetual alliance, and, while granting full legisla-
tive autonomy to the colonies singly or combined,
should prevent the people of either country from
ever forgetting that the Americans were English.
There was at least a chance that this noble policy
might succeed, and until the trial should have been
made he would not willingly consent to a step that
seemed certain to wreck the empire his genius had
won for England. But death now stepped in to
simplify the situation in the old ruthless way.

The Duke of Richmond, anxious to bring matters to an issue, gave notice that on the 7th of
April he should move that the royal fleets and
armies should be instantly withdrawn from America, and peace be made on whatever terms Congress might see fit to accept. Such at least was
the practical purport of the motion. For such an
Death of Chat-ham. unconditional surrender Chatham was
not yet ready, and on the appointed day
he got up from his sick-bed and came into the
House of Lords to argue against the motion.
Wrapped in flannel bandages and leaning upon
crutches, his dark eyes in their brilliancy enhan-
cing the pallor of his careworn face, as he entered
the House, supported on the one side by his son-
in-law, Lord Mahon, and on the other by that
younger son who was so soon to add fresh glory to
the name of William Pitt, the peers all started to

their feet, and remained standing until he had taken his place. In broken sentences, with strange flashes of the eloquence which had once held captive ear and heart, he protested against the hasty adoption of a measure which simply prostrated the dignity of England before its ancient enemy, the House of Bourbon. The Duke of Richmond's answer, reverently and delicately worded, urged that while the magic of Chatham's name could work anything short of miracles, yet only a miracle could now relieve them from the dire necessity of abandoning America. The earl rose to reply, but his overwrought frame gave way, and he sank in a swoon upon the floor. All business was at once adjourned. The peers, with eager sympathy, came crowding up to offer assistance, and the unconscious statesman was carried in the arms of his friends to a house near by, whence in a few days he was removed to his home at Hayes. There, after lingering between life and death for several weeks, on the 11th of May, and in the seventieth year of his age, Lord Chatham breathed his last.

The man thus struck down, like a soldier at his post, was one whom Americans no less than Englishmen have delighted to honour. The personal fascination which he exerted in his lifetime is something we can no longer know; but as the field of modern history expands till it covers the globe, we find ourselves better able than his contemporaries to comprehend the part which he played His prodigious greatness. at one of the most critical moments of the career of mankind. For simple magnitude, the preponderance of the English race in the world has come now to be the most striking fact in human history; and when we consider all that is implied in this growing preponderance of an industrial civilization over other civilizations of relatively archaic and militant type, we find reason to believe that among historic events it is the most teeming with mighty consequences to be witnessed by a distant future. With no other historic personage are the beginnings of this supremacy of the English race so closely associated as with the elder William Pitt. It was he who planned the victories which gave England the dominion of the sea, and which, rescuing India from the anarchy of centuries, prepared it to become the seat of a new civilization, at once the apt pupil and the suggestive teacher of modern Europe. It was he who, by driving the French from America, cleared the way for the peaceful overflow of our industrial civilization through the valley of the Mississippi; saving us from the political dangers which chronic warfare might otherwise have entailed, and insuring us the ultimate control of the fairest part of this continent. To his valiant and skilful lieutenants by sea and land, to such great men as Hawke, and Clive, and Wolfe, belong the credit of executing the details; it was the genius of Pitt that conceived and superintended the prodigious scheme as a connected whole. Alone among the Englishmen of his time, Pitt looked with prophetic gaze into the mysterious future of colonial history, and saw the meaning of the creation of a new and greater Europe in the outlying regions of the earth; and through his triumphs it was decided that this new

and greater Europe should become for the most
part a new and greater England, — a world of self-
government, and of freedom of thought and speech.
While his political vision thus embraced the utter-
most parts of the globe, his action in the centre of
Europe helped to bring about results the importance of which we are now beginning to appreciate.
From the wreck of all Germany in that horrible
war of religion which filled one third of the seventeenth century, a new Protestant power had slowly
emerged and grown apace, till in Pitt's time — for
various reasons, dynastic, personal, and political —
it had drawn down upon itself the vengeance of all
the reactionary countries of Europe. Had the coalition succeeded, the only considerable Protestant
power on the continent would have been destroyed,
and the anarchy which had followed the Thirty
Years' War might have been renewed. The stupid
George II., who could see in Prussia nothing but a
rival of Hanover, was already preparing to join the
alliance against Frederick, when Pitt overruled
him, and threw the weight of England into the
other side of the scale. The same act which thus
averted the destruction of Prussia secured to England a most efficient ally in her struggle with
France. Of this wise policy we now see the fruits
in that renovated German Empire which has come
to be the strongest power on the continent of Europe, which is daily establishing fresh bonds of
sympathy with the people of the United States, and
whose political interests are daily growing more
and more visibly identical with those of Great
Britain. As in days to come the solidarity of the

Teutonic race in its three great nationalities — America, England, and Germany — becomes more and more clearly manifest, the more will the student of history be impressed with the wonderful fact that the founding of modern Germany, the maritime supremacy of England, and the winning of the Mississippi valley for English - speaking America were but the different phases of one historic event, coherent parts of the one vast conception which marks its author as the grandest of modern statesmen. As the lapse of time carries us far enough from the eighteenth century to study it in its true proportions, the figure of Chatham in the annals of the Teutonic race will appear no less great and commanding than the figure of Charlemagne a thousand years before.

But Chatham is interesting to Americans not only as the eloquent defender in our revolutionary struggle, not only as standing in the forefront of that vast future in which we are to play so important a part, but also as the first British statesman whose political thinking was of a truly American type. Pitt was above all things the man of the people, and it has been well said that his title of the "Great Commoner" marks in itself a political revolution. When the king and the Old Whig lords sought to withstand him in the cabinet, he could say with truth, "It is the people who have sent me here." He was the first to discover the fact that the development of trade and manufactures, due chiefly to the colonial expansion of England, had brought into existence an important class of society, for which neither the

Tory nor the Old Whig schemes of government had made provision. He was the first to see the absurdity of such towns as Leeds and Manchester going without representation, and he began in 1745 the agitation for parliamentary reform which was first successful in 1832. In the celebrated case of Wilkes, while openly expressing his detestation of the man, he successfully defended the rights of constituencies against the tyranny of the House of Commons. Against the fierce opposition of Lord Mansfield, he maintained inviolate the liberty of every Englishman to publish his opinions. He overthrew the abuse of arbitrary imprisonment by general warrants. He ended the chronic troubles of Scotland by taking the Highlanders into his confidence and raising regiments from them for the regular army. In this intense devotion to liberty and to the rights of man, Pitt was actuated as much by his earnest, sympathetic nature as by the clearness and breadth of his intelligence. In his austere purity of character, as in his intensity of conviction, he was an enigma to sceptical and frivolous people in his own time. Cromwell or Milton would have understood him much better than did Horace Walpole, to whom his haughty mien and soaring language seemed like theatrical affectation. But this grandiose bearing was nothing but the natural expression of that elevation of soul which, lighted by a rich poetic imagination and fired by the glow of passion beneath, made his eloquence the most impressive that has ever been heard in England. He was soaring in outward demeanour only as his mind habitually dwelt with strong emotion upon great thoughts and noble deeds. He was the incarnation of all that is lofty and aspiring in human nature, and his sublime figure, raised above the grave in the northern transept of Westminster Abbey, with its eager outstretched arm, still seems to be urging on his countrymen in the path of duty and of glory.

By the death of Chatham the obstacles which had beset the king were suddenly removed. On the morning after the pathetic scene in the House of Lords, he wrote with ill-concealed glee to North, "May not the political exit of Lord Chatham incline you to continue at the head of my affairs?" North was very unwilling to remain, but it was difficult to find any one who could form a government in his place. Among the New Whigs, now that Chatham was gone, Lord Shelburne was the most prominent; but he was a man who, in spite of great talents, never succeeded in winning the confidence either of the politicians or of the people. He was a warm friend to the American cause, but no one supposed him equal to the difficult task which Chatham would have undertaken, of pacifying the American people. The Old Whigs, under Lord Rockingham, had committed themselves to the full independence of the United States, and for this the people of England were not yet prepared. Under the circumstances, there seemed to be nothing for Lord North to do but remain in office. The king was delighted,

Lord North
remains in
power.

and his party appeared to have gained strength from the indignation aroused by the alliance of the Americans with France. It was strengthened still more by the positive refusal of Congress to treat with the commissioners sent over by Lord North. The commissioners arrived in America in June, and remained until October, without effecting anything. Congress refused to entertain any propositions whatever from Great Britain until the independence of the United States should first be acknowledged. Copies of Lord North's conciliatory bills were published by order of Congress, and scattered broadcast over the country. They were everywhere greeted with derision; at one town in Rhode Island they were publicly burned under a gallows which had been erected for the occasion. After fruitlessly trying all the devices of flattery and intrigue, the commissioners lost their temper; and just before sailing for England they issued a farewell manifesto, in which they threatened the American people with exemplary punishment for their contumacy. The conduct of the war, they said, was now to be changed; these obstinate rebels were to be made to suffer the extremes of distress, and no mercy was to be shown them. Congress instantly published this document, and it was received with somewhat more derision than the conciliatory bills had been. Under the circumstances of that day, the threat could have but one meaning. It meant arson along the coasts at the hands of the British fleet, and murder on the frontiers at the hands of Indian auxil-

His commissioners in America fail to accomplish anything.

iaries. The commissioners sought to justify their manifesto before Parliament, and one of them vehemently declared that if all hell could be let loose against these rebels, he should approve of the measure. "The proclamation," said he, "certainly does mean a war of desolation : it can mean nothing else." Lord Rockingham denounced the policy of the manifesto, and few were found in Parliament willing to support it openly. This barbarous policy, however, was neither more nor less than that which Lord George Germain had deliberately made up his mind to pursue for the remainder of the war. Giving up the problem of conquering the Americans by systematic warfare, he thought it worth while to do as much damage and inflict as much suffering as possible, in the hope that by and by the spirit of the people might be broken and their patience worn out. No policy could be more repugnant to the amiable soul of Lord North, but his false position obliged him passively to sanction much that he did not like. Besides this plan for tiring out the people, it was designed to conduct a systematic expedition against Virginia and the Carolinas, in order to detach these states from the rest of the confederacy. Should it be found necessary, after all, to acknowledge the independence of the United States, it seemed worth while at least to cut down their territory as much as possible, and save to the British Crown these rich countries of rice, and indigo, and tobacco. Such was the plan now proposed by Germain, and adopted by the ministry of which he was a member.

CHAPTER IX.

VALLEY FORGE.

LORD GEORGE GERMAIN'S scheme for tiring out the Americans could not seem altogether hopeless. Though from a military point of view the honours of the war thus far remained with them, yet the losses and suffering had been very great. The disturbance of trade was felt even more severely in America than in England, and it was further exacerbated by the evils of a depreciated currency. The country had entered into the war heavily handicapped by the voluntary stoppage of importation which had prevailed for several years. The war had cut off New England from the Newfoundland fisheries and the trade with the West Indies, and the coasting trade had been nearly annihilated by British cruisers. The problem of managing the expenses of a great war was something quite new to the Americans, and the consequent waste and extravagance were complicated and enhanced by the curse of paper money. Congress, as a mere advisory body, could only recommend to the various states the measures of taxation which were deemed necessary for the support of the army. It had no authority to raise taxes in any state, nor had it any power to constrain the government of a state

Distress in America.

to raise taxes. The states were accordingly all
delinquent, and there was no resource left for Congress but to issue its promissory notes. Congress
already owed more than forty million dollars, and
during the first half of the year 1778 the issues of
paper money amounted to twenty-three millions.
The depreciation had already become alarming,
and the most zealous law-making was of course
powerless to stop it.

Until toward the close of the Revolutionary War,
indeed, the United States had no regularly organized government. At the time of the Declaration
of Independence a committee had been appointed
by Congress to prepare articles of confederation,
to be submitted to the states for their approval.
These articles were ready by the summer of 1778,
but it was not until the spring of 1781 that all the
states had signed them. While the thirteen dis-
tinct sovereignties in the United States were visible in clear outline, the central government was something very shadowy and
ill-defined. Under these circumstances, the military efficiency of the people was reduced to a min-
imum. The country never put forth more than
a small fraction of its available strength. Everything suffered from the want of organization. In
spite of the popular ardour, which never seems to
have been deficient when opportunities came for
testing it, there was almost as much difficulty in
keeping up the numbers of the army by enlistment
as in providing equipment, sustenance, and pay
for the soldiers when once enlisted. The army of
80,000 men, which Congress had devised in the

Lack of or-
ganization.

preceding year, had never existed except on paper. The action of Congress had not, indeed, been barren of results, but it had fallen far short of the end proposed. During the campaigns of 1777 the army of Washington had never exceeded 11,000 men ; while of the 20,000 or more who witnessed the surrender of Burgoyne, at least half were local militia, assembled merely to meet the exigencies of the moment. The whole country, indeed, cherished such a horror of armies that it was unjust even to the necessary instrument by which its independence was to be won ; and it sympathized with Congress in the niggardly policy which, by discouraging pensions, endangered the future of brave and skilful officers who were devoting the best years of their lives to the public service. Washington's earnest efforts to secure for retired officers the promise of half pay for life succeeded only in obtaining it for the term of seven years. The excessive dread of a standing army made it difficult to procure long enlistments, and the frequent changes in the militia, besides being ruinous to discipline, entailed a sad waste of equipments and an interruption of agriculture which added much to the burdens of the people.

Besides these evils, for which no one in particular was to blame, since they resulted so directly from the general state of the country, the army suffered under other drawbacks, which were immediately traceable to the incapacity of Congress. Just as afterwards, in the War of Secession, the soldiers had often to pay the penalty for the sins of the politicians. A single specimen of the ill-timed meddling of Congress may serve as an example.

Vexatious meddling of Congress. At one of the most critical moments of the year 1777, Congress made a complete change in the commissariat, which had hitherto been efficiently managed by a single officer, Colonel Joseph Trumbull. Two commissary-generals were now appointed, one of whom was to superintend the purchase and the other the issue of supplies; and the subordinate officers of the department were to be accountable, not to their superiors, but directly to Congress. This was done in spite of the earnest opposition of Washington, and the immediate result was just what he expected. Colonel Trumbull, who had been retained as commissary-general for purchases, being unable to do his work properly without controlling his subordinate officers, soon resigned his place. The department was filled up with men selected without reference to fitness, and straightway fell into hopeless confusion, whereby the movements of the armies were grievously crippled for the rest of the season. On the 22d of December Washington was actually prevented from executing a most promising movement against General Howe, because two brigades had become mutinous for want of food. For three days they had gone without bread, and for two days without meat. The quartermaster's department was in no better condition. The dreadful sufferings of

Sufferings at Valley Forge. Washington's army at Valley Forge have called forth the pity and the admiration of historians; but the point of the story is lost unless we realize that this misery resulted from gross mismanagement rather than from the poverty of the country. As the poor soldiers marched on the 17th of December to their winter quarters, their route could be traced on the snow by the blood that oozed from bare, frost-bitten feet; yet at the same moment, says Gordon, "hogsheads of shoes, stockings, and clothing were lying at different places on the roads and in the woods, perishing for want of teams, or of money to pay the teamsters." On the 23d, Washington informed Congress that he had in camp 2,898 men "unfit for duty, because they are barefoot, and otherwise naked." For want of blankets, many were fain " to sit up all night by fires, instead of taking comfortable rest in a natural and common way." Cold and hunger daily added many to the sick-list; and in the crowded hospitals, which were for the most part mere log-huts or frail wigwams woven of twisted boughs, men sometimes died for want of straw to put between themselves and the frozen ground on which they lay. In the deficiency of oxen and draft-horses, gallant men volunteered to serve as beasts of burden, and, yoking themselves to wagons, dragged into camp such meagre supplies as they could obtain for their sick and exhausted comrades. So great was the distress that there were times when, in case of an attack by the enemy, scarcely two thousand men could have been got under arms. When one thinks of these sad consequences wrought by a negligent quartermaster and a deranged commissariat, one is strongly reminded of the remark once made by the eccentric Charles Lee, when with caustic alliteration he described Congress as " a stable of stupid cattle that stumbled at every step."

The mischief did not end, however, with the demoralization of the departments that were charged with supplying the army. In the appointment and promotion of general officers, Congress often acted upon principles which, if consistently carried out, would have ruined the efficiency of any army that ever existed. For absurdly irrelevant political reasons, brave and well-tried officers were passed by, and juniors, comparatively little known, were promoted over their heads. The case of Benedict Arnold was the most conspicuous and flagrant example of this. After his good name had been destroyed by his treason, it became customary for historians to cite the restiveness of Arnold under such treatment as one more proof of his innate wickedness. But Arnold was not the only officer who was sensitive about his rank. In June, 1777, it was rumoured about Washington's camp that a Frenchman named Ducoudray was about to be appointed to the chief command of the artillery, with the rank of major-general. Congress was continually beset with applications from vagrant foreign officers in quest of adventure; and such appointments as this were sometimes made, no doubt, in that provincial spirit which it has taken Americans so long to outgrow, and which sees all things European in rose-colour. As soon as the report concerning Ducoudray reached the camp, Generals Greene, Sullivan, and Knox each wrote a letter to Congress, proffering their resignations in case the

(margin note: Promoting officers for non-military reasons.*)*

report were true; and the three letters were dated on the same day. Congress was very angry at this, and the three generals were abused without stint. The affair, however, was more serious than Congress had supposed, and the contemplated appointment of Ducoudray was not made. The language of John Adams with reference to matters of this sort was more pungent than wise, and it gave clear expression to the principles upon which Congress too often acted. This "delicate point of honour" he stigmatized as "one of the most putrid corruptions of absolute monarchy." He would be glad to see Congress elect all the general officers annually; and if some great men should be obliged to go home in conseqence of this, he did not believe the country would be ruined! The jealousy with which the several states insisted upon "a share of the general officers" in proportion to their respective quotas of troops, he characterized as a just and sound policy. It was upon this principle, he confessed, that many promotions had been made; and if the generals were so unreasonable as not to like it, they must "abide the consequences of their discontent." Such expressions of feeling, in which John Adams found many sympathizers, bear curious testimony to the intense distrust with which our poor little army was regarded on account of the monarchical tendencies supposed to be necessarily inherent in a military organization. This policy, which seemed so "sound" to John Adams, was simply an attempt to apply to the regimen of the army a set of principles fit only for the organization

Absurd talk of John Adams.

of political assemblies; and if it had been consistently adopted, it is probable that Lord George Germaine's scheme of tiring the Americans out would have succeeded beyond his most sanguine expectations.

But the most dangerous ground upon which Congress ventured during the whole course of the war was connected with the dark intrigues of those officers who wished to have Washington removed from the chief command that Gates might be put in his place. We have seen how successful Gates had been in supplanting Schuyler on the eve of victory. Without having been under fire or directing any important operation, Gates had carried off the laurels of the northern campaign. From many persons, no doubt, he got credit even for what had happened before he joined the army, on the 19th of August. His appointment dated from the 2d, before either the victory of Stark or the discomfiture of St. Leger; and it was easy for people to put dates together uncritically, and say that before the 2d of August Burgoyne had continued to advance into the country, and nothing could check him until after Gates had been appointed to command. The very air rang with the praises of Gates, and his weak head was not unnaturally turned with so much applause. In his dispatches announcing the surrender of Burgoyne, he not only forgot to mention the names of Arnold and Morgan, who had won for him the decisive victory, but he even seemed to forget that he was serving under a commander-in-chief, for he sent his dispatches directly

Gates is puffed up with success,

to Congress, leaving Washington to learn of the event through hearsay. Thirteen days after the surrender, Washington wrote to Gates, congratulating him upon his success. "At the same time," said the letter, "I cannot but regret that a matter of such magnitude, and so interesting to our general operations, should have reached me by report only, or through the channels of letters not bearing that authenticity which the importance of it required, and which it would have received by a line over your signature stating the simple fact."

But, worse than this, Gates kept his victorious army idle at Saratoga after the whole line of the Hudson was cleared of the enemy, and would not send reinforcements to Washington. Congress so far upheld him in this as to order that Washington should not detach more than 2,500 men from the northern army without consulting Gates and Governor Clinton. It was only with difficulty that Washington, by sending Colonel Hamilton with a special message, succeeded in getting and shows back Morgan with his riflemen. When symptoms of insubordination. reinforcements finally did arrive, it was tion. too late. Had they come more promptly, Howe would probably have been unable to take the forts on the Delaware, without control of which he could not have stayed in Philadelphia. But the blame for the loss of the forts was by many people thrown upon Washington, whose recent defeats at Brandywine and Germantown were now commonly contrasted with the victories at the North.

The moment seemed propitious for Gates to try his peculiar strategy once more, and displace

Washington as he had already displaced Schuyler. Assistants were not wanting for this dirty work. Among the foreign adventurers then with the army was one Thomas Conway, an Irishman, who had been for a long time in the French service, and, coming over to America, had taken part in the Pennsylvania campaign. Washington had opposed Conway's claim for undue promotion, and the latter at once threw himself with such energy into the faction then forming against the commander-in-chief that it soon came to be known as the "Conway Cabal." The other principal members of the cabal were Thomas Mifflin, the quartermaster-general, and James Lovell, a delegate from Massachusetts, who had been Schuyler's bitterest enemy in Congress. It was at one time reported that Samuel Adams was in sympathy with the cabal, and the charge has been repeated by many historians, but it seems to have originated in a malicious story set on foot by some of the friends of John Hancock. At the beginning of the war, Hancock, whose overweening vanity often marred his usefulness, had hoped to be made commander-in-chief, and he never forgave Samuel Adams for preferring Washington for that position. In the autumn of 1777, Hancock resigned his position as president of Congress, and was succeeded by Henry Laurens, of South Carolina. On the day when Hancock took leave of Congress, a motion was made to present him with the thanks of that body in acknowledgment of his admirable discharge of his duty; but the New England delegates, who had not been altogether satisfied with

The Conway Cabal.

him, defeated the motion on general grounds, and established the principle that it was injudicious to pass such complimentary votes in the case of any president. This action threw Hancock into a rage, which was chiefly directed against Samuel Adams as the most prominent member of the delegation; and after his return to Boston it soon became evident that he had resolved to break with his old friend and patron. Artful stories, designed to injure Adams, were in many instances traced to persons who were in close relation with Hancock. After the fall of the cabal, no more deadly stab could be dealt to the reputation of any man than to insinuate that he had given it aid or sympathy; and there is good ground for believing that such reports concerning Adams were industriously circulated by unscrupulous partisans of the angry Hancock. The story was revived at a later date by the friends of Hamilton, on the occasion of the schism between Hamilton and John Adams, but it has not been well sustained. The most plausible falsehoods, however, are those which are based upon misconstrued facts; and it is certain that Samuel Adams had not only favoured the appointment of Gates in the North, but he had sometimes spoken with impatience of the so-called Fabian policy of Washington. In this he was like many other ardent patriots whose military knowledge was far from commensurate with their zeal. His cousin, John Adams, was even more outspoken. He declared himself "sick of Fabian systems." "My toast," he said, "is a short and violent war;" and he complained of the reverent affection which the people felt for Washington as an "idolatry" dangerous to American liberty. It was by working upon such impatient moods as these, in which high-minded men like the Adamses sometimes indulged, that unscrupulous men like Gates hoped to attain their ends.

The first-fruits of the cabal in Congress were seen in the reorganization of the Board of War in November, 1777. Mifflin was chosen a member of the board, and Gates was made its president, with permission to serve in the field should occasion require it. Gates was thus, in a certain sense, placed over Washington's head; and soon afterward Conway was made inspector-general of the army, with the rank of major-general. In view of Washington's well-known opinions, the appointments of Mifflin and Conway might be regarded as an open declaration of hostility on the part of Congress.

Some weeks before, in regard to the rumour that Conway was to be promoted, Washington had written, " It will be impossible for me to be of any further service, if such insuperable difficulties are thrown in my way." Such language might easily be understood as a conditional threat of resignation, and Conway's appointment was probably urged by the conspirators with the express intention of forcing Washington to resign. Should this affront prove ineffectual, they hoped, by dint of anonymous letters and base innuendoes, to make the commander's place too hot for him. It was asserted that Washington's army had all through the year outnumbered Howe's more than three to one. The distress

Attempts to injure Washington.

of the soldiers was laid at his door; the sole result, if not the sole object, of his many marches, according to James Lovell, was to wear out their shoes and stockings. An anonymous letter to Patrick Henry, then governor of Virginia, dated from York, where Congress was sitting, observed: "We have wisdom, virtue, and strength enough to save us, if they could be called into action. The northern army has shown us what Americans are capable of doing with a general at their head. The spirit of the southern army is no way inferior to the spirit of the northern. A Gates, a Lee, or a Conway would in a few weeks render them an irresistible body of men. Some of the contents of this letter ought to be made public, in order to awaken, enlighten, and alarm our country." Henry sent this letter to Washington, who instantly recognized the well-known handwriting of Dr. Benjamin Rush. Another anonymous letter, sent to President Laurens, was still more emphatic: "It is a very great reproach to America to say there is only one general in it. The great success to the northward was owing to a change of commanders; and the southern army would have been alike successful if a similar change had taken place. The people of America have been guilty of idolatry by making a man their God, and the God of heaven and earth will convince them by woful experience that he is only a man; for no good can be expected from our army until Baal and his worshippers are banished from camp." This mischievous letter was addressed to Congress, but, instead of laying it before that body, the high-minded Laurens sent it directly to Washington. But the commander-in-chief was forewarned, and neither treacherous missives like these, nor the direct affronts of Congress, were allowed to disturb his equanimity. Just before leaving Saratoga, Gates received from Conway a letter Conway's letter to Gates. containing an allusion to Washington so terse and pointed as to be easily remembered and quoted, and Gates showed this letter to his young confidant and aid-de-camp, Wilkinson. A few days afterward, when Wilkinson had reached York with the dispatches relating to Burgoyne's surrender, he fell in with a member of Lord Stirling's staff, and under the genial stimulus of Monongahela whiskey repeated the malicious sentence. Thus it came to Stirling's ears, and he straightway communicated it to Washington by letter, saying that he should always deem it his duty to expose such wicked duplicity. Thus armed, Washington simply sent to Conway the following brief note : —

"Sir, — A letter which I received last night contained the following paragraph : 'In a letter from General Conway to General Gates, he says, *Heaven has determined to save your country, or a weak General and bad counsellors would have ruined it.*' I am, sir, your humble servant,

George Washington."

Conway knew not what sort of answer to make to this startling note. When Mifflin heard of it, he wrote at once to Gates, telling him that an extract from one of Conway's letters had fallen into Washington's hands, and advising him to take better care of his papers in future. All the plot-

ters were seriously alarmed ; for their scheme was
one which would not bear the light for a moment,
and Washington's curt letter left them quite in
the dark as to the extent of his knowledge.
" There is scarcely a man living," protested Gates,
" who takes greater care of his papers than I do.
I never fail to lock them up, and keep the key in
my pocket." One thing was clear : there must be
no delay in ascertaining how much Washington
knew and where he got his knowledge. After
four anxious days it occurred to Gates that it must
have been Washington's aid-de-camp, Hamilton,
who had stealthily gained access to his papers
during his short visit to the northern camp.
Filled with this idea, Gates chuckled as he thought
he saw a way of diverting attention from the subject matter of the letters to the mode in which
Washington had got possession of their contents.
He sat down and wrote to the comman-
der-in-chief, saying he had learned that Gates's letter to Washington.
some of Conway's confidential letters
to himself had come into his excellency's hands:
such letters must have been copied by stealth, and
he hoped his excellency would assist him in un-
earthing the wretch who prowled about and did
such wicked things, for obviously it was unsafe to
have such creatures in the camp; they might disclose precious secrets to the enemy. And so important did the matter seem that he sent a dupli-
cate of the present letter to Congress, in order that
every imaginable means might be adopted for
detecting the culprit without a moment's delay.
The purpose of this elaborate artifice was to create

in Congress, which as yet knew nothing of the
matter, an impression unfavourable to Washington,
by making it appear that he encouraged his aids-
de-camp in prying into the portfolios of other generals.   For, thought Gates, it is as clear as day
that Hamilton was the man; nobody else could
have done it.

But Gates's silly glee was short-lived. Washington discerned at a glance the treacherous purpose
of the letter, and foiled it by the simple expedi-
Washington's ent of telling the plain truth. "Your
reply.   letter," he replied, "came to my hand
a few days ago, and, to my great surprise, informed
me that a copy of it had been sent to Congress, for
what reason I find myself unable to account; but
as some end was doubtless intended to be answered
by it, I am laid under the disagreeable necessity
of returning my answer through the same channel,
lest any member of that honourable body should
harbour an unfavourable suspicion of my having
practised some indirect means to come at the contents of the confidential letters between you and
General Conway."   After this ominous prelude,
Washington went on to relate how Wilkinson had
babbled over his cups, and a certain sentence from
one of Conway's letters had thereupon been trans-
mitted to him by Lord Stirling.   He had communicated this discovery to Conway, to let that officer
know that his intriguing disposition was observed
and watched.   He had mentioned this to no one
else but Lafayette, for he thought it indiscreet to
let scandals arise in the army, and thereby "afford
a gleam of hope to the enemy." He had not

known that Conway was in correspondence with
Gates, and had even supposed that Wilkinson's
information was given with Gates's sanction, and
with friendly intent to forearm him against a secret enemy. "But in this," he disdainfully adds,
"as in other matters of late, I have found myself
mistaken."

So the schemer had overreached himself. It
was not Washington's aid-de-camp who had pried,
but it was Gates's own aid who had blabbed. But
for Gates's treacherous letter Washington would
not even have suspected him; and, to crown all,
he had only himself to thank for rashly blazoning
before Congress a matter so little to his credit,
and which Washington, in his generous discretion,
would forever have kept secret. Amid this discomfiture, however, a single ray of hope could be
discerned. It appeared that Washington had
known nothing beyond the one sentence which
had come to him as quoted in conversation by
Wilkinson. A downright falsehood
might now clear up the whole affair, Gates tries,
unsuccess-
fully, to save
and make Wilkinson the scapegoat for himself by
lying;
all the others. Gates accordingly wrote
again to Washington, denying his intimacy with
Conway, declaring that he had never received but
a single letter from him, and solemnly protest-
ing that this letter contained no such paragraph
as that of which Washington had been informed.
The information received through Wilkinson he
denounced as a villainous slander. But these lies
were too transparent to deceive any one, for in his
first letter Gates had implicitly admitted the exist-

ence of several letters between himself and Conway, and his manifest perturbation of spirit had
shown that these letters contained remarks that he
would not for the world have had Washington see.
A cold and contemptuous reply from Washington
made all this clear, and put Gates in a very un-
comfortable position, from which there was no retreat.

When the matter came to the ears of Wilkinson,
who had just been appointed secretary of the
Board of War, and was on his way to Congress,
his youthful blood boiled at once. He wrote bom-
bastic letters to everybody, and challenged Gates
to deadly combat. A meeting was arranged for
sunrise, behind the Episcopal church at York,
with pistols. At the appointed hour, when all had
arrived on the ground, the old general requested,
through his second, an interview with his young
antagonist, walked up a back street with him,
burst into tears, called him his dear
boy, and denied that he had ever made
any injurious remarks about him.

but is success-
ful, as usual,
in keeping
from under
fire.

Wilkinson's wrath was thus assuaged
for a moment, only to blaze forth presently with
fresh violence, when he made inquiries of Washington, and was allowed to read the very letter
in which his general had slandered him. He instantly wrote a letter to Congress, accusing Gates
of treachery and falsehood, and resigned his position on the Board of War.

These revelations strengthened Washington in
proportion as they showed the malice and duplicity of his enemies. About this time a pamphlet

was published in London, and republished in New York, containing letters which purported to have been written by Washington to members of his family, and to have been found in the possession of a mulatto servant taken prisoner at Fort Lee. The letters, if genuine, would have proved their author to be a traitor to the American cause; but they were so bunglingly con- The forged letters. cocted that every one knew them to be a forgery, and their only effect was to strengthen Washington still more, while throwing further discredit upon the cabal, with which many persons were inclined to connect them.

The army and the people were now becoming incensed at the plotters, and the press began to ridicule them, while the reputation of Gates suf- fered greatly in Congress as the indications of his real character were brought to light. All that was needed to complete the discomfiture of the cabal was a military fiasco, and this was soon forthcoming. In order to detach Scheme for invading Can- Lafayette from Washington, a winter ada. expedition against Canada was devised by the Board of War. Lafayette, a mere boy, scarcely twenty years old, was invited to take the com- mand, with Conway for his chief lieutenant. It was said that the French population of Canada would be sure to welcome the high-born French- man as their deliverer from the British yoke; and it was further thought that the veteran Irish schemer might persuade his young commander to join the cabal, and bring to it such support as might be gained from the French alliance, then

about to be completed. Congress was persuaded
to authorize the expedition, and Washington was
not consulted in the matter.

But Lafayette knew his own mind better than
was supposed. He would not accept the command
until he had obtained Washington's consent, and
then he made it an indispensable condition that
Baron de Kalb, who outranked Conway, should
accompany the expedition. These preliminaries
having been arranged, the young general went to
_{The dinner at} York for his instructions. There he
_{York.}   found Gates, surrounded by schemers
and sycophants, seated at a very different kind of
dinner from that to which Lafayette had lately
been used at Valley Forge. Hilarious with wine,
the company welcomed the new guest with accla-
mations. He was duly flattered and toasted, and
a glorious campaign was predicted. Gates assured
him that on reaching Albany he would find 3,000
regulars ready to march, while powerful assistance
was to be expected from the valiant Stark with
his redoubtable Green Mountain Boys. The marquis listened with placid composure till his papers
were brought him, and he felt it to be time to go.
Then rising as if for a speech, while all eyes were
turned upon him and breathless silence filled the
room, he reminded the company that there was
one toast which, in the generous excitement of
the occasion, they had forgotten to drink, and he
begged leave to propose the health of the com-
_{Lafayette's} mander-in-chief of the armies of the
_{toast.}   United States. The deep silence became
still deeper. None dared refused the toast, " but

some merely raised their glasses to their lips, while others cautiously put them down untasted." With the politest of bows and a scarcely perceptible shrug of the shoulder, the new commander of the northern army left the room, and mounted his horse to start for his headquarters at Albany.

When he got there, he found neither troops, supplies, nor equipments in readiness. Of the army to which Burgoyne had surrendered, the militia had long since gone home, while most of the regulars had been withdrawn to Valley Forge or the highlands of the Hudson. Instead of 3,000 regulars which Gates had promised, barely 1,200 could be found, and these were in no wise clothed or equipped for a winter march through the wilderness. Between carousing and backbiting, the new Board of War had no time left to attend to its duties. Not an inch of the country but was known to Schuyler, Lincoln, and Arnold, and they assured Lafayette that an invasion of Canada, under the circumstances, would be worthy of Don Quixote. In view of the French alliance, moreover, the conquest of Canada had even ceased to seem desirable to the Americans; for when peace should be concluded the French might insist upon retaining it, in compensation for their services. The men of New England greatly preferred Great Britain to France as a neighbour, and accordingly Stark, with his formidable Green Mountain Boys, felt no interest whatever in the enterprise, and not a dozen volunteers could be got together for love or money.

The fiasco was so complete, and the scheme itself so emphatically condemned by public opinion, that Congress awoke from its infatuation. Lafayette and Kalb were glad to return to Valley Forge. Conway, who stayed behind, became indignant with Congress over some fancied slight, and sent a conditional threat of resignation, which, to his unspeakable amazement, was accepted uncondi-

Downfall of the cabal.

tionally. In vain he urged that he had not meant exactly what he said, having lost the nice use of English during his long stay in France. His entreaties and objurgations fell upon deaf ears. In Congress the day of the cabal was over. Mifflin and Gates were removed from the Board of War. The latter was sent to take charge of the forts on the Hudson, and cautioned against forgetting that he was to report to the commander-in-chief. The cabal and its deeds having become the subject of common gossip, such friends as it had mustered now began stoutly to deny their connection with it. Conway himself was dangerously wounded a few months afterward in a duel with General Cadwallader, and, believing himself to be on his death-bed, he wrote a very humble letter to Washington, expressing his sincere grief for having ever done or said anything with intent to injure so great and good a man. His wound proved not to be mortal, but on his recovery, finding himself generally despised and shunned, he returned to France, and American history knew him no more.

Had Lord George Germain been privy to the secrets of the Conway cabal, his hope of wearing out the American cause would have been sensibly strengthened. There was really more danger in such intrigues than in an exhausted treasury, a half-starved army, and defeat on the field. The people felt it to be so, and the events of the winter left a stain upon *Decline of the Continental Congress.* the reputation of the Continental Congress from which it never fully recovered. Congress had already lost the high personal consideration to which it was entitled at the outset. Such men as Franklin, Washington, Jefferson, Henry, Jay, and Rutledge were now serving in other capacities. The legislatures of the several states afforded a more promising career for able men than the Continental Congress, which had neither courts nor magistrates, nor any recognized position of sovereignty. The meetings of Congress were often attended by no more than ten or twelve members. Curious symptoms were visible which seemed to show that the sentiment of union between the states was weaker than it had been two years before. Instead of the phrase " people of the United States," one begins, in 1778, to hear of " inhabitants of these Confederated States." In the absence of any central sovereignty which could serve as the symbol of union, it began to be feared that the new nation might after all be conquered through its lack of political cohesion. Such fears came to cloud the rejoicings over the victory of Saratoga, as, at the end of 1777, the Continental Congress began visibly to lose its place in public esteem, and sink, step by step, into the utter degradation and impotence which was to overwhelm it before another ten years should have expired.

As the defeat of the Conway cabal marked the beginning of the decline of Congress, it marked at the same time the rise of Washington to a higher place in the hearts of the people than he had ever held before.   As the silly intrigues against him recoiled upon their authors, men began to realize that it was far more upon his consummate sagacity and unselfish patriotism than upon anything that Congress could do that the country rested its hopes of success in the great enterprise which it had undertaken.   As the nullity of Congress made it ever more apparent that the country as a whole was without a government, Washington stood forth more and more conspicuously as the living symbol of the union of the states.   In him and his work were centred the common hopes and the common interests of all the American people.   There was no need of clothing him with extraordinary powers.   During the last years of the war he came, through sheer weight of personal character, to wield an influence like that which Perikles had wielded over the Athenians. He was all-powerful because he was "first in the hearts of his countrymen."   Few men, since history began, had ever occupied so lofty a position ; none ever made a more disinterested use of power. His arduous labours taught him to appreciate, better than any one else, the weakness entailed upon the country by the want of a stable central government.   But when the war was over, and the political problem came into the foreground, instead of using this knowledge to make himself personally indispensable to the country, he bent all the weight

Increasing influence of Washington.

of his character and experience toward securing the adoption of such a federal constitution as should make anything like a dictatorship forever unnecessary and impossible.

CHAPTER X

DURING the dreary winter at Valley Forge, Washington busied himself in improving the organization of his army. The fall of the Conway cabal removed many obstacles. Greene was persuaded, somewhat against his wishes, to serve as quartermaster-general, and forthwith the duties of that important office were discharged with zeal and promptness. Conway's resignation opened the way for a most auspicious change in the inspectorship of the army. Of all the foreign officers who served under Washington during the War

Baron Friedrich von Steuben. for Independence, the Baron von Steuben was in many respects the most important. Member of a noble family which for five centuries had been distinguished in the local annals of Magdeburg, Steuben was one of the best educated and most experienced soldiers of Germany. His grandfather, an able theologian, was well known as the author of a critical treatise on the New Testament. His uncle, an eminent mathematician, had been the inventor of a new system of fortification. His father had seen half a century of honourable service in the corps of engineers. He had himself held the rank of first lieutenant at the beginning of the Seven Years'

War, and after excellent service in the battles of
Prague, Rossbach, and Kunersdorf he was raised
to a position on the staff of Frederick the Great.
At the end of the war, when the thrifty king reduced his army, and Blücher with other officers
afterward famous left the service, Steuben retired
to private life, with the honorary rank of General
of the Circle of Swabia. For more than ten years
he was grand marshal to the Prince of Hohenzol-
lern-Hechingen. Then he went travelling about
Europe, until in the spring of 1777 he arrived in
Paris, and became acquainted with Franklin and
Beaumarchais.

The American alliance was already secretly contemplated by the French ministry, and the astute
Vergennes, knowing that the chief defect of our
armies lay in their want of organization and discipline, saw in the scientific German soldier an efficient instrument for remedying the evil. After
much hesitation Steuben was persuaded to undertake the task. That his arrival upon the scene
might excite no heart-burning among the American officers, the honorary rank which he held in
Germany was translated by Vergennes into the
rank of lieutenant-general, which the Americans
would at once recognize as more eminent than any
position existing in their own army except that of
the commander-in-chief.

Knowing no English, Steuben took with him as
secretary and interpreter the youthful
Pierre Duponceau, afterward famous as Steuben
arrives in
America,
a lawyer, and still more famous as a
philologist. One day, on shipboard, this gay young

Frenchman laid a wager that he would kiss the first Yankee girl he should meet on landing. So as they came ashore at Portsmouth on a frosty December day, he gravely stepped up to a pretty New Hampshire maiden who was passing by, and told her that before leaving his native land to fight for American freedom he had taken a vow to ask, in earnest of victory, a kiss from the first lady he should meet. The prayer of chivalry found favour in the eyes of the fair Puritan, and the token of success was granted.

At Boston John Hancock furnished the party with sleighs, drivers, and saddle-horses for the inland journey of more than four hundred miles to York. During this cheerful journey, which it took three weeks to perform, Steuben's heart was warmed toward his new country by the reminiscences of the Seven Years' War which he frequently encountered. The name of Frederick was deservedly popular in America, and his familiar features decorated the sign-board of many a wayside inn, while on the coffee-room walls hung quaint prints with doggerel verses commemorating Rossbach and Leuthen along with and visits Congress at York. Louisburg and Quebec. On arriving at York, the German general was received by Congress with distinguished honours; and this time the confidence given to a trained European soldier turned out to be well deserved. Throughout the war Steuben proved no less faithful than capable. He came to feel a genuine love for his adopted country, and after the war was over, retiring to the romantic woodland near Oris-

kany, where so many families of German lineage
were already settled, and where the state of New
York presented him with a farm of sixteen thousand acres in acknowledgment of his services, he
lived the quiet life of a country gentleman until
his death in 1794. A little village some twelve
miles north of the site of old Fort Stanwix still
bears his name and marks the position of his estate.

After his interview with Congress, Steuben repaired at once to Valley Forge, where Washington was not slow in recognizing his ability; nor
was Steuben, on the other hand, at a loss to per-
ceive, in the ragged and motley army which he
passed in review, the existence of soldierly qualities which needed nothing so much as training.
Disregarding the English prejudice which looked
upon the drilling of soldiers as work fit only for
sergeants, he took musket in hand and showed
what was to be done. Alert and untiring, he
worked from morning till night in showing the
men how to advance, retreat, or change front without falling into disorder, — how to per- Steuben at
form, in short, all the rapid and accu- Valley Forge.
rate movements for which the Prussian army had
become so famous. It was a revelation to the
American troops. Generals, colonels, and captains were fired by the contagion of his example
and his tremendous enthusiasm, and for several
months the camp was converted into a training-
school, in which masters and pupils worked with
incessant and furious energy. Steuben was struck
with the quickness with which the common soldiers

learned their lessons. He had a harmlessly chol-
eric temper, which was part of his overflowing
vigour, and sometimes, when drilling an awkward
squad, he would exhaust his stock of French and
German oaths, and shout for his aid to come and
curse the blockheads in English. " Viens, mon
ami Walker," he would say, — " viens, mon bon
ami. Sacre-bleu! Gott-vertamn de gaucherie of
dese badauts. Je ne puis plus ; I can curse dem
no more ! " Yet in an incredibly short time, as
he afterward wrote, these awkward fellows had
acquired a military air, had learned how to carry
their arms, and knew how to form into column,
deploy, and execute manœuvres with precision.
In May, 1778, after three months of such work,
Steuben was appointed inspector - general of the
army, with the rank and pay of major-general.
The reforms which he introduced were so far-
reaching that after a year they were said to have
saved more than 800,000 French livres to the
United States. No accounts had been kept of
arms and accoutrements, and owing to the careless
good-nature which allowed every recruit to carry
home his musket as a keepsake, there had been a
loss of from five to eight thousand muskets annually. During the first year of Steuben's inspectorship less than twenty muskets were lost. Half
of the arms at Valley Forge were found by Steuben without bayonets. The American soldier had
no faith in this weapon, because he did not know
how to use it ; when he did not throw it away, he
adapted it to culinary purposes, holding on its
point the beef which he roasted before his camp-

fire. Yet in little more than a year after Steuben's arrival we shall see an American column,
without firing a gun, storm the works at Stony
Point in one of the most spirited bayonet charges
known to history.

Besides all this, it was Steuben who first taught
the American army to understand the value of an
efficient staff. The want of such a staff had been
severely felt at the battle of Brandywine ; but before the end of the war Washington had become
provided with a staff that Frederick need not have
despised. While busy with all these laborious reforms, the good baron found time to prepare a new
code of discipline and tactics, based on Prussian
experience, but adapted to the peculiar Steuben's man-
conditions of American warfare ; and ual of tactics.
this excellent manual held its place, long after the
death of its author, as the Blue Book of our army.
In this adaptation of means to ends, Steuben
proved himself to be no martinet, but a thorough
military scholar ; he was able not only to teach,
but to learn. And in the art of warfare there was
one lesson which Europe now learned from America. In woodland fights with the Indians, it had
been found desirable to act in loose columns, which
could easily separate to fall behind trees and reu-
nite at brief notice ; and in this way there had
been developed a kind of light infantry peculiar to
America, and especially adapted for skirmishing.
It was light infantry of this sort that, in the hands
of Arnold and Morgan, had twice won the day
in the Saratoga campaign. Reduced to scientific
shape by Steuben, and absorbed, with all the other

military knowledge of the age, by Napoleon, these light-infantry tactics have come to play a great part on the European battlefields of the nineteenth century.

Thus from the terrible winter at Valley Forge, in which the accumulated evils of congressional mismanagement had done their best to destroy the army, it came forth, nevertheless, stronger in organization and bolder in spirit than ever before. On the part of the enemy nothing had been done to molest it. The position at Valley Forge was a strong one, and Sir William Howe found it easier to loiter in Philadelphia than to play a strategic game against Washington in the depths of an American winter. When Franklin at Paris first heard the news that Howe had taken Philadelphia, knowing well how slight was the military value of the conquest, he observed that it would be more correct to say that Philadelphia had taken General Howe.

Sir William Howe resigns his command. And so it turned out, in more ways than one; for his conduct in going there at all was roundly blamed by the opposition in Parliament, and not a word was said in his behalf by Lord George Germain. The campaign of 1777 had been such a bungling piece of work that none of the chief actors, save Burgoyne, was willing frankly to assume his share of responsibility for it. Sir William Howe did not care to disclose the secret of his peculiar obligations to the traitor Lee; and it would have ruined Lord George Germain to have told the story of the dispatch that never was sent. Lord George, who was never noted for generosity, sought to screen himself by throwing

the blame for everything indiscriminately upon the
two generals.   Burgoyne, who sat in Parliament,
defended himself ably and candidly ; and when
Howe heard what was going on, he sent in his resignation, in order that he too might go home and
defend himself.   Besides this, he had grown sick
of the war, and was more than ever convinced
that it must end in failure.   On the 18th of May,
Philadelphia was the scene of a grand farewell
banquet, called the *Mischianza*, — a strange med-
ley combining the modern parade with the mediæval tournament, wherein seven silk-clad   The Mischi-
knights of the Blended Rose and seven ·anza·
more of the Burning Mountain did amicably break
lances in honour of fourteen blooming damsels
dressed in Turkish costume, while triumphal
arches, surmounted by effigies of Fame, displayed
inscriptions commemorating in fulsome Latin and
French the glories of the departing general.   In
these curious festivities, savouring more strongly
of Bruges in the fifteenth century than of Philadelphia in the eighteenth, it was long after remembered that the most prominent parts were taken by
the ill-starred Major André and the beautiful Miss
Margaret Shippen, who was soon to become the
wife of Benedict Arnold.   With such farewell cere-
monies Sir William Howe set sail for England,
and Sir Henry Clinton took his place as commander-in-chief of the British armies in America.

Washington's position at Valley Forge had held
the British in check through the winter.   They had
derived no advantage from the possession of the
"rebel capital," for such poor work as Congress

could do was as well done from York as from Phil-
The British
evacuate Phil-
adelphia, June
18, 1778. adelphia, and the political life of the
United States was diffused from one end
of the country to the other.   The place
was worthless as a basis for military operations.   It
was harder to defend and harder to supply with
food than the insular city of New York; and,
moreover, a powerful French fleet, under Count
d'Estaing, was approaching the American coast.
With the control of the Delaware imperilled, Philadelphia would soon become untenable, and, in accordance with instructions received from the ministry, Sir Henry Clinton prepared to evacuate the
place and concentrate his forces at New York.   His
first intention was to go by water; but finding
that he had not transports enough for his whole
army, together with the Tory refugees who had put
themselves under his protection, he changed his
plan.   The Tories, to the number of 3,000, with
their personal effects, were sent on in the fleet,
while the army, encumbered with twelve miles of
baggage wagons, began its retreat across New Jersey.   On the morning of the 18th of June, 1778,
the rear-guard of the British marched out of Phil-
'adelphia, and before sunset the American advance
marched in and took possession of the city.   General Arnold, whose crippled leg did not allow him
to take the field, was put in command, and after a
Arnold takes
command at
Philadelphia. fortnight both Congress and the state
government returned.   Of the Tories
who remained behind, twenty-five were
indicted, under the laws of Pennsylvania, for the
crime of offering aid to the enemy.   Two Quakers,

who had actually conducted a party of British to a midnight attack upon an American outpost, were found guilty of treason and hanged. The other twenty-three were either acquitted or pardoned. Across the river, seventeen Tories, convicted of treason under the laws of New Jersey, all received pardon from the governor.

The British retreat from Philadelphia was regarded by the Americans as equivalent to a victory, and Washington was anxious to enhance the moral effect of it by a sudden blow which should cripple Sir Henry Clinton's army. In force he was about equal to the enemy, both armies now numbering about 15,000, while in equipment and discipline his men were better off than ever before. Unfortunately, the American army had just received one addition which went far to neutralize these advantages. The mischief-maker Lee had returned. In the preceding summer the British Major-General Prescott had been captured in Rhode Island, and after a tedious negotiation of nine months Lee was exchanged for him. He arrived at Valley Forge in May, and as Washington had found a lenient inter- Return of Charles Lee. pretation for his outrageous conduct before his capture, while nothing whatever was known of his treasonable plot with the Howes, he naturally came back unquestioned to his old position as senior major-general of the army. It was a dangerous situation for the Americans to have such high command entrusted to such a villain.

When Philadelphia was evacuated, Lee first tried to throw Washington off on a false scent

by alleging reasons for believing that Clinton did
not intend to retreat across New Jersey. Failing
in this, he found reasons as plentiful as blackber-
ries why the British army should not be followed
up and harassed on its retreat. Then
when Washington decided that an attack must be made he grew sulky, and
refused to conduct it. Washington was marching
more rapidly than Clinton, on a line nearly parallel with him, to the northward, so that by the
time the British general reached Allentown he
found his adversary getting in front of him upon
his line of retreat. Clinton had nothing to gain
by fighting, if he could possibly avoid it, and accordingly he turned to the right, following the
road which ran through Monmouth and Middletown to Sandy Hook. Washington now detached
a force of about 5,000 men to advance swiftly and
cut off the enemy's rear, while he designed to
come up and support the operation with the rest
of his army. To Lee, as second in rank, the command of this advanced party properly belonged;
but he declined to take it, on the ground that it
was sure to be defeated, and Washington entrusted the movement to the youthful Lafayette,
of the soundness of whose judgment he had already seen many proofs. But in the course of the
night it occurred to Lee, whatever his miserable
purpose may have been, that perhaps he might
best accomplish it, after all, by taking the field.
So he told Washington, next morning, that he
had changed his mind, and was anxious to take
the command which he had just declined. With

Washington pursues the British.

extraordinary forbearance Washington granted his request, and arranged the affair with such tact as not to wound the feelings of Lafayette, who thus, unfortunately, lost the direction of the movement.

On the night of June 27th the left wing of the British army, 8,000 strong, commanded by Lord Cornwallis, encamped near Monmouth Court House, on the road from Allentown. The right wing, of about equal strength, and composed chiefly of Hessians under Knyphausen, lay just beyond the Court House on the road to Middletown. In order of march the right wing took the lead, convoying the immense baggage train. The left wing, following in the rear, was the His plan of part exposed to danger, and with it attack. stayed Sir Henry Clinton. The American advance under Lee, 6,000 strong, lay about five miles northeast of the British line, and Washington, with the main body, was only three miles behind. Lee's orders from Washington were positive and explicit. He was to gain the flank of the British left wing and attack it vigorously, while Washington was to come up and complete its discomfiture. Lee's force was ample, in quantity and quality, for the task assigned it, and there was fair ground for hope that the flower of the British army might thus be cut off and captured or destroyed. Since the war began there had hardly been such a golden opportunity.

Sunday, the 28th of June, was a day of fiery heat, the thermometer showing 96° in the shade. Early in the morning Clinton moved cautiously.

Knyphausen made all haste forward on the Middletown road, and the left wing followed till it
had passed more than a mile beyond
Monmouth Court House, when it found
itself outflanked on the north by the
American columns.   Lee had advanced from
Freehold church by the main road, crossing two
deep ravines upon causeways; and now, while his
left wing was folding about Cornwallis on the
north, occupying superior ground, his centre, under Wayne, was close behind, and his right, under
Lafayette, had already passed the Court House,
and was threatening the other end of the British
line on the south.   Cornwallis instantly changed
front to meet the danger on the north, and a detachment was thrown down the road toward the
Court House to check Lafayette.   The British
position was one of extreme peril, but the behaviour of the American commander now became very
extraordinary.   When Wayne was beginning his
attack, he was ordered by Lee to hold back and
simply make a feint, as the main attack was to
be made in another quarter.   While Wayne was
wondering at this, the British troops coming down
the road were seen directing their march so as to
come between Wayne and Lafayette.   It would
be easy to check them, but the marquis had no
sooner started than Lee ordered him back, mur-
muring about its being impossible to stand against
British soldiers.   Lafayette's suspicions were now
aroused, and he sent a dispatch in all
haste to Washington, saying that his
presence in the field was sorely needed.   The

Battle of Mon-
mouth, June
28, 1778.

Lee's shame-
ful retreat.

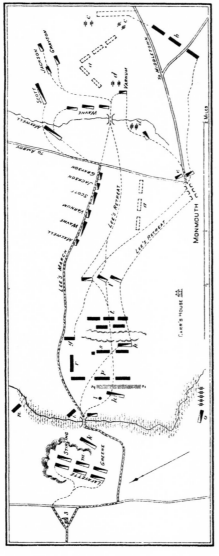

BATTLE OF MONMOUTH. JUNE 28, 1778.

a Position occupied by the British the night before the battle.
b British detachment moving towards Monmouth.
c British batteries.
d Captain Oswald's American batteries.
e American troops formed near the court-house.
f First position taken by Gen. Lee in his retreat.
g Attack by a party of British in the woods.
h Positions taken by General Lee.
i British detachment.
k Last position of the retreating troops.
m Army formed by Gen. Washington after he met Gen. Lee retreating.
n British detachment.
p Principal action.
r First position of the British after the action.
s Second position.
t British passed the night after the battle.
1 Where Washington met Lee retreating.
2 Hedge-row.
o American battery.
3 Meeting-house.

army was bewildered. Fighting had hardly begun, but their position was obviously so good that the failure to make prompt use of it suggested some unknown danger. One of the divisions on the left was now ordered back by Lee, and the others, seeing this retrograde movement, and understanding it as the prelude to a general retreat, began likewise to fall back. All thus retreated, though without flurry or disorder, to the high ground just east of the second ravine which they had crossed in their advance. All the advantage of their offensive movement was thus thrown away without a struggle, but the position they had now reached was excellent for a defensive fight. To the amazement of everybody, Lee ordered the retreat to be continued across the marshy ravine. As they crowded upon the causeway the ranks began to fall into some disorder. Many sank exhausted from the heat. No one could tell from what they were fleeing, and the exultant ardour with which they had begun to enfold the British line gave place to bitter disappointment, which vented itself in passionate curses. So they hurried on, with increasing disorder, till they approached the brink of the westerly ravine, where their craven commander met Washington riding up, pale with anger, looking like an avenging deity.

"What is the meaning of all this?" shouted Washington. His tone was so fierce and his look so threatening that the traitor shook in his stirrups, and could make no answer. When the question was repeated with yet greater fierceness, and further emphasized by a tremendous oath, he flew

into a rage, and complained at having been sent
out to beard the whole British army. "I am very
sorry," said Washington, "that you undertook the
command, if you did not mean to fight." Lee replied that he did not think it prudent to bring on
a general engagement, which was, however, precisely what he had been sent out to do. "Whatever your opinions may have been," said Washington sharply, "I expected my orders
to be obeyed;" and with these words
he wheeled about to stop the retreat

Washington
retrieves the
situation.

and form a new front. There was not a moment
to lose, for the British were within a mile of them,
and their fire began before the line of battle could
be formed. To throw a mass of disorderly fugitives in the face of advancing reinforcements, as
Lee had been on the point of doing, was to endan-
ger the organization of the whole force. It was
now that the admirable results of Steuben's teach-
ing were to be seen. The retreating soldiers immediately wheeled and formed under fire with as
much coolness and precision as they could have
shown on parade, and while they stopped the
enemy's progress, Washington rode back and
brought up the main body of his army. On some
heights to the left of the enemy Greene placed a
battery which enfiladed their lines, while Wayne
attacked them vigorously in front. After a brave
resistance, the British were driven back upon the
second ravine which Lee had crossed in the morning's advance. Washington now sent word to
Steuben, who was a couple of miles in the rear,
telling him to bring up three brigades and press

the retreating enemy. Some time before this he
had again met Lee and ordered him to the rear,
for his suspicion was now thoroughly aroused. As
the traitor rode away from the field he met Steuben advancing, and tried to work one final piece
of mischief. He tried to persuade Steuben to
halt, alleging that he must have misunderstood
Washington's orders; but the worthy baron was
not to be trifled with, and doggedly kept on his
way. The British were driven in some confusion
across the ravine, and were just making a fresh
stand on the high ground east of it when night put
an end to the strife. Washington sent out parties to attack them on both flanks as soon as day
should dawn; but Clinton withdrew in the night,
leaving his wounded behind, and by daybreak had
joined Knyphausen on the heights of Middletown,
whither it was useless to follow him.

The British loss in the battle of Monmouth was
about 416, and the American loss was 362. On
both sides there were many deaths from sunstroke.
The battle has usually been claimed as a victory
for the Americans; and so it was in a certain
sense, as they drove the enemy from the field.
Strategically considered, however, Lord Stanhope
is quite right in calling it a drawn battle. The
purpose for which Washington undertook it was
foiled by the treachery of Lee. Never- It was a drawn
theless, in view of the promptness with battle.
which Washington turned defeat into victory, and
of the greatly increased efficiency which it showed
in the soldiers, the moral advantage was doubtless
with the Americans. It deepened the impression

produced by the recovery of Philadelphia, it silenced the cavillers against Washington, and its effect upon Clinton's army was disheartening. More than 2,000 of his men, chiefly Hessians, deserted in the course of the following week.

During the night after the battle, the behaviour of Lee was the theme of excited discussion among the American officers. By the next day, having recovered his self-possession, he wrote a petulant letter to Washington, demanding an apology for his language on the battlefield. Washington's reply was as follows: —

"SIR, — I received your letter, expressed, as I conceive, in terms highly improper. I am not conscious of making use of any very singular expressions at the time of meeting you, as you intimate. What I recollect to have said was dictated by duty and warranted by the occasion. As soon as circumstances will permit, you shall have an opportunity of justifying yourself to the army, to Congress, to America, and to the world in general; or of convincing them that you were guilty of a breach of orders, and of misbehaviour before the enemy on the 28th instant, in not attacking them as you had been directed, and in making an unnecessary, disorderly, and shameful retreat."

To this terrible letter Lee sent the following impudent answer: "You cannot afford me greater pleasure than in giving me the opportunity of showing to America the sufficiency of her respective servants. I trust that temporary power of office and the tinsel dignity attending it will not

be able, by all the mists they can raise, to obfus-
cate the bright rays of truth." Wash-   <small>Trial and sen-</small>
ington replied by putting Lee under   <small>tence of Lee.</small>
arrest. A court-martial was at once convened,
before which he was charged with disobedience of
orders in not attacking the enemy, with misbehaviour on the field in making an unnecessary and
shameful retreat, and, lastly, with gross disrespect
to the commander-in-chief. After a painstaking
trial, which lasted more than a month, he was
found guilty on all three charges, and suspended
from command in the army *for the term of one
year.*

This absurdly inadequate sentence is an example of the extreme and sometimes ill-judged humanity which has been wont to characterize judicial proceedings in America. Many a European
soldier has been ruthlessly shot for less serious
misconduct and on less convincing evidence. A
general can be guilty of no blacker crime than
knowingly to betray his trust on the field of battle. But in Lee's case, the very enormity of his
crime went far to screen him from the punishment
which it deserved. People are usually slow to believe in criminality that goes far beyond the ordinary wickedness of the society in which they live.
If a candidate for Congress is accused of bribery
or embezzlement, we unfortunately find it easy to
believe the charge; but if he were to be accused
of attempting to poison his rival, we should find it
very hard indeed to believe it. In the France of
Catherine de' Medici or the Italy of Cæsar Borgia,
the one accusation would have been as credible as

the other, but we have gone far toward outgrowing some of the grosser forms of crime. In American history, as in modern English history, instances of downright treason have been very rare; and in proportion as we are impressed with their ineffable wickedness are we slow to admit the possibility of their occurrence. In ancient Greece and in mediæval Italy there were many Benedict Arnolds; in the United States a single plot for surrendering a stronghold to the enemy has consigned its author to a solitary immortality of infamy. But unless the proof of Arnold's treason had been absolutely irrefragable, many persons would have refused to believe it. In like manner, people were slow to believe that Lee could have been so deliberately wicked as to plan the defeat of the army in which he held so high a command, and some historians have preferred to regard his conduct as wholly unintelligible, rather than adopt the only clue by which it can be explained. He might have been bewildered, he might have been afraid, he might have been crazy, it was suggested; and to the latter hypothesis his well-known eccentricity gave some countenance. It was well for the court-martial to give him the benefit of the doubt, but in any case it should have been obvious that he had proved himself *permanently* unfit for a command.

Historians for a long time imitated the clemency of the court-martial by speaking of the " waywardness " of General Lee. Nearly eighty years elapsed before the discovery of that document which obliges us to put the worst interpretation

upon his acts, while it enables us clearly to understand the motives which prompted them.   Lee was
nothing but a selfish adventurer.   He
had no faith in the principles for which
the Americans were fighting, or indeed

Lee's charac-
ter and
schemes.

in any principles.   He came here to advance his
own fortunes, and hoped to be made commander-
in-chief.   Disappointed in this, he began at once
to look with hatred and envy upon Washington,
and sought to thwart his purposes, while at the
same time he intrigued with the enemy.   He became infatuated with the idea of playing some
such part in the American Revolution as Monk
had played in the Restoration of Charles II.   This
explains his conduct in the autumn of 1776, when
he refused to march to the support of Washington.   Should Washington be defeated and captured, then Lee, as next in command and at the
head of a separate army, might negotiate for
peace.   His conduct as prisoner in New York,
first in soliciting an interview with Congress, then
in giving aid and counsel to the enemy, is all to be
explained in the same way.   And his behaviour in
the Monmouth campaign was part and parcel of
the same crooked policy.   Lord North's commissioners had just arrived from England to offer
terms to the Americans, but in the exultation over
Saratoga and the French alliance, now increased
by the recovery of Philadelphia, there was little
hope of their effecting anything.   The spirits of
these Yankees, thought Lee, must not be suffered
to rise too high, else they will never listen to reason.   So he wished to build a bridge of gold for

Clinton to retreat by; and when he found it impossible to prevent an attack, his second thoughts led him to take command, in order to keep the game in his own hands. Should Washington now incur defeat by adopting a course which Lee had emphatically condemned as impracticable, the impatient prejudices upon which the cabal had played might be revived. The downfall of Washington would perhaps be easy to compass; and the schemer would thus not only enjoy the humiliation of the man whom he so bitterly hated, but he might fairly hope to succeed him in the chief command, and thus have an opportunity of bringing the war to a " glorious " end through a negotiation with Lord North's commissioners. Such thoughts as these were, in all probability, at the bottom of Lee's extraordinary behaviour at Monmouth. They were the impracticable schemes of a vain, egotistical dreamer. That Washington and Chatham, had that great statesman been still alive, might have brought the war to an honourable close through open and frank negotiation was perhaps not impossible. That such a man as Lee, by paltering with agents of Lord North, should effect anything but mischief and confusion was inconceivable. But selfishness is always incompatible with sound judgment, and Lee's wild schemes were quite in keeping with his character. The method he adopted for carrying them out was equally so. It would have been impossible for a man of strong military instincts to have relaxed his clutch upon an enemy in the field, as Lee did at the battle of Monmouth. If Arnold had been there that day, with his head never so full of treason, an irresistible impulse would doubtless have led him to attack the enemy tooth and nail, and the treason would have waited till the morrow.

As usually happens in such cases, the selfish schemer overreached himself. Washington won a victory, after all; the treachery was detected, and the traitor disgraced. Maddened by the destruction of his air-castles, Lee now began writing scurrilous articles in the newspapers. He could not hear Washington's name mentioned without losing his temper, and his venomous tongue at length got him into a duel with Colonel Laurens, one of Washington's aids and son of the president of Congress. He came out of the affair with nothing worse than a wound in the side; but when, a little later, he wrote an angry letter to Con-   Lee's expulsion from the army. gress, he was summarily expelled from the army. "Ah, I see," he said, aiming a Parthian shot at Washington, "if you wish to become a great general in America, you must learn to grow tobacco;" and so he retired to a plantation which he had in the Shenandoah valley. He lived to behold the triumph of the cause which he had done so much to injure, and in October, 1782, he died in a mean public-house in Philadelphia, friendless and alone. His last   His death. wish was that he might not be buried in consecrated ground, or within a mile of any church or meeting-house, because he had kept so much bad company in this world that he did not choose to continue it in the next. But in this he was not allowed to have his way. He was buried in the cemetery of Christ Church in Philadelphia, and many worthy citizens came to the funeral.

When Washington, after the battle of Monmouth, saw that it was useless further to molest Clinton's retreat, he marched straight for the Hudson river, and on the 20th of July he encamped at White Plains, while his adversary took refuge in New York. The opposing armies occupied the same ground as in the autumn of 1776 ; but the Americans were now the aggressive party. Howe's object in 1776 was the capture of Washington's army; Clinton's object in 1778 was limited to keeping possession of New York. There was now a chance for testing the worth of the French alliance. With the aid of a powerful French fleet, it might be possible to capture Clinton's army, and thus end the war at a blow. But this was not to be. The French fleet of twelve ships-of-the-line and six frigates, commanded by the Count d'Estaing, sailed from Toulon on the 13th of April, and after a tedious struggle with head-winds arrived at the mouth of the Delaware on the 8th of July, just too late to intercept Lord Howe's squadron. The fleet contained a land force of 4,000 men, and brought over M. Gérard, the first minister from France to the United States. Finding nothing to do on the Delaware, the count proceeded to Sandy Hook, where he was boarded by Washington's aids, Laurens and Hamilton, and a council of war was held. As the British fleet in the harbour consisted of only six ships-of-the-line, with several frigates and gun-

The situation at New York.

boats, it seemed obvious that it might be destroyed
or captured by Estaing's superior force, and then
Clinton would be entrapped in the island city.
But this plan was defeated by a strange obstacle.
Though the harbour of New York is one of the
finest in the world, it has, like most harbours situated at the mouths of great rivers, a bar at the
entrance, which in 1778 was far more troublesome
than it is to-day. Since that time the bar has
shifted its position and been partially worn away,
so that the largest ships can now freely   The French
enter, except at low tide. But when   fleet unable to
the American pilots examined Estaing's   bour.
two largest ships, which carried eighty and ninety
guns respectively, they declared it unsafe, even at
high tide, for them to venture upon the bar. The
enterprise was accordingly abandoned, but in its
stead another one was undertaken, which, if successful, might prove hardly less decisive than the
capture of New York.

After their expulsion from Boston in the first
year of the war, the British never regained their
foothold upon the mainland of New England.
But in December, 1776, the island which gives its
name to the state of Rhode Island had been seized
by Lord Percy, and the enemy had occupied it
ever since. From its commanding position at the
entrance to the Sound, it assisted them in threatening the Connecticut coast; and on the other
hand, should occasion require, it might even enable
them to threaten Boston with an overland attack.
After Lord Percy's departure for England in the
spring of 1777, the command devolved upon Major

General Richard Prescott, an unmitigated brute.

General Prescott at Newport.

Under his rule no citizen of Newport was safe in his own house. He not only arrested people and threw them into jail without assigning any reason, but he encouraged his soldiers in plundering houses and offering gross insults to ladies, as well as in cutting down shade-trees and wantonly defacing the beautiful lawns. A great loud-voiced, irascible fellow, swelling with the sense of his own importance, if he chanced to meet with a Quaker who failed to take off his hat, he would seize him by the collar and knock his head against the wall, or strike him over the shoulders with the big gnarled stick which he usually carried. One night in July, as this petty tyrant was sleeping at a country house about five miles from Newport, a party of soldiers rowed over from the mainland in boats, under the guns of three British frigates, and, taking the general out of bed, carried him off in his nightgown. He was sent to Washington's headquarters on the Hudson. As he passed through the village of Lebanon, in Connecticut, he stopped to dine at an old inn kept by one Captain Alden. He was politely received, and in the course of the meal Mrs. Alden set upon the table a dish of succotash, whereupon Prescott, not knowing the delicious dish, roared, " What do you mean by offering me this hog's food ? " and threw it all upon the floor. The good woman retreated in tears to the kitchen, and presently her husband, coming in with a stout horsewhip, dealt with the boor as he deserved. When Prescott was exchanged for General Lee, in

April, 1778, he resumed the command at Newport, but was soon superseded by the amiable and
accomplished Sir Robert Pigott, under whom the
garrison was increased to 6,000 men.

New York and Newport were now the only places
held by the enemy in the United States, and the
capture of either, with its army of occupation,
would be an event of prime importance. As soon
as the enterprise was suggested, the New England
militia began to muster in force, Mas-
sachusetts sending a strong contingent   <small>Attempt to
capture the
British garri-
son at New-
port.</small>
under John Hancock. General Sullivan had been in command at Providence since April. Washington now sent him
1,500 picked men of his Continental troops, with
Greene, who was born hard by and knew every
inch of the island; with Glover, of amphibious
renown; and Lafayette, who was a kinsman of the
Count d'Estaing. The New England yeomanry
soon swelled this force to about 9,000, and with
the 4,000 French regulars and the fleet, it might
well be hoped that General Pigott would quickly
be brought to surrender.

The expedition failed through the inefficient co-
operation of the French and the insubordination
of the yeomanry. Estaing arrived off the harbour
of Newport on the 29th of July, and had a conference with Sullivan. It was agreed that the
Americans should land upon the east side of the
island while the French were landing upon the
west side, thus intervening between the main garrison at Newport and a strong detachment which
was stationed on Butts Hill, at the northern end

of the island. By such a movement this detachment might be isolated and captured, to begin
with. But General Pigott, divining the purpose
of the allies, withdrew the detachment, and concentrated all his forces in and around the city.
At this moment the French troops were landing
upon Conanicut island, intending to cross to the
Sullivan seizes
Butts Hill. north of Newport on the morrow, according to the agreement. Sullivan
did not wait for them, but seeing the commanding position on Butts Hill evacuated, he rightly
pushed across the channel and seized it, while at
the same time he informed Estaing of his reasons
for doing so. The count, not understanding the
situation, was somewhat offended at what he
deemed undue haste on the part of Sullivan, but
thus far nothing had happened to disturb the execution of their scheme. He had only to continue landing his troops and blockade the southern
end of the island with his fleet, and Sir Robert
Pigott was doomed. But the next day Lord Howe
appeared off Point Judith, with thirteen ships-of-
the-line, seven frigates, and several small vessels,
and Estaing, reëmbarking the troops he had landed
on Conanicut, straightway put out to sea to engage
him. For two days the hostile fleets manœuvred
for the weather-gage, and just as they were getting ready for action there came up a terrific
storm, which scattered them far and wide. In-
Naval battle
prevented by
storm. stead of trying to destroy one another,
each had to bend all his energies to sav-
ing himself. So fierce was the storm
that it was remembered in local tradition as lately

as 1850 as " the Great Storm." Windows in the
town were incrusted with salt blown up in the
ocean spray. Great trees were torn up by the roots,
and much shipping was destroyed along the coast.

It was not until the 20th of August that Estaing brought in his squadron, somewhat damaged
from the storm. He now insisted upon going to
Boston to refit, in accordance with general instructions received from the ministry before leaving
home. It was urged in vain by Greene and Lafayette that the vessels could be repaired as easily
in Narragansett Bay as in Boston har-
bour; that by the voyage around Cape
Cod, in his crippled condition, he would
only incur additional risk; that by staying he
would strictly fulfil the spirit of his instructions;
that an army had been brought here, and stores
collected, in reliance upon his aid; that if the expedition were to be ruined through his failure to
coöperate, it would sully the honour of France
and give rise to hard feelings in America; and
finally, that even if he felt constrained, in spite
of sound arguments, to go and refit at Boston,
there was no earthly reason for his taking the
4,000 French soldiers with him. The count was
quite disposed to yield to these sensible remon-
strances, but on calling a council of war he found
himself overruled by his officers. Estaing was
not himself a naval officer, but a lieutenant-general in the army, and it has been said that the
officers of his fleet, vexed at having a land-lubber
put over them, were glad of a chance to thwart
him in his plans. However this may have been, it

*Estaing goes
to Boston, to
refit his ships.*

was voted that the letter of the royal instructions must be blindly adhered to, and so on the 23d Estaing weighed anchor for Boston, taking the land forces with him, and leaving General Sullivan in the lurch.

Great was the exasperation in the American camp. Sullivan's vexation found indiscreet expression in a general order, in which he hoped the event would prove America " able to procure that by her own arms which her allies refuse to assist in obtaining." But the insubordination of the

Yeomanry go
home in dis-
gust.

volunteers now came in to complicate the matter. Some 3,000 of them, despairing of success and impatient at being kept from home in harvest time, marched away in disgust and went about their business, thus reducing Sullivan's army to the same size as that of the enemy. The investment of Newport, by land had already been completed, but the speedy success of the enterprise depended upon a superiority of force, and in case of British reinforcements arriving from New York the American situation would become dangerous. Upon these grounds, Sullivan, on the 28th, decided to retreat to the strong position at Butts Hill, and await events. Lafayette mounted his horse and rode the seventy miles to Boston in seven hours, to beg his kinsman to return as soon as possible. Estaing despaired of getting his ships ready for many days, but, catching a spark of the young man's enthusiasm, he offered to bring up his troops by land. Fired with fresh hope, the young marquis spurred back as fast as he had come, but when he arrived

on the scene of action all was over. As soon as
Sullivan's retreat was perceived the whole British
army gave chase. After the Americans had retired to their lines on Butts Hill, Sir Robert Pigott
tried to carry their position by storm, and there
ensued an obstinate fight, in which the $\quad$ Battle of
conditions were in many respects sim- Butts Hill,
ilar to those of Bunker Hill; but this $\quad$ Aug. 29, 1778.
time the Americans had powder enough, and the
British were totally defeated. This slaughter of
their brave men was useless. The next day Sullivan received a dispatch from Washington, with
the news that Clinton had started from New York
with 5,000 men to reinforce Sir Robert Pigott.
Under these circumstances, it was rightly thought
best to abandon the island. The services of General Glover, who had taken Washington's army
across the East River after the defeat of Long
Island, and across the Delaware before the victory of Trenton, were called into requi- The enter-
sition, and all the men and stores were prise aban-
ferried safely to the mainland; Lafay- doned.
ette arriving from Boston just in time to bring off
the pickets and covering-parties. The next day
Clinton arrived with his 5,000 men, and the siege
of Newport was over.

The failure of this enterprise excited much indignation, and seemed to justify the distrust with
which so many people regarded the French alliance. In Boston the ill-feeling found vent in a
riot on the wharves between French and American
sailors, and throughout New England there was

loud discontent. It required all Washington's tact
to keep peace between the ill-yoked allies.   When
Congress passed a politic resolution approving the
course of the French commander, it met with no
cordial assent from the people.   When,
in November, Estaing took his fleet to
the West Indies, for purposes solely
French, the feeling was one of lively disgust, which
was heightened by an indiscreet proclamation of
the count inviting the people of Canada to return
to their old allegiance.   For the American people
regarded the work of Pitt as final, and at no time
during the war did their feeling against Great
Britain rise to such a point as to make them willing to see the French restored to their old position
on this continent.   The sagacious Vergennes understood this so well that Estaing's proclamation
found little favour in his eyes.   But it served none
the less to irritate the Americans, and especially
the people of New England.

So far as the departure of the fleet for the West
Indies was concerned, the American complaints
were not wholly reasonable ; for the operations of
the French in that quarter helped materially to
diminish the force which Great Britain could spare
for the war in the United States.   On the very day
of Estaing's departure, Sir Henry Clinton was
obliged to send 5,000 men from New York to take
part in the West India campaign.   This new pressure put upon England by the necessity of warding
off French attack went on increasing.   In 1779
England had 314,000 men under arms in various
parts of the world, but she had so many points to

Unpopularity of the French alliance.

defend that it was difficult for her to maintain a
sufficient force in America. In the autumn of that
year, Sir Henry Clinton did not regard his position in New York as secure enough to justify him
any longer in sparing troops for the occupation of
Newport, and the island was accordingly
evacuated. From this time till the end
of the war, the only point which the
British succeeded in holding, north of Virginia,
was the city of New York. After the Rhode Island campaign of 1778, no further operations occurred at the North between the two principal
armies which could properly be said to constitute
a campaign. Clinton's resources were too slender
for him to do anything but hold New York. Washington's resources were too slender for him to do
anything but sit and watch Clinton. While the
two commanders-in-chief thus held each other at
bay, the rapid and violent work of the war was
going on in the southern states, conducted by subordinate officers. During much of this time Washington's army formed a cordon about Manhattan
Island, from Danbury in Connecticut to Elizabeth-
town in New Jersey, and thus blockaded the enemy. But while there were no decisive military
operations in the northern states during this period, many interesting and important events occurred which demand consideration before we go
on to treat of the great southern campaigns which
ended the war.

Stagnation of
the war in the
northern
states.

CHAPTER XI.

WAR ON THE FRONTIER.

THE barbarous border fighting of the Revolutionary War was largely due to the fact that powerful tribes of wild Indians still confronted us on every part of our steadily advancing frontier. They would have tortured and scalped our backwoodsmen even if we had had no quarrel with George III., and there could be no lasting peace until they were crushed completely. When the war broke out, their alliance with the British was natural, but the truculent spirit which sought to put that savage alliance to the worst uses was something which it would not be fair to ascribe to the British commanders in general; it must be charged to the account of Lord George Germain and a few unworthy men who were willing to be his tools.

In the summer of 1778 this horrible border warfare became the most conspicuous feature of the struggle, and has afforded themes for poetry and romance, in which the figures of the principal actors are seen in a lurid light. One of these figures is of such importance as to deserve especial mention. Joseph Brant, or Thayendanegea, was perhaps the greatest Indian of whom we have any knowledge; cer-

Joseph Brant, missionary and war-chief.

tainly the history of the red men presents no more
many-sided and interesting character. A pure-
blooded Mohawk, descended from a line of distinguished chiefs,[1] in early boyhood he became a favourite with Sir William Johnson, and the laughing
black eyes of his handsome sister, Molly Brant, so
fascinated the rough baronet that he took her to
Johnson Hall as his wife, after the Indian fashion.
Sir William believed that Indians could be tamed
and taught the arts of civilized life, and he laboured
with great energy, and not without some success,
in this difficult task. The young Thayendanegea
was sent to be educated at the school in Lebanon,
Connecticut, which was afterwards transferred to
New Hampshire and developed into Dartmouth
College. At this school he not only became expert
in the use of the English language, in which he
learned to write with elegance and force, but he
also acquired some inkling of general literature
and history. He became a member of the Episcopal Church, and after leaving school he was for
some time engaged in missionary work among the
Mohawks, and translated the Prayer-Book and
parts of the New Testament into his native language. He was a man of earnest and serious character, and his devotion to the church endured

[1] He has been sometimes described incorrectly as a half-breed,
and even as a son of Sir William Johnson. His father was a Mohawk, of the Wolf clan, and son of one of the five chiefs who
visited the court of Queen Anne in 1710. The name is sometimes
wrongly written "Brandt." The Indian name is pronounced as
if written "Thayendanauga," with accent on penult. Brant was
not a sachem. His eminence was personal, not official. See
Morgan, *League of the Iroquois,* p. 103.

throughout his life. Some years after the peace of 1783, the first Episcopal church ever built in Upper Canada was erected by Joseph Brant, from funds which he had collected for the purpose while on a visit to England. But with this character of devout missionary and earnest student Thayenda-negea combined, in curious contrast, the attributes of an Iroquois war-chief developed to the highest degree of efficiency. There was no accomplishment prized by Indian braves in which he did not outshine all his fellows. He was early called to take the war-path. In the fierce struggle with Pontiac he fought with great distinction on the English side, and at the beginning of the War of Independence he was one of the most conspicuous of Iroquois war-chiefs.

It was the most trying time that had ever come to these haughty lords of the wilderness, and called for all the valour and diplomacy which they could summon. Brant was equal to the occasion, and no chieftain ever fought a losing cause with greater spirit than he. We have seen how at Oriskany he came near turning the scale against us in one of the critical moments of a great campaign. From the St. Lawrence to the Susquehanna his name became a name of terror. Equally skilful and zealous, now in planning the silent night march and deadly ambush, now in preaching the gospel of peace, he reminds one of some newly re-claimed Frisian or Norman warrior of the Carolin-gian age. But in the eighteenth century the incongruity is more striking than in the tenth, in so far as the traits of the barbarian are more vividly projected against the background of a higher civilization. It is odd to think of Thayendanegea, who could outyell any of his tribe on the battlefield, sitting at table with Burke and Sheridan, and behaving with the modest grace of an English gentleman. The tincture of civilization he had acquired, moreover, was by no means superficial. Though engaged in many a murderous attack, his conduct was not marked by the ferocity so characteristic of the Iroquois. Though he sometimes approved the slaying of prisoners on grounds of public policy, he was flatly opposed to torture, and never would allow it. He often went out of his way to rescue women and children from the tomahawk, and the instances of his magnanimity toward suppliant enemies were very numerous.

At the beginning of the war the influence of the Johnsons had kept all the Six Nations on the side of the Crown, except the Oneidas and Tuscaroras, who were prevailed upon by New England missionaries to maintain an attitude of neutrality. The Indians in general were quite incapable of understanding the issue involved in the contest, but Brant had some comprehension of it, and looked at the matter with Tory eyes. The loyalists in central New York were numerous, but the patriot party was the stronger, and such fierce enmities were aroused in this frontier society that most of the Tories were obliged to abandon their homes and flee to the wilds of western New York and Upper Canada, where they made the beginnings of the first English settlement in that country. There, under

The Tories of western New York.

their leaders, the Johnsons, with Colonel John Butler and his son Walter, they had their headquarters at Fort Niagara, where they were joined by Brant with his Mohawks. Secure in the possession of that remote stronghold, they made it the starting-point of their frequent and terrible excursions against the communities which had cast them forth. These rough frontiersmen, many of them Scotch Highlanders of the old stripe, whose raiding and reaving propensities had been little changed by their life in an American wilderness, were in every way fit comrades for their dusky allies. Clothed in blankets and moccasins, decked with beads and feathers, and hideous in war-paint, it was not easy to distinguish them from the stalwart barbarians whose fiendish cruelties they often imitated and sometimes surpassed. Border tradition tells of an Indian who, after murdering a young mother with her three children, as they sat by the evening fireside, was moved to pity by the sight of a little infant sweetly smiling at him from its cradle ; but his Tory comrade picked up the babe with the point of his bayonet, and, as he held it writhing in mid-air, exclaimed, " Is not this also a d—d rebel ? " There are many tales of like import, and whether always true or not they seem to show the reputation which these wretched men had won. The Tory leaders took less pains than Thayendanegea to prevent useless slaughter, and some of the atrocities permitted by Walter Butler have never been outdone in the history of savage warfare.

During the year 1778 the frontier became the

scene of misery such as had not been witnessed
since the time of Pontiac. Early in July there
came a blow at which the whole country stood
aghast. The valley of Wyoming, situated in
northeastern Pennsylvania, where the Susquehanna
makes its way through a huge cleft in
the mountains, had become celebrated The valley of Wyoming and
for the unrivalled fertility and beauty its settlers from Connecticut.
which, like the fatal gift of some un-
friendly power, served only to make it an occasion
of strife. The lovely spot lay within the limits of
the charter of Connecticut, granted in 1662, according to which that colony or plantation was to extend westward to the Pacific Ocean. It also lay
within the limits of the charter of 1681, by which
the proprietary colony of Pennsylvania had been
founded. About one hundred people from Connecticut had settled in Wyoming in 1762, but
within a year this little settlement was wiped out
in blood and fire by the Delaware Indians. In
1768 some Pennsylvanians began to settle in the
valley, but they were soon ousted by a second detachment of Yankees, and for three years a min-
iature war was kept up, with varying fortunes,
until at last the Connecticut men, under Zebulon
Butler and Lazarus Stewart, were victorious. In
1771 the question was referred to the law-officers
of the Crown, and the claim of Connecticut was
sustained. Settlers now began to come rapidly, —
the forerunners of that great New England migra-
tion which in these latter days has founded so
many thriving states in the West. By the year
1778 the population of the valley exceeded 3,000,

distributed in several pleasant hamlets, with town-meetings, schools and churches, and all the characteristics of New England orderliness and thrift. Most of the people were from Connecticut, and were enthusiastic and devoted patriots, but in 1776 a few settlers from the Hudson valley had come in, and, exhibiting Tory sympathies, were soon after expelled. Here was an excellent opportunity for the loyalist border ruffians to wreak summary vengeance upon their enemies. Here was a settlement peculiarly exposed in position, regarded with no friendly eyes by its Pennsylvania neighbours, and, moreover, ill provided with defenders, for it had sent the best part of its trained militia to serve in Washington's army.

These circumstances did not escape the keen eye of Colonel John Butler, and in June, 1778, he took the war-path from Niagara, with a company of his own rangers, a regiment of Johnson's Greens, and a band of Senecas; in all about 1,200 men. Reaching the Susquehanna, they glided down the swift stream in bark canoes, landed a little above the doomed settlement, and began their work of murder and pillage. Conster-

Massacre at Wyoming, July 3, 1778.

nation filled the valley. The women and children were huddled in a block-house, and Colonel Zebulon Butler, with 300 men, went out to meet the enemy. There seemed to be no choice but to fight, though the odds were so desperate. As the enemy came in sight, late in the afternoon of July 3d, the patriots charged upon them, and for about an hour there was a fierce struggle, till, overwhelmed by weight of numbers, the little band of defenders broke and fled. Some made their way to the fort, and a few escaped to the mountains, but nearly all were overtaken and slain, save such as were reserved for the horrors of the night. The second anniversary of independence was ushered in with dreadful orgies in the valley of Wyoming. Some of the prisoners were burned at the stake, some were laid upon hot embers and held down with pitchforks till they died, some were hacked with knives. Sixteen poor fellows were arranged in a circle, while an old half-breed hag, known as Queen Esther, and supposed to be a granddaughter of the famous Frontenac, danced slowly around the ring, shrieking a death-song as she slew them one after the other with her tomahawk.

The next day, when the fort surrendered, no more lives were taken, but the Indians plundered and burned all the houses, while the inhabitants fled to the woods or to the nearest settlements on the Lehigh and Delaware, and the vale of Wyoming was for a time abandoned. Dreadful sufferings attended the flight. A hundred women and children perished of fatigue and starvation in trying to cross the swamp, which has since been known to this day as the "Shades of Death." Several children were born in that fearful spot, only to die there with their unhappy mothers. Such horrors needed no exaggeration in the telling, yet from the confused reports of the fugitives, magnified by popular rumour, a tale of wholesale slaughter went abroad which was even worse than the reality, but which careful research has long since completely disproved.

The popular reputation of Brant as an incarnate demon rests largely upon the part which he was formerly supposed to have taken in the devastation of Wyoming. But the " monster Brant," who figures so conspicuously in Campbell's celebrated poem, was not even present on this occasion. Thayendanegea was at that time at Niagara. It was not long, however, before he was concerned

Massacre at Cherry Valley, Nov. 10.

in a bloody affair in which Walter Butler was principal. The village of Cherry Valley, in central New York, was destroyed on the 10th of November by a party of 700 Tories and Indians. All the houses were burned, and about fifty of the inhabitants murdered, without regard to age or sex.[1] Many other atrocious things were done in the course of this year; but the affairs of Wyoming and Cherry Valley made a deeper impression than any of the others. Among the victims there were many refined gentlemen and ladies, well known in the northern states, and this was especially the case of Cherry Valley.

Washington made up his mind that exemplary vengeance must be taken, and the source of the evil extinguished as far as possible. An army of

Sullivan's expedition.

5,000 men was sent out in the summer of 1779, with instructions to lay waste the country of the hostile Iroquois and capture the nest of Tory miscreants at Fort Niagara. The command of the expedition was offered to

---

[1] It has been shown that on this occasion Thayendanegea did what he could to restrain the ferocity of his savage followers. See Stone's *Life of Brant,* i. 379–381.

Gates, and when he testily declined it, as requiring too much hard work from a man of his years, it was given to Sullivan. To prepare such an army for penetrating to a depth of four hundred miles through the forest was no light task; and before they had reached the Iroquois country, Brant had sacked the town of Minisink and annihilated a force of militia sent to oppose him. Yet the expedition was well timed for the purpose of destroying the growing crops of the enemy. The army advanced in two divisions. The right wing, under General James Clinton, proceeded up the valley of the Mohawk as far as Canajoharie, and then turned to the southwest; while the left wing, under Sullivan himself, ascended the Susquehanna. On the 22d of August the two columns met at Tioga, and one week later they found the enemy at Newtown, on the site of the present town of Elmira, — 1,500 Tories and Indians, led by Sir John Johnson in person, with both the Butlers and Thayendanegea. In the battle which ensued, the enemy was routed with great slaughter, while the American loss was less than fifty. No further resistance was made, but the army was annoyed in every possible way, and stragglers were now and then caught and tortured to death. On one occasion, a young lieutenant, named Boyd, was captured while leading a scouting party, and fell into the hands of one of the Butlers, who threatened to give him up to torture unless he should disclose whatever he knew of General Sullivan's plans. On his refusal, he was given into the hands of a Seneca demon,

Battle of Newtown, Aug. 29, 1779.

named Little Beard; and after being hacked and plucked to pieces with a refinement of cruelty which the pen refuses to describe, his torments were ended by disembowelling.

Such horrors served only to exasperate the American troops, and while they do not seem to have taken life unnecessarily, they certainly carried out their orders with great zeal and thoroughness. The Iroquois tribes were so far advanced in the agricultural stage of development that they were much more dependent upon their crops than upon the chase for subsistence; and they had besides learned some of the arts of civilization from their white neighbours. Their long wigwams were

Devastation of the Iroquois country. beginning to give place to framed houses, with chimneys; their extensive fields were planted with corn and beans; and their orchards yielded apples, pears, and peaches in immense profusion. All this prosperity was now brought to an end. From Tioga the American army marched through the entire country of the Cayugas and Senecas, laying waste the cornfields, burning the houses, and cutting down all the fruit-trees. More than forty villages, the largest containing 128 houses, were razed to the ground. So terrible a vengeance had not overtaken the Long House since the days of Frontenac. The region thus devastated had come to be the most important domain of the Confederacy, which never recovered from the blow thus inflicted. The winter of 1779–80 was one of the coldest ever known in America, — so cold that the harbour of New York was frozen solid enough to bear troops and artillery,[1] while the British in the city, deprived of the aid of their fleet, spent the winter in daily dread of attack. During this extreme season the houseless Cayugas and Senecas were overtaken by famine and pestilence, and the diminution in their numbers was never afterwards made good. The stronghold at Niagara, however, was not wrested from Thayendanegea. That part of Sullivan's expedition was a failure. From increasing sickness among the soldiers and want of proper food, he deemed it impracticable to take his large force beyond the Genesee river, and accordingly he turned back toward the seaboard, arriving in New Jersey at the end of October, after a total march of more than seven hundred miles.

Though so much harrying had been done, the snake was only scotched, after all. Nothing short of the complete annihilation of the savage enemy would have put a stop to his inroads. Before winter was over dire vengeance fell upon the Oneidas, who were now regarded by their brethren as traitors to the Confederacy; they were utterly crushed by Thayendanegea. For two years more the tomahawk and firebrand were busy in the Mohawk valley. It was a reign of terror. Block-houses were erected in every neighbourhood, into which forty or fifty families could crowd together at the first note of alarm. The farmers ploughed and harvested in companies, keeping their rifles within easy reach, while pickets and scouts peered in every direction

Reign of terror in the Mohawk valley.

[1] Cannon were wheeled on the solid ice from Staten Island to the city. See Stone's *Life of Brant,* ii. 54.

for signs of the stealthy foe. In battles with the militia, of which there were several, the enemy, with his greatly weakened force, was now generally worsted; but nothing could exceed the boldness of his raids. On one or two occasions he came within a few miles of Albany. Once a small party of Tories actually found their way into the city, with intent to assassinate General Schuyler, and came very near succeeding. In no other part of the United States did the war entail so much suffering as on the New York border. During the five years ending with 1781, the population of Tryon county was reduced by two thirds of its amount, and in the remaining third there were more than three hundred widows and two thousand orphan children.

This cruel warfare, so damaging to the New York frontier settlements and so fatal to the Six Nations, was really part of a desultory conflict which raged at intervals from north to south along our whole western border, and resulted in the total overthrow of British authority beyond the

The wilderness beyond the Alleghanies. Alleghanies. The vast region between these mountains and the Mississippi river — a territory more than twice as large as the German Empire — was at that time an almost unbroken wilderness. A few French towns garrisoned by British troops, as at Natchez, Kaskaskia, and Cahokia on the Mississippi river, at Vincennes, on the Wabash, and at Detroit, sufficed to represent the sovereignty of George III., and to exercise a very dubious control over the wild tribes that roamed through these primeval solitudes. When the thirteen colonies declared themselves independent of the British Crown, the ownership of this western territory was for the moment left undecided. Portions of it were claimed by Massachusetts, Connecticut, New York, Virginia, North Carolina, and Georgia, on the strength of their old charters or of their relations with the Indian tribes. Little respect, however, was paid to the quaint terminology of charters framed in an age when almost nothing was known of American geography; and it was virtually left for circumstances to determine to whom the western country should belong. It was now very fortunate for the United States that the policy of Pitt had wrested this all-important territory from the French. For to conquer from the British enemy so remote a region was feasible ; but to have sought to obtain it from a power with which we were forming an alliance would have been difcult indeed.

The commanding approach to this territory was by the town and fortress of Pittsburgh, the " Gateway of the West," from which, through the Ohio river and its tributary streams, an army might penetrate with comparative ease to any part of the vast Mississippi valley. The possession of this gateway had for some years been a subject of dispute between Pennsylvania and Virginia. Though the question was ultimately settled in favour of Pennsylvania, yet for the present Virginia, which had the longest arm, kept her hold upon the commanding

Rivalry between Pennsylvania and Virginia for the possession of Fort Pitt.

citadel. To Virginia its possession was then a matter of peculiar importance, for her population had already begun to overflow its mountain barriers, and, pressing down the Ohio valley, had made the beginnings of the state of Kentucky. Virginia and North Carolina, lying farther westward than any of the other old states, were naturally the first to send colonies across the Alleghanies. It was not long before the beginning of the war that Daniel Boone had explored the Kentucky river, and that Virginia surveyors had gone down the Ohio as far as the present site of Louisville. Conflicts ensued with the Indians, so fierce and deadly that this region was long known as the " Dark and Bloody Ground."

During this troubled period, the hostile feeling between Pennsylvania and Virginia was nourished by the conflicting interests of the people of those two colonies in respect to the western country and its wild inhabitants. The Virginians entered the country as settlers, with intent to take possession of the soil and keep the Indians at a distance; but there were many people in Pennsylvania who reaped large profits from trade with the savages, and therefore did not wish to see them dispossessed of their border forests and driven westward. The Virginia frontiersmen were angry with the Pennsylvania traders for selling rifles and powder to the redskins, and buying from them horses stolen from white men. This, they alleged, was practically inciting the Indians to deeds of plunder and outrage. In the spring of 1774, there seemed to be serious danger of an outbreak of hostilities at

Fort Pitt, when the attention of Virginia was all at once absorbed in a brief but hard-fought war, which had a most important bearing upon the issue of the American struggle for independence.

This border war of 1774 has sometimes been known as " Cresap's War," but more recently, and with less impropriety, as " Lord Dunmore's War." It was conducted under the general direction of the Earl of Dunmore, last royal governor of Virginia ; and in the political excitement of the time there were some who believed that he actually contrived to stir up the war out of malice aforethought, in order to hamper the Virginians in their impending struggle with the mother-country. Dunmore's agent, or lieutenant, in western Virginia, Dr. John Connolly, was a violent and unscrupulous man, whose arrogance was as likely to be directed against friendly as against hostile Indians, and it was supposed that he acted under the earl's secret orders with intent to bring on a war. But the charge is ill-supported and quite improbable. According to some writers, the true cause of the war was the slaying of the whole family of the friendly chief Logan, and doubtless this event furnished the occasion for the outbreak of hostilities. It was conspicuous in a series of outrages that had been going on for years, such as are always apt to occur on the frontier between advancing civilization and resisting barbarism. John Logan, or Tagahjutè, was of Cayuga descent, a chief of the Mingos, a brave and honest man, of fine and stately presence. He had always been kind and hospitable to the English settlers,

Lord Dunmore's War, 1774.

perhaps in accordance with the traditional policy
of his Iroquois forefathers, — a tradition which by
1774 had lost much of its strength.   In April of
that year some Indian depredations occurred on
the upper Ohio, which led Dr. Connolly to issue
instructions, warning the settlers to be on their
guard, as an attack from the Shawnees was to be
Logan and   apprehended.   Captain Michael Cresap
Cresap.   was a pioneer from Maryland, a brave
man and sterling patriot ; but as for the Indians,
his feelings toward them were like those of most
backwoodsmen.   Cresap not unnaturally interpreted the instructions from Dunmore's lieutenant
as equivalent to a declaration of war, and he proceeded forthwith to slay and scalp some friendly
Shawnees.   As is apt to be the case with reprisals
and other unreasoning forms of popular vengeance,
the blow fell in the wrong quarter, and innocent
people were made scapegoats for the guilty.   Cresap's party next started off to attack Logan's camp
at Yellow Creek; but presently bethinking themselves of Logan's well-known friendliness toward
the whites, as they argued with one another, they
repented of their purpose, and turned their steps
in another direction.   But hard by the Mingo
encampment a wretch named Greathouse had set
up a whiskey shop, and thither, on the last day of
April, repaired Logan's family, nine thirsty barbarians, male and female, old and young.   When
they had become dead drunk, Greathouse and two
or three of his cronies illustrated their peculiar
view of the purport of Connolly's instructions by
butchering them all in cold blood.   The Indians

of the border needed no stronger provocation for rushing to arms. Within a few days Logan's men had taken a dozen scalps, half of them from young children. Mingos and Shawnees were joined by Wyandots, Delawares, and Senecas, and the dismal tale of blazing cabins and murdered women was renewed all along the frontier. It was in vain that Lord Dunmore and his lieutenant disclaimed responsibility for the massacre at Yellow Creek. The blame was by all the Indians and many of the whites laid upon Cresap, whose name has been handed down to posterity as that of the arch-villain in this rough border romance. The pathetic speech of the bereaved Logan to Dunmore's envoy, John Gibson, was preserved and immortalized by Jefferson in his "Notes on Virginia," and has been declaimed by thousands of American school-boys. In his comments Jefferson spoke of Cresap as " a man infamous for the many murders he had committed upon these injured people." Jefferson here simply gave voice to the tradition which had started into full life as early as June, 1774, when Sir William Johnson wrote that " a certain Mr. Cressop had trepanned and murdered forty Indians on the Ohio, . . . and that the unworthy author of this wanton act is fled." The charge made by Jefferson was answered at the time, but continued to live on in tradition, until finally disposed of in 1851 by Brantz Mayer.[1] The origin of the misconception is doubtless to be traced to the insignificance of

---

[1] In a paper read before the Maryland Historical Society. See also his *Logan and Cresap*, Albany, 1867. The story is well told by Mr. Theodore Roosevelt, in his admirable book, *The Winning*

Greathouse. In trying to shield himself, Connolly deposed Cresap from command, but he was presently reinstated by Lord Dunmore.

In June of the next year, Captain Cresap marched to Cambridge at the head of 130 Maryland riflemen ; but during the early autumn he was seized with illness, and while making his way homeward Death of
Cresap. died at New York, at the age of thirty-three. His grave is still to be seen in Trinity churchyard, near the door of the north transept. The Indian chief with whose name his has so long been associated was some time afterwards tomahawked by a brother Indian, in the course of a drunken affray.

The war thus ushered in by the Yellow Creek massacre was an event of cardinal importance in the history of our western frontier. It was ended by the decisive battle at Point Pleasant, on the Great Kanawha (October 10, 1774), in which the Indians, under the famous Shawnee chief Cornstalk, were totally defeated by the backwoodsmen under Andrew Lewis. This defeat so cowed the Battle of
Point Pleasant
and its conse-
quences. Indians that they were fain to purchase peace by surrendering all their claims upon the hunting-grounds south of the Ohio. It kept the northwestern tribes comparatively quiet during the first two years of the Revolutionary War, and thus opened the way for white settlers to rush into Kentucky. The four years

of the West, New York, 1889. Though I leave the present chapter mainly as it was written in 1883, I have, in revising it for publication, derived one or two valuable hints from Mr. Roosevelt's work.

following the battle of Point Pleasant saw remarkable and portentous changes on the frontier. It was just at the beginning of Lord Dunmore's war that Parliament passed the Quebec Act, of which the practical effect, had it ever been enforced, would have been the extension of Canada southward to the Ohio river. In contravention of old charters, it would have deprived the American colonies of the great northwestern territory. But the events that followed upon Lord Dunmore's war soon rendered this part of the Quebec Act a nullity.

In 1775, Richard Henderson of North Carolina purchased from the Cherokees the tract between the Kentucky and Cumberland rivers, and at the same time Boonesborough and Harrodsburg were founded by Daniel Boone and James Harrod. As a party of these bold backwoodsmen were encamping near the sources of the southern fork of the Licking, they heard the news of the victory which ushered in the War of Independence, and forthwith gave the name of Lexington to the place of their encampment, on which a thriving city now stands. These new settlements were not long in organizing themselves into a state, which they called Transylvania. Courts were instituted, laws enacted, and a militia enrolled, and a delegate was sent to the Continental Congress; but finding that Virginia still claimèd their allegiance, they yielded their pretensions to autonomy, and were organized for the present as a county of the mother state. The so-called " county " of Kentucky, comprising the whole of the present state of that name, with an area one fourth larger than that of Scotland, was indeed of formidable dimensions for a county.

The settlement of Tennessee was going on at and of eastern the same time. The movement of pop-
Tennessee. ulation for some time had a southwest-
ward trend along the great valleys inclosed by the Appalachian ranges, so that frontiersmen from Pennsylvania found their way down the Shenan-doah, and thence the stream of Virginian migra-tion reached the Watauga, the Holston, and the French Broad, in the midst of the most magnifi-cent scenery east of the Rocky Mountains. At the same time there was a westward movement from North Carolina across the Great Smoky range, and the defeat of the Regulators by Gov-ernor Tryon at the battle of the Alamance in 1771 no doubt did much to give strength and volume to this movement. The way was prepared in 1770 by James Robertson, who penetrated the wilder-ness as far as the banks of the Watauga. Forts were soon erected there and on the Nolichucky. The settlement grew apace, and soon came into conflict with the most warlike and powerful of the southern tribes of Indians. The Cherokees, like the Iroquois at the North, had fought on the Eng-lish side in the Seven Years' War, and had ren-dered some service, though of small value, at the capture of Fort Duquesne. Early in the Revolu-tionary War fierce feuds with the encroaching set-tlers led them to take sides with the British, and in company with Tory guerrillas they ravaged the frontier. In 1776, the Watauga settlement was

attacked, and invasions were made into Georgia and South Carolina. But the blow re- coiled upon the Cherokees. Their country was laid waste by troops from the Carolinas, under Andrew Williamson and Griffith Rutherford; their attack upon the Watauga settlement was defeated by James Robertson and John Sevier; and in 1777 they were forced to make treaties renouncing for the most part their claims upon the territory between the Tennessee and the Cumberland rivers.

Defeat of the Cherokees on the Watauga.

Robertson and Sevier were the most commanding and picturesque figures in Tennessee history until Andrew Jackson came upon the scene ; and their military successes, moreover, like those of " Old Hickory," were of the utmost importance to the whole country. This was especially true of their victory at the Watauga ; for had the settlement there been swept away by the savages, it would have uncovered the great Wilderness Road to Lexington and Harrodsburg, and the Kentucky settlement, thus fatally isolated, would very likely have had to be abandoned. The Watauga victory thus helped to secure in 1776 the ground won two years before at the Great Kanawha.[1]

Its consequences.

Such were the beginnings of Kentucky and Tennessee, and such was the progress already made to the west of the mountains, when the next and longest step was taken by George Rogers Clark. During the years 1776 and 1777,

George Rogers Clark.

[1] This point has been well elucidated by Mr. Roosevelt in his *Winning of the West*, vol. i. pp. 240, 306.

Colonel Henry Hamilton, the British commander at Detroit, was busily engaged in preparing a general attack of Indian tribes upon the northwestern frontier. Such concerted action among these barbarians was difficult to organize, and the moral effect of Lord Dunmore's war doubtless served to postpone it. There were isolated assaults, however, upon Boonesborough and Wheeling and in the neighbourhood of Pittsburgh. While Hamilton was thus scheming and intriguing, a gallant young Virginian was preparing a most effective counter - stroke. In the late autumn of 1777, George Rogers Clark, then just twenty-five years old, was making his way back from Kentucky along the Wilderness Road, and heard with exultation the news of Burgoyne's surrender. Clark was a man of bold originality. He had been well educated by that excellent Scotch school-master, Donald Robertson, among whose pupils was James Madison. In 1772, Clark was practising the profession of a land surveyor upon the upper Ohio, and he rendered valuable service as a scout in the campaign of the Great Kanawha. For skill in woodcraft, as for indomitable perseverance and courage, he had few equals. He was a man of picturesque and stately presence, like an old Norse viking, tall and massive, with ruddy cheeks, auburn hair, and piercing blue eyes sunk deep under thick yellow brows.

When he heard of the " convention " of Saratoga, Clark was meditating a stroke as momentous in the annals of the Mississippi valley as Burgoyne's overthrow in the annals of the Hudson.

He had sent spies through the Illinois country, without giving them any inkling of his purpose, and from what he could gather from their reports he had made up his mind that by a bold and sudden movement the whole region could be secured and the British commander checkmated. On arriving in Virginia, he laid his scheme before Governor Patrick Henry; and Jefferson, Wythe, and Madison were also taken into his confidence. The plan met with warm approval; but as secrecy and dispatch were indispensable, it would not do to consult the legislature, and little could be done beyond authorizing the adventurous young man to raise a force of 350 men and collect material of war at Pittsburgh. People supposed that his object was merely to defend the Kentucky settlements. Clark had a hard winter's work in enlisting men, but at length in May, 1778, having collected a flotilla of boats and a few pieces of light artillery, he started from Pittsburgh with 180 picked riflemen, and rowed swiftly down the Ohio river a thousand miles to its junction with the Mississippi. The British garrison at Kaskaskia had been removed, to strengthen the posts at Detroit and Niagara, and the town was an easy prey. Hiding his boats in a creek, Clark marched across the prairie, and seized the place without resistance. The French inhabitants were not ill-disposed toward the change, especially when they heard of the new alliance between the United States and Louis XVI., and Clark showed consummate skill in playing upon their feelings. Cahokia and two other neighbour-

Clark's conquest of the northwestern territory, 1778.

ing villages were easily persuaded to submit, and
the Catholic priest Gibault volunteered to carry
Clark's proposals to Vincennes, on the Wabash;
upon receiving the message this important post
likewise submitted. As Clark had secured the
friendship of the Spanish commandant at St.
Louis, he felt secure from molestation for the
present, and sent a party home to Virginia with
the news of his bloodless conquest. The territory
north of the Ohio was thus annexed to Virginia as
the "county" of Illinois, and a force of 500 men
was raised for its defence.

When these proceedings came to the ears of
Colonel Hamilton at Detroit, he started out with a
little army of about 500 men, regulars, Tories, and
Indians, and after a march of seventy days through
the primeval forest reached Vincennes, and took
possession of it. He spent the winter intriguing
with the Indian tribes, and threatened the Spanish
governor at St. Louis with dire vengeance if he
should lend aid or countenance to the nefarious
proceedings of the American rebels. Meanwhile,
the crafty Virginian was busily at work. Sending
a few boats, with light artillery and provisions, to
ascend the Ohio and Wabash, Clark started overland from Kaskaskia with 130 men;
and after an arduous winter march of
sixteen days across the drowned lands
in what is now the state of Illinois, he appeared
before Vincennes in time to pick up his boats and
cannon. In the evening of February 23d the town
surrendered, and the townspeople willingly assisted
in the assault upon the fort. After a brisk can-

Capture of
Vincennes,
Feb. 23, 1779.

nonade and musket-fire for twenty hours, Hamilton surrendered at discretion, and British authority in this region was forever at an end.[1] An expedition descending from Pittsburgh in boats had already captured Natchez and ousted the British from the lower Mississippi. Shortly after, the Cherokees and other Indians whom Hamilton had incited to take the war-path were overwhelmed by Colonel Shelby, and on the upper Ohio and Alleghany the Indian country was so thoroughly devastated by Colonel Brodhead that all along the frontier there reigned a profound peace, instead of the carnival of burning and scalping which the British commander had contemplated.

The stream of immigration now began to flow steadily. Fort Jefferson was established on the Mississippi river to guard the mouth of the Ohio. Another fortress, higher up on the beautiful river which La Salle had discovered and Clark had conquered, became the site of Louisville, so named in honour of our ally, the French king. James Robertson again appeared on the scene, and became the foremost pioneer in middle Tennessee, as he had already led the colonization of the eastern part of that great state. On a bold bluff on the southern bank of the Cumberland river, Robertson founded a city, which took its name from the gallant General Nash, who fell in the battle of Germantown; and among the cities of the fair South there is to-day none more thriving than Nashville. Thus by degrees was our

Settlement of middle Tennessee.

[1] Mr. Roosevelt's account of Clark's expedition (vol. ii. pp. 31-90) is extremely graphic and spirited.

grasp firmly fastened upon the western country, and year by year grew stronger.

In the gallery of our national heroes, George Rogers Clark deserves a conspicuous and honourable place. It was due to his boldness and sagacity that when our commissioners at Paris, in 1782, were engaged in their difficult and delicate work of thwarting our not too friendly French ally, while arranging terms of peace with the British enemy, the fortified posts on the Mississippi and the Wabash were held by American garrisons. Possession is said to be nine points in the law, and while Spain and France were intriguing to keep us out of the Mississippi valley, we were in possession of it. The military enterprise of Clark was crowned by the diplomacy of Jay.[1] The four cardinal events in the history of our western frontier during the Revolution are : (1) the defeat of the Shawnees and their allies at Point Pleasant in 1774; (2) the defeat of the Cherokees on the Watauga in 1776; (3) Clark's conquest of the Illinois country in 1778–79; (4) the detection and thwarting of the French diplomacy in 1782 by Jay. When Washington took command of the Continental army at Cambridge, in 1775, the population and jurisdiction of the thirteen united commonwealths scarcely reached beyond the Alleghanies; it was due to the series of events here briefly recounted that when he laid down his command at Annapolis, in 1783, the domain of the independent United States was bounded on the west by the Mississippi river.

Importance of Clark's conquest.

[1] See my *Critical Period of American History*, chap. i.

Clark's last years were spent in poverty and obscurity at his sister's home, near Louisville, where he died in 1818. It was his younger brother, William Clark, who in company with Meriwether Lewis made the famous expedition to the Columbia river in 1804, thus giving the United States a hold upon Oregon.

To return to our story, — Lord George Germain's plan for breaking the spirit of the Americans, in so far as it depended upon the barbarous aid which his Indian allies could render, had not thus far proved very successful. Terrible damage had been wrought on the frontier, especially in Pennsylvania and New York, but the net result had been to weaken the Indians and loosen the hold of the British upon the continent, while the American position was on the whole <small>Marauding ex-</small> strengthened. The warfare which the <small>peditions.</small> British themselves conducted in the north after the Newport campaign, degenerated into a series of marauding expeditions unworthy of civilized soldiers. They seem to have learned a bad lesson from their savage allies. While Sir Henry Clinton's force was beleaguered in New York, he now and then found opportunities for detaching some small force by sea, to burn and plunder defence-less villages on the coast, in accordance with Lord George's instructions. During the autumn of 1778 the pretty island of Martha's Vineyard was plundered from end to end, the towns of New Bedford and Fair Haven, with all the shipping in their harbours, were burned, and similar havoc was wrought on the coast of New Jersey. At Old Tappan some American dragoons, asleep in a barn, were captured by Sir Charles Grey's troops, — and thirty-seven of them were bayoneted in cold blood. Fifty-five light infantry belonging to Pulaski's legion were similarly surprised at night by Captain Ferguson and all but five were massacred. In May, 1779, General Mathews was sent with 2,500 men to Virginia, where he sacked the towns of Portsmouth and Norfolk, with cruelties worthy of a mediæval freebooter. Every house was burned to the ground, many unarmed citizens were murdered, and delicate ladies were abandoned to the diabolical passions of a brutal soldiery. In July the enterprising Tryon conducted a raiding expedition along the coast of Connecticut. At New Haven he burned the ships in the harbour and two or three streets of warehouses, and slew several citizens ; his intention was to burn the whole town, but the neighbouring yeomanry quickly swarmed in and drove the British to their ships. Next day the British landed at Fairfield and utterly destroyed it. Next they burned Green Farms and then Norwalk. After this, just as they were about to proceed against New London, they were suddenly recalled to New York by bad news.

Tryon's proceedings, July, 1779.

In so far as these barbarous raids had any assignable military purpose, it was hoped that they might induce Washington to weaken his force at the Highlands by sending troops into Connecticut to protect private property and chastise .the marauders. After the destruction of the Highland

forts in October, 1777, the defence of this most
important position had been entrusted to the powerful fortifications lately erected at West Point.
A little lower down the river two small but very
strong forts, at Stony Point on the right
bank and at Verplanck's Point on the
left, guarded the entrance to the Highlands. While the fort at Stony Point
was building, Sir Henry Clinton came up the river
and captured it, and then, with the aid of its batteries, subdued the opposite citadel also. Stony
Point was a rocky promontory washed on three
sides by the waters of the Hudson. It was separated from the mainland by a deep morass, over
which ran a narrow causeway that was covered at
high tide, but might be crossed when the water
was low. This natural stronghold was armed with
heavy batteries which commanded the morass, with
its causeway, and the river; and the British garrisoned it with six hundred men, and built two
additional lines of fortification, rendering it well-
nigh impregnable.

The acquisition of this spot seemed like the
auspicious beginning of a summer campaign for
Clinton's army, which had been cooped up in New
York ever since the battle of Monmouth. To
have kept on and captured West Point would
have gone a long way toward retrieving the disaster of Saratoga, but Washington's force was so
well disposed that Clinton did not venture to attempt so much as this. Such hopes, moreover, as
he may have based upon the Connecticut raids
proved entirely delusive. Washington's method

*Clinton cap-
tures the for-
tress at Stony
Point, May 31,
1779.*

of relieving Connecticut and destroying Clinton's scheme was different from what was expected. Among his generals was one whom the soldiers called " Mad Anthony " for his desperate bravery, but there was much more method than madness about Anthony Wayne. For the union of impetuous valour with a quick eye and a cool head, he was second to none. Twelve hundred light infantry were put at his disposal. Every dog within three miles was slaughtered, that no indiscreet bark might alarm the garrison. Not a gun was loaded, lest some untimely shot betray the approaching column. The bayonet was now to be put to more warlike use than the roasting of meat before a camp-fire. At midnight of the 15th of July the Americans crossed the causeway at low tide, and were close upon the outworks before their advance was discovered. The garrison sprang to arms, and a heavy fire was opened from the batteries, but Wayne's rush was rapid and

The storming of Stony Point, July 16, 1779.

sure. In two solid columns the Americans came up the slope so swiftly that the grape - shot made few victims. Shoulder to shoulder, in resistless mass, like the Theban phalanx of Epaminondas, they pressed over the works, heedless of obstacles, and within a few minutes the garrison surrendered at discretion. In this assault the Americans lost fifteen killed, and eighty-three wounded, and the British sixty-three killed. The rest of the garrison, 553 in number, including the wounded, were made prisoners, and not a man was killed in cold blood, though the shameful scenes in Virginia were fresh in men's memories, and

the embers of Fairfield and Norwalk still smoul-
dered. The contemporary British historian Stedman praises Wayne for his humanity, and thinks
that he " would have been fully justified in putting the garrison to the sword ; " but certainly no
laws or usages of war that have ever obtained in
America would have justified such a barbarous
proceeding, and Stedman's remark simply bears
unconscious testimony to the higher degree of humanity which American civilization had reached as
compared with the civilization of Europe.

The capture of Stony Point served the desired
purpose of relieving Connecticut, but the Americans held it but three days. Clinton Evacuation of
at once drew his forces together and Stony Point.
came up the Hudson, hoping to entice Washington into risking a battle for the sake of keeping his hold upon Stony Point. But Washington
knew better than to do so. In case of defeat he
would run risk of losing the far more important
position at West Point. He was not the man
to hazard his main citadel for the sake of an outpost. Finding that it would take more men than
he could spare to defend Stony Point against a
combined attack by land and water he ordered it
to be evacuated. The works were all destroyed,
and the garrison, with the cannon and stores, withdrawn into the Highlands. Sir Henry took possession of the place and held it for some time, but
did not venture to advance against Washington.
To give the British general a wholesome sense of
his adversary's vigilance, a blow was struck in an
unexpected quarter. At Paulus Hook, on the site

of the present Jersey City, the British had a very strong fort. The "Hook" was a long low neck of land reaching out into the Hudson. A sandy isthmus, severed by a barely fordable creek, connected it with the mainland. Within the line of the creek, a deep ditch had been dug across the whole isthmus, and this could only be crossed by means of a drawbridge. Within the ditch were two lines of intrenchments. The place was garrisoned by 500 men, but relying on the strength of their works and their distance from the American lines, the garrison had grown somewhat careless. This fact was made known to Washington by Major Henry Lee, who volunteered to surprise the fort. On the night of the 18th of August, at the head of 300 picked men, Lee crossed the creek which divided Paulus Hook from the mainland. A foraging expedition had been sent out in the course of the day, and as the Americans approached they were at first mistaken by the sentinels for the foragers returning. Favoured by this mistake, they surmounted all the obstacles and got possession of the fort in a twinkling. Alarm guns, quickly answered by the ships in the river and the forts on the New York side, warned them to retreat as fast as they had come, but not until Lee had secured 159 prisoners, whom he carried off safely to the Highlands, losing of his own men only two killed and three wounded. This exploit, worthy of the good Lord James Douglas, has no military significance save for its example of skill and boldness; but it deserves mention for the personal interest

Henry Lee's exploit at Paulus Hook.

which must ever attach to its author. In the youthful correspondence of Washington mention is made of a "Lowland Beauty" for whom he entertained an unrequited passion. This lady married a member of the illustrious Virginian family to which Richard Henry Lee belonged. Her son, the hero of Paulus Hook, was always a favourite with Washington, and for his dashing exploits in the later years of the revolutionary war became endeared to the American people as "Light Horse Harry." His noble son, Robert Edward Lee, must be ranked among the foremost generals of modern times.

CHAPTER XII.

WAR ON THE OCEAN.

UNTIL the war of independence the Americans had no navy of their own, such maritime expeditions as that against Louisburg having been undertaken with the aid of British ships. When the war broke out, one of the chief advantages possessed by the British, in their offensive operations, was their entire control of the American waters. Not only were all the coast towns exposed to their sudden attack, but on the broad deep rivers they were sometimes able to penetrate to a considerable distance inland, and by means of their ships they could safely transport men and stores from point to point. Their armies always rested upon the fleets as bases of operations, and soon lost their efficiency when severed from these bases. General Howe was not safe in Philadelphia until his brother had gained control of the Delaware river, and Burgoyne's army invited capture as soon as its connection with the lakes was cut off. From first to last, the events of the war illustrated this dependence of the army upon the fleet. On the retreat from Lexington, it was only the ships that finally saved Lord Percy's weary troops from capture ; at Yorktown, it was only the momentary loss of

Importance of the control of the water.

naval superiority that made escape impossible for Cornwallis. For want of a navy, General Washington could not hold the island of New York in 1776; and for a like reason, in 1778, after the enemy had been reduced to the defensive, he could not prudently undertake its recapture. It was through lack of effective naval aid that the Newport expedition failed; and the atrocities of 1779, in Virginia and Connecticut, bore sad testimony to the defenceless condition of our coasts.

Early in the war this crying want was earnestly considered by Congress, and efforts were made to repair it by the construction of a navy and the equipment of private cruisers. But the construction of a regular navy, which alone could serve the purpose, was beset with even greater difficulties than those which attended the organization of a permanent army. There was, indeed, no lack of good material, whether for ships or for seamen. New England, in particular, with its great length of seacoast and its extensive fisheries, had always possessed a considerable merchant marine, and nourished a hardy race of seafaring people. How formidable they could become in naval warfare, Great Britain was destined, nearly forty years afterward, to find out, to her astonishment and chagrin. But the absence of a central government was even more seriously felt in naval than in military affairs. The action of Congress was feeble, un- Feeble action intelligent, and vacillating. The " ma- of Congress. rine committees," " navy boards," and " boards of admiralty," to which the work of creating a navy was entrusted, were so often changed in their composition and in their functions that it was difficult for any piece of work to be carried out in accordance with its original design. As there was a total absence of system in the department of admiralty, so there was utter looseness of discipline in the service. There were the same wranglings about rank as in the army, and the consequences were even more pernicious. It was difficult to enlist good crews, because of the uncertainty arising from the general want of system. The risks encountered were excessive, because of the overwhelming preponderance of the enemy from the outset. Of thirteen new cruisers laid down in the autumn of 1775, only six ever succeeded in getting out to sea. During the war one ship-of-the-line was built, — the America 74; but she was given to the king of France while yet on the stocks. Between 1775 and 1783, there were twenty small frigates and twenty-one sloops-of-war in the service. Of these, fifteen frigates and ten sloops-of-war were either captured by the enemy, or destroyed to prevent their falling into the enemy's hands. The armaments of these ships were very light; the largest of them, the Bon Homme Richard, was constructed for a thirty-eight, but her heaviest guns were only twelve-pounders.

Yet in spite of this light force, weak discipline, and unsteady management, the little American navy did some very good work in the course of the war, and it was efficiently helped by a multitude of private cruisers, just as the Continental army often got valuable aid from the militia. Before the French alliance

American and British cruisers.

more than six hundred British vessels had fallen prey to the American cruisers, and so venturesome were these swift little craft that they even hovered around the coast of England, and merchant vessels going from one British port to another needed the protection of a convoy. During the same period, about nine hundred American vessels were taken by British cruisers; so that the damaging power of the American marine seems to have amounted to about two thirds that of such part of the British marine as could be devoted to the injury of American shipping. The damage inflicted upon the Americans was the more serious, for it well-nigh ruined the New England fisheries and the coasting trade. On the other hand, the American cruisers caused marine insurance in England to rise to a far higher point than had ever before been known; and we learn from a letter of Silas Deane to Robert Morris that, shortly before the alliance between France and the United States, the docks on the Thames were crowded with French vessels loading with British goods that sought the shelter of a neutral flag.

In one respect the value of this work of the American cruisers was incalculable. It familiarized Europe with the sight of the American flag in European waters. It was of great importance that Europe should think of the new republic not as merely the theme of distant rumours, but as a maritime power, able to defend itself within sight of the British coasts; and in this re- <small>Wickes and</small> spect it would be difficult to overrate the <small>Conyngham.</small> services rendered by the heroic captains who first

carried the stars and stripes across the ocean, and
bearded the lion in his native lair.   Of these gallant fellows, Lambert Wickes was the first, and his
ship, the Reprisal 16, was the first American war
vessel to visit the eastern shores of the Atlantic.
After a brilliant cruise in the summer of 1777,
she foundered off the banks of Newfoundland,
with the loss of all on board.   Next came Gustavus
Conyngham, with the Surprise and the Revenge,
which in the same summer took so many prizes in
the North Sea and the British Channel that insurance rose as high as twenty-five per cent., and in
some instances ten per cent. was demanded for the
short passage between Dover and Calais.   But the
fame of both these captains was soon eclipsed by

Paul Jones.   that of John Paul Jones, a Scotch sailor,
who from boyhood had been engaged in
the Virginia trade, and in 1773 had gone to Virginia to live.   When war broke out Jones offered
his services to Congress, and in October, 1776, his
name appears as eighteenth in the list of captains
in the new navy.   From the outset he was distinguished for skill and bravery, and in 1778, being
then thirty years old, he was sent, with the Ranger
18, to prowl about the British coasts.   In this
little ship he made a successful cruise in the Irish
Channel, burned some of the shipping in the port
of Whitehaven, in Cumberland, and in a fierce
fight off Carrickfergus captured the British sloop-
of-war Drake 20 ; losing only eight men in killed
and wounded, while the Drake lost forty-two.
With the Drake and several merchant prizes,
Jones made his way to Brest, and sent the Ran-

ger home to America, while he remained to take
command of a more considerable expedition that
was fitting out for the following year. Along
with the other duties of Franklin, as minister of
the United States at the French court, Franklin's
was joined a general superintendence of supervision of maritime
maritime affairs. He was a sort of affairs.
agent plenipotentiary of Congress in all matters
relating to the navy. He had authority from Congress to issue letters of marque, and exercised it
freely, while imposing restrictions that were characteristic of his magnanimous spirit. In 1779, he
issued instructions to all American cruisers that,
in whatsoever part of the sea they might happen to
meet the great discoverer Captain Cook, they were
to forget the temporary quarrel in which they were
fighting, and not merely suffer him to pass unmolested, but offer him every aid and service in their
power; since it would ill beseem Americans to lift
their hands against one who had earned the rever-
ence and gratitude of all mankind. So in the instructions given to Paul Jones, he ordered him not
to burn defenceless towns on the British coast except in case of military necessity, and in such case
he was to give notice, so that the women and children, with the sick and aged inhabitants, might
be removed betimes.

The expedition of which Paul Jones took command in the summer of 1779 was designed for a
signal "demonstration" upon the coasts of Great
Britain. The object of the British raids in Virginia and Connecticut was partly to terrify the
Americans by a bold and savage assertion of the

ubiquity of British power. The expedition of Paul Jones was to serve as a sort of counter-irritant. The confused and indefinite character of the American naval service at that time could not have a better illustration than is to be found in the details of the little squadron with which he was called upon to undertake his perilous task. The flagship was an old Indiaman named the Duras, purchased by the French government and fitted up for the occasion. In compliment to the author of Poor Richard's maxims, her name was changed to the Bon Homme Richard. She was an exceedingly clumsy affair, with swelling bows and a tower-like poop such as characterized the ships of the seventeenth century. She was now pierced for a thirty-eight-gun frigate, but as there was delay in procuring the eighteen-pounders suited for such a craft, her main deck was armed with twelve-pounders instead. In the gun-room below, Captain Jones had twelve portholes cut, in which he mounted six old eighteens, that could be shifted from side to side as occasion required. Leaving these eighteens out of the account, the force of the Bon Homme Richard was about equal to that of a thirty-two-gun frigate. This singular vessel was manned by a crew as nondescript as herself, — a motley gang of sailors and marines from nearly every country in Europe, with half a dozen Malays into the bargain. To these a hundred New England men were afterwards added, bringing up the whole number to 380. For this flagship three consorts were supplied, under the direction of the French government. The Pallas,

Jones's squadron.

a merchant vessel pierced for the occasion, was thus transformed into a thirty-two-gun frigate; the Vengeance and Cerf were of smaller calibre. All these ships were French built. To these Franklin added the Alliance 32, which happened to be in a French port at the time. The Alliance, lately built at Salisbury, in Massachusetts, and named in honour of the treaty between France and the United States, was a swift and beautiful ship, one of the finest in the American navy. Unfortunately, it was thought desirable to pay a further compliment to our new allies by appointing a French captain to command her, and this step gave rise to so much discontent and insubordination as well-nigh to destroy her efficiency. Nor had Captain Landais done anything to merit such distinction; he was simply an adventurer, seeking notoriety in the American service.

The ships in this motley squadron were not privateers. The Alliance was a regular member of our navy. The French-built ships were regarded as loaned to the United States, and were to resume their French nationality after the termination of the cruise; but they were all duly commissioned by Franklin, under the powers delegated to him by Congress. For the time being, they were part of the American navy and subject to its regulations. Their commodore, Paul Jones, has often been spoken of as a privateer, sometimes as a pirate, but he was as much a regular captain in our navy as Greene was a regular general in our army. Though, however, there could be no doubt as to the legitimate naval

Jones's cruise on the British coast.

character of the expedition, a more ill-assorted or disorderly squadron was perhaps never sent to sea. The summer was spent in cruising about the British coasts, and many prizes were taken; but the insubordination of the French commanders was so gross that during a large part of the time the ships were scattered in all directions, and Jones was left to cruise alone. On the 17th of September, having got his fleet together, he entered the Frith of Forth, and came within gunshot of Leith, which he intended to attack and capture. Sir Walter Scott, then a school-boy at Edinburgh, has given, in the introduction to " Waverley," a graphic description of the excitement which was felt upon that occasion. But, as Scott says, " a steady and powerful west wind settled the matter by sweeping Paul Jones and his vessels out of the Frith of Forth." Four days later, the Bon Homme Richard and the Vengeance entered the river Humber, and destroyed several vessels. On the 23d, the Alliance and Pallas having come up, a British fleet He meets a of forty sail was descried off Flambor-British fleet off Flambor-ough Head. They were merchant ves-ough Head. sels bound for the Baltic, under convoy of the Serapis 44, Captain Pearson, and the Countess of Scarborough 20, Captain Piercy. Captain Jones instantly gave chase, ordering his consorts to follow and form in line of battle; but the Alliance disobeyed and ran off to some distance, for a time disconcerting the Pallas, which could not understand the discrepancy between the signals and the movements. The British merchant ships crowded all sail to get out of the way, but the two frigates accepted Jones's challenge, and came up to fight. The Countess of Scarborough was very inferior in size and armament to the Pallas, while on the other hand the Serapis was much more powerful than the Bon Homme Richard. She was a two-decker, mounting twenty eighteen-pounders below, and twenty nine-pounders above, with ten six-pounders on her quarter-deck and fore-castle; so that she could throw 300 pounds of metal on a broadside. The Bon Homme Richard, with her six eighteens, could indeed throw 312 pounds on a broadside, but her weight of metal was very badly distributed among light guns. Without her eighteens, she could throw only 204 pounds on a broadside, being thus inferior to her opponent by one third. The Serapis had a crew of 320 well-trained British sailors, and she was a new and fast ship, perfect in all her appointments.

The fight began at half past seven o'clock, on a dark, cloudy evening, in very smooth water. The two principal opponents delivered their entire broadsides at the same moment. At this first fire, two of the old eighteens in the American frigate burst, killing a dozen men. After this disaster, no one had confidence enough in such guns to fire them again, so that the Bon Homme Richard was at once reduced to two thirds the force of her antagonist, and in ordinary fight must soon have been overcome. A brisk cannonade was kept up for an hour, while the two ships manœuvred for a raking position. The Serapis, being much the bet-ter sailer, was passing across her adversary's bows,

Terrific fight between the Serapis and the Bon Homme Rich-ard, Sept. 23, 1779.

with very little elbow-room, when Jones succeeded in running his vessel into her just aft of her weather beam. For a moment all firing ceased on both ships, and Captain Pearson called out, "Have you struck your colours?" "I have not yet begun to fight," replied Captain Jones. For a moment the ships separated, the Serapis running ahead almost in a line with the Bon Homme Richard. The Serapis now put her helm hard down and was box-hauled, in order to luff up athwart her adversary's bow, and thus regain her raking position; but the Bon Homme Richard changed her tack, and presently, in a dense cloud of smoke, the two ships came together again, the British bowsprit passing over the high old-fashioned poop of the American vessel. This was just what Jones desired, and as he stood there on his quarter-deck he seized a stout rope, and lashed the enemy's jib-boom to his mizzen-mast. Thus tied fast, the pressure of the light wind brought the ships alongside, the head of the one lying opposite the stern of the other. Grappling-hooks were now thrown into the quarter of the Serapis, and with repeated lashings fore and aft the two monsters were held together in deadly embrace. So close did they lie that their yards were interlocked, and some of the guns of the Serapis became useless for want of room to use the rammers. The advantage of her superior armament was thus in some measure lost, while her advantage in quickness of movement was entirely neutralized. Still her heavy guns at this short range did frightful execution, and the main deck of the Bon Homme Richard was soon covered with mangled and dying men, while her timbers were badly shivered and many cannon were knocked from their carriages. Unable to bear this terrible fire, the Americans crowded upon the upper deck in such numbers as easily to defeat the British attempts to board. Parties of marksmen, climbing into the rigging, cleared the enemy's tops, and shot down every man upon the Serapis who ventured from under cover. Hand-grenades were thrown into her port-holes to slay the gunners; and presently one bold fellow, crawling out to the very end of the Bon Homme Richard's main-yard, just over the main hatchway of the Serapis, dropped one of these mischievous missiles through the hatchway, where it ignited a row of cartridges that were lying upon the main deck. The explosion ran swiftly along the line, as through a pack of gigantic fire-crackers. More than twenty men were blown into fragments, their heads, arms, and legs flying in every direction, while forty others were disabled. With the havoc already wrought by the guns, the Serapis had now lost two fifths of her crew, and her fire perceptibly slackened; so that the Americans were able to go below and work their guns again, pouring into the British port-holes a storm of grape and canister which made an awful carnage.

It was now ten o'clock. All this while the Alliance had kept out of the fight, but the Pallas had attacked the Countess of Scarborough, and after a brisk cannonade compelled her to surrender. The Alliance now came down, and stupidly poured a raking volley along the decks of the two chief combatants, doing impartial damage to friend and foe. Warning shouts went up from the Bon Homme Richard, and her commander called out to Captain Landais to fall upon the farther side of the Serapis and board her. The Frenchman replied that he would do so, but instead he ran his ship off a couple of miles to leeward, and comfortably awaited the end of the battle. By this time the Serapis was on fire in several places, so that part of her crew had to leave their guns, and bend all their energies to extinguishing the flames. The American ship was in still worse plight; she had not only been burning for half an hour, but so many holes had been shot in her hull that she began to sink. She had more than a hundred British prisoners below decks, and these men were now set free and marshalled at the pumps. Few guns were worked on either ship, and the rest of the fight between the two exhausted combatants was a mere question of dogged tenacity. At last Captain Jones, with his own hands, directed a couple of guns against the enemy's mainmast, and just as it was threatening to fall she surrendered. The gallant British commander stood almost alone on the main deck of his ship, in the midst of an awful scene of death; while of his few men who remained unhurt, most had sunk down, panting and overcome with fatigue. No sooner were the ships cut asunder than the tottering mainmast of the Serapis went overboard, carrying with it the mizzen topmast and all the mizzen rigging. The Bon Homme Richard was with difficulty kept afloat till morning, and all night long fresh men from her consorts were hard at work fighting the flames, while the wounded were being carried off. At ten o'clock next morning she sank.

Thus ended one of the most obstinate and murderous struggles recorded in naval history. Of the men engaged, more than half were killed or badly wounded, and few got off without some scar or bruise to carry   Effect of Jones's victory.
as a memento of this dreadful night. From a merely military point of view, this first considerable fight between British and American frigates had perhaps no great significance. But the moral effect, in Europe, of such a victory within sight of the British coast was prodigious. The King of France made Paul Jones a knight of the order of merit, and from the Empress of Russia he received the ribbon of St. Anne. The King of Denmark settled a pension on him, while throughout Europe his exploit was told and told again in the gazettes, and at the drinking-tables on street corners. On his arrival in Holland, whither he went with his prizes a fortnight after the battle, the British government peremptorily demanded that he should be given up, to be hanged as a pirate. The sympathies of the Dutch were decidedly with the Americans; but as they were not quite ready to go to war with England, a tardy notice was given to Jones, after ten weeks, that he had better quit the country. Though chased by a British fleet, he got safely to France in December, and after various adventures, lasting through the ensuing year, he reached Philadelphia early in 1781. On inquiry into the extraordinary behaviour of Captain

Landais, some doubt as to his sanity arose, so that he was not shot for disobedience of orders, but simply discharged from the navy. Paul Jones was put in command of the America 74, but the war was so nearly ended that he did not get to sea again, and Congress presented his ship to the King of France. In 1788, he passed into the Russian service with the rank of rear-admiral. He died in Paris, in 1792, in the forty-fifth year of his age.

Here the question naturally arises, Why should the King of Denmark and the Empress of Russia have felt so much interest in the victory of Paul Jones as to confer distinguished honours upon him for winning it? The answer, at which we shall presently arrive, will forcibly disclose to us the extent to which, by the end of the year 1779, the whole civilized world had become involved in the quarrel between England and her revolted colonies. As at the bridge of Concord the embattled farmers of Massachusetts had once fired a shot heard round the world, so those last guns aimed by Paul Jones against the mainmast of the Serapis aroused an echo of which the reverberations were not to cease until it should be shown that henceforth nobler principles of international law must prevail upon the high seas than had ever yet been acknowledged. We have now to trace the origin and progress of the remarkable complication of affairs which at length, during the year 1780, brought all the other maritime powers of Europe into an attitude of hostility toward Great Britain.

For not until we have duly comprehended this can we understand the world-wide significance of our Revolutionary War, or estimate aright the bearings of the events which led to that grand twofold consummation, — the recognition of the independence of the United States, and the overthrow of the personal government of George III. in England.

Paul Jones was not the only enemy who hovered about the British coast in the summer of 1779. In June of that year, Spain declared war against England, but without recognizing the independence of the United States, or entering into an alliance with us. From the beginning, Count Vergennes had sought Spanish aid in his plans for supporting the Americans, but anything like cordial coöperation between Spain and France in such an undertaking was impossible, for their interests were in many respects directly opposite. So far as mere hatred toward England was concerned, Spain doubtless went even farther than France. Spain had not forgotten that she had once been mistress of the seas, or that it was England which had ousted her from this supremacy in the days of Queen Elizabeth. Of England, as the greatest of Protestant and constitutional powers, as the chief defender of political and religious liberty, priest-ridden and king-ridden Spain was the natural enemy. She had also, like France, the recollection of injuries lately suffered in the Seven Years' War to urge her to a policy of revenge. And to crown all, in the event of a successful war, she might hope to

Relations of Spain to France and England.

regain Jamaica, or the Floridas, or Minorca, or, above all, Gibraltar, that impregnable stronghold, the possession of which by England had for more than sixty years made Spaniards blush for shame. On the other hand, Spain regarded the Americans with a hatred probably not less rancorous than that which she felt toward the British. The mere existence of these English colonies in North America was a perpetual reminder of the days when the papal edict granting this continent to Spain had been set at naught by heretical cruisers and explorers. The obnoxious principles of civil and religious liberty were represented here with even greater emphasis than in England. In Mexico and South America the Spanish crown had still a vast colonial empire; and it was rightly foreseen that a successful revolt of the English colonies would furnish a dangerous precedent for the Spanish colonies to follow. Spain was, moreover, the chief upholder of the old system of commercial monopoly; and here her interests were directly opposed to those of France, which, since it had been deprived of its colonial empire, saw in the general overthrow of commercial monopoly the surest way of regaining its share in the trade of the world.

Under the influence of these conflicting motives, the conduct of Spain was marked for a time by hesitation and double-dealing. Between his various wishes and fears, the Spanish prime minister,

Intrigues of Spain. Florida Blanca, knew not what course to pursue. When he heard of the alliance between France and the United States, which was undertaken against his advice to Vergennes, his wrath knew no bounds. It was a treaty, he said, "worthy of Don Quixote." At first he intrigued with the British government, offering his services as mediator between England and France. Lord Weymouth, the British minister for foreign affairs, refused to enter into any negotiation so long as France should extend aid to "the rebel colonies." To the covert threat of the wily Spaniard, that if the war were to continue his royal master would doubtless feel compelled to take part with one side or the other, Lord Weymouth replied that the independence of the United States would prove fatal to the continuance of Spanish control over Mexico and South America; and he suggested, accordingly, that the true interest of Spain lay in forming an alliance with Great Britain. While this secret discussion was going on, Florida Blanca also sounded Vergennes, proposing that peace should be made on such terms as to allow the British to retain possession, of Rhode Island and New York. This, he thought, would prevent the formation of an American Union, and would sow the seeds of everlasting dissension between Great Britain and the American States, whereby the energies of the English race would be frittered away in internecine conflict, leaving room for Spain to expand itself. But Vergennes would not hear of this. France had recognized the independence of the thirteen States, and had explicitly and publicly agreed to carry on the war until that independence should be acknowledged by England; and from that position she could not

easily retreat. At the same time Vergennes inti-
mated that France was in no way bound to protect the American claim to the Ohio
valley, and was far from desiring that
the people of the United States should
control the whole of North America. Upon this
suggestion the Spanish court finally acted. After
six months more of diplomatic fencing, a treaty
was concluded in April, 1779, between France and
Spain, whereby it was agreed that these two powers should undertake a concerted invasion of England. For this undertaking, France was to furnish the land force, while both powers were to
raise as great a naval armament as possible.
France was to assist Spain in recovering Minorca
and the Floridas, and if Newfoundland could be
conquered, its fisheries were to be monopolized by
the two parties to this treaty. Neither power was
to make peace on any terms until England should
have surrendered Gibraltar to Spain.

This convention brought Spain into the lists
against England without bringing her directly
into alliance with the United States. She was left
free to negotiate with Congress at her own good
pleasure, and might ask for the whole Mississippi
valley, if she chose, in return for her assistance.
Gerard, the French minister at Philadelphia,
sought to persuade Congress to give up the fisheries and relinquish all claim to the territory west of
the Alleghanies. There were hot debates on this
subject in 1779, and indeed the situation of affairs
was sufficiently complicated to call for the exercise
of skilful diplomacy. As the treaty between

*Treaty be-
tween Spain
and France,
April, 1779.*

France and Spain became known in America, it was felt to be in some respects inconsistent with the prior convention between France and the United States. In that convention it had been stipulated that neither party should make peace with Great Britain without the consent of the other. In the convention between France and Spain it was agreed that neither party should make peace until Great Britain should surrender Gibraltar. But the Americans rightly felt that, should Great Britain be found willing to concede their independence, they were in no wise bound to keep up the war for the sole purpose of helping France to conquer Gibraltar for a power which had never owed them any good will, and was at this very moment hoping to cut down their territory. The proposal to exclude America as well as Great Britain from the fisheries excited loud indignation in New England.

Meanwhile, the new allies had gone energetically to work. Early in 1779, a French fleet had captured the British settlements in Senegambia, and made a vigorous though unsuccessful assault upon the island of Jersey. In June, war was declared by Spain so suddenly that England was quite taken by surprise. Florida Blanca had lied with so grave a face that Lord North had not been looking out for such a step. In August, the allied French and Spanish fleets, numbering more than sixty ships-of-the-line, with a full complement of frigates, entered the English Channel, with intent to repeat the experiment of the Invincible Armada; while a

French and Spanish fleets attempt an invasion of England, Aug., 1779.

French army lay at Havre, ready to cross at the first opportunity. To oppose this formidable force, Admiral Hardy was able to get together only thirty-eight ships-of-the-line, with the ordinary proportion of frigates. There was a panic in England, and the militia were called out. But owing to dissensions between the French and Spanish admirals and serious illness in the crews, nothing whatever was accomplished, and the great fleet retired crestfallen from the channel. Everybody blamed everybody else, while an immense sum of money had been spent upon a wretched fiasco. In America, however, the allies were more successful. Galvez, the Spanish governor of Louisiana, captured Baton Rouge and Mobile, with their British garrisons, and preparations were made for the siege of Pensacola, to complete the conquest of West Florida. In the West Indies, the islands of Grenada and St. Vincent were captured by Estaing. The moment that war was declared by Spain, there was begun that siege of Gibraltar which, for the heroic defence, as well as for its long duration of nearly four years, has had no parallel in the annals of modern warfare.

It was only through maritime expeditions that the two new allies could directly assail England with any hope of success; but here on the sea her natural superiority was not long in asserting itself. Great efforts were made to increase the strength of the navy, and in December, 1779, the command of the fleet in the West Indies was given to a man who among English sailors ranks with Blake and Hawke, on a plane inferior only to that occupied

by Nelson. The brilliant career of Sir George
Rodney began in the Seven Years' War, _{Sir George}
in the course of which he bombarded _{Rodney.}
Havre, thus warding off a projected invasion of
England, and moreover captured several islands in
the West Indies. It was Pitt who first discerned
his genius, and put him into a position in which
he could win victories. After the peace of 1763
he became a member of Parliament, but lost all
he had in gambling, and fled to France to get rid
of his creditors. When war broke out between
France and England in 1778, the venerable Marshal de Biron loaned him enough money to save
him from the Marshalsea or the Fleet, and he returned to England to be appointed to the chief
command in the West Indies. A vain and unscrupulous man, as many called him, he was none the
less a most skilful and indomitable captain. He
was ordered, on his way to the West Indies, to relieve Gibraltar, which was beginning to suffer the
horrors of famine, and never was such a task more
brilliantly performed. First, he had the good fortune to fall in with fifteen Spanish ships, loaded
with provisions and under the convoy of seven war
vessels, and all this fleet he captured. Then, at
Cape St. Vincent, on a dark and stormy night, he
gave chase to a Spanish fleet of eleven ships-of-the-
line and two frigates, and in a sharp fight captured
or destroyed all but four of them without losing
one of his own ships. He thus reached Gibraltar,
and after passing up to the fortress the welcome
cargoes of the fifteen merchant prizes went on to
the West Indies, where his presence turned the

scale against the allies. A powerful French fleet
under Count de Guichen was cruising in those waters ; and it was hoped that this fleet would soon
be able to come to New York and coöperate with
Washington in an attempt to regain that city. But
the arrival of Rodney changed all this, and the
Count de Guichen, after being worsted in battle,
sailed away for France, while Rodney proceeded
to New York, to relieve Sir Henry Clinton and foil
the projects of Washington.

That very supremacy upon the sea, however,
which enabled England to defy the combined fleets
of France and Spain served, in its immediate consequences, only to involve her in fresh difficulties.

Rights of
neutrals upon
the sea.

By the arrogant and indiscriminate
manner in which she exercised the right
of search, she soon succeeded in uniting
against her all the neutral nations of Europe ; and
a principle of international law was laid down
which in our own time has become fully established, and must in future essentially limit the
areas over which wars are likely to extend. This
new principle of international law related to the
rights of merchant vessels belonging to neutral
powers in time of war. In early times it was held
that if one country went to war with another, its
right to prey upon its enemy's commerce was virtually unlimited. If it found its enemy's goods
carried in a ship belonging to some neutral power,
it had a right to seize and confiscate them ; and in
days when hostility was the rule and peace the ex-
ception, when warfare was deemed honourable and
commerce ignoble, and when the usages of war

were rough and unscrupulous, the neutral ship itself, which carried the goods, was very likely to be
confiscated also. As the neutral power whose
ship was seized would be sure to resent such behaviour, it followed that any war between two maritime powers was likely to spread, until it involved
every other power which possessed any merchant
shipping or did any business upon the high seas.
With a view to confining such evils within as narrow a limit as possible, the maritime code known
as the Consolato del Mare, which represented the
commercial interests of the Middle Ages, and was
generally accepted as of the highest authority in
maritime affairs, recognized the right of confiscating an enemy's goods found in a neutral ship, but
did not recognize the right of confiscating the neutral ship. In the Middle Ages maritime warfare
played a subordinate part; but after The Consolato
colonies had been planted in America del Mare.
and the East Indies by the great maritime nations
of Western Europe, the demand for fixed rules,
whereby the usages of such warfare should be regulated, soon came to be of transcendent importance.
England and the Netherlands, as powers with whom
industrial considerations were of the first consequence and military considerations only secondary,
adhered firmly to the rule of the Consolato del
Mare as the most liberal rule then in existence.
France and Spain, as preëminently militant powers, caring more for the means of annoying an enemy than for the interests of commerce in general,
asserted the principle that neutral ships detected
in carrying an enemy's goods were themselves law-

ful subjects for seizure. France, however, did not hold this doctrine so firmly as Spain. Here, as in so many other respects France showed herself more advanced in civilization than Spain, while less advanced than England and the Netherlands. In 1655, by a treaty between Cromwell and Mazarin, France accepted the English rule; in 1681, under the retrograde government of Louis XIV., she went back to her ancient practice; in 1744, she again adopted the English rule, while Spain kept on with her old custom, until sharply called to account by Russia in 1780.

Until the middle of the eighteenth century, the most liberal doctrines respecting maritime warfare had concerned themselves only with the protection of neutral ships. It had never occurred to anybody to maintain that the goods of an enemy should be guaranteed against scrutiny and seizure by the mere fact of their being carried on a neutral ship. That any belligerent could seize its antagonist's property, if found on a neutral ship, was the doctrine laid down alike by Vattel and Bynkershoek, the chief French and Dutch authorities on maritime law. In acting upon this principle, therefore, at the time of our Revolutionary War, England acted strictly in accordance with the recognized maritime law of Europe. She was not, as some American writers seem to have supposed, introducing a new principle of aggression, in virtue of her position as chief among maritime powers. In stopping the defenceless merchant vessels of neutral or friendly powers, compelling them to show their bills of lading, searching their

holds if need be, subjecting them to a hateful in-
quisition and vexatious delays, she did no more
than every maritime nation had been in the habit
of doing, and even less than Spain claimed the
right to do. It was quite natural, too, that England should insist upon retaining this privilege,
as something which no great naval power could
afford to dispense with; for obviously, if in time
of war your enemy can go on trading with everybody but yourself and can even receive timber
and provisions from people not concerned in the
struggle, your means of crippling him are very
materially diminished.

Such reasoning seemed conclusive everywhere
in Europe until after the middle of the eighteenth
century. At that time, however, the unexampled
naval preponderance of England began to lead
other nations to take a new view of the case. By
the maintenance of the old rule, England could
damage other nations much more than they could
damage her. Other nations, accordingly, began
to feel that it would be a good thing if the flag of
a neutral ship might be held to protect any merchandise whatsoever that she might happen to
have on board. This modern doctrine, that free
ships make free goods, was first suggested by
Prussia in 1752. Such a view naturally commended itself to a nation which had a Prussian doc-
considerable number of merchantmen trine: free
ships make
afloat, without any navy fit to protect free goods.
them; and it was accordingly likely to find favour
in the eyes of such nations as Denmark, Sweden,
Russia, and the United States. But, more than

this, it was a view entirely in accordance with the philosophic tendencies of the age. The great humanitarian movement, which in our time has borne rich and ample fruit, and which has tended in every practicable way to diminish the occasions for warfare and to restrict its scope, had its first brilliant literary representatives among the clear-sighted and enthusiastic French philosophers of the eighteenth century. The liberal tendencies in politics, which hitherto England alone had represented practically, were caught up in France, as soon as the dismal and protracted tyranny of Louis XIV. had come to an end, with an eagerness that partook of fanaticism. English political ideas, without being thoroughly comprehended in their practical bearings, were seized and generalized by Montesquieu and Turgot, and a host of lesser writers, until they acquired a width of scope and a genial interest which exercised a prodigious influence upon the thought of Continental Europe. Never in any age, perhaps, since the days when Sokrates talked to enchanted crowds upon street corners in Athens, did men of broad philosophic

Influence of the French philosophers. ideas come so closely into contact with men absorbed in the pursuit of life's immediate ends as at the time when all Paris rushed to kiss the hand of Voltaire, and when ladies of the court went to sleep with the last *brochure* of Diderot or Helvetius under their pillows. The generous " enthusiasm of humanity," which revealed itself in every line of the writings of these great men, played an important part in the political history of the eighteenth century. It was an age of crowned philosophers and benevolent despots. Joseph of Austria, Frederick of Prussia, and Catherine of Russia, in their several ways, furnished illustrations of this tendency. Catherine, who wrote letters to Voltaire, and admired Fox above all other English statesmen, set almost as much store by free thought as by free love, and her interest in the amelioration of mankind in general was second only to her particular interest in the humiliation of the Turk. The idea of taking the lead in a general movement for the liberation of maritime commerce was sure to prove congenial to her enlightened mind, and her action would have great weight with England, which at that time, isolated from all European sympathy, was especially desirous of an alliance with Russia, and especially anxious to avoid offending her.

At the beginning of 1778, Sir James Harris, afterward Earl of Malmesbury, was sent as ambassador to St. Petersburg, with instructions to leave no stone unturned to secure an offensive and defensive alliance between Russia and Great Britian, in order to offset and neutralize the alliance between France and the United States. Negotiations to this end were kept up as long as the war lasted, but they proved fruitless. While Catherine coquetted and temporized, the Prussian ambassador had her ear, and his advice was unfavourable to such an alliance. For the England of Pitt the great Frederick felt sympathy and gratitude; for the England of George III. he had nothing but hatred, and his counsels went far to

Great Britain wishes to secure an alliance with Russia.

steady Catherine, if ever she showed signs of wavering. The weight of France was of course thrown into the same scale, and for four years the Russian court was the scene of brisk and multifarious intrigues. Harris said that his very valets were offered bribes by busybodies who wished to get a look at his papers ; and when he went out, leaving his secretary writing, he used to lock him up, not through doubts of his fidelity, but lest he should thoughtlessly leave the door ajar. From Prince Potemkin, one of Catherine's lovers whose favour Harris courted, he learned that nothing short of the cession of Minorca would induce the empress to enter into the desired alliance. Russia was already taking advantage of the situation to overrun and annex the Crimea, and the maritime outlook thus acquired made her eager to secure some naval station on the Mediterranean. Minorca was England's to give. She had won it in the war of the Spanish Succession, and for seventy years it had been one of the brightest jewels in her imperial crown. Together with Gibraltar it had given her that firm grasp upon the Mediterranean which — strengthened in later times by Importance of Minorca. the acquisition of Malta, Cyprus, and the isthmus of Suez — has gone far toward making that vast inland sea an English lake. So great a value did England set upon Minorca that when, in the Seven Years' War, it was lost for a moment, through an error of judgment on the part of Admiral Byng, the British people were seized with a bloodthirsty frenzy, and one of the foulest judicial murders known to history was

committed when that gallant commander was shot
on his own quarter-deck. Yet even this island,
by which England set such store, she was now
ready to surrender in exchange for the help of
Russia against her revolted colonies and the House
of Bourbon. It was not, however, until 1781 that
the offer of Minorca was made, and then Catherine had so far acceded to the general combination
against England that she could not but refuse it.
That such an offer should ever have been made
shows how important an alliance with Russia
seemed to England at the moment when France
and Spain were leagued against her, and all the
neutral powers looked on her with hostile eyes.
We can thus the better appreciate the significance
of the step which Russia was now to take with
reference to the great question of maritime law
which was beginning to agitate the civilized world.

In the summer of 1778, the French government,
with intent to curb the depredations of British
cruisers, issued a proclamation adopting the Prussian doctrine of 1752, that free ships make free
goods, and Vergennes took occasion to France adopts
suggest that Catherine should put her- the Prussian doctrine.
self at the head of a league of neutral
powers for the purpose of protecting neutral commerce all over the world. For the moment no decided action was taken, but the idea was one of
those broad ideas in which the empress delighted.
Count Panin, her principal minister, who was
strongly in sympathy with the King of Prussia,
insisted upon the necessity of protecting the commerce of minor powers against England, which

since 1763 had become the great naval bully of the world. England was doubtless acting in strict accordance with time-honoured custom, but circumstances had changed, and the law must be changed to meet them. The first great war since 1763 was now showing that England could destroy the commerce of all the rest of the world, without any fear of retaliation except through a universal war. During the summers of 1778 and 1779, Prussian, Swedish, Danish, and Dutch ships were continually overhauled by British cruisers, and robbed of cargoes which they were carrying to France. Such gross outrages upon private property, however sanctioned by laws of war that had grown up in a barbarous age, awakened general indignation throughout Europe; and from whatever quarter complaints poured in, Vergennes and Frederick took good care that they should be laid before the Empress of Russia, until presently she came to look upon herself as the champion of little states and oppressed tradesmen.

The British depredations were, moreover, apt to be characterized by an arrogance which, while it rendered them all the more exasperating, sometimes transcended the limits of aggression prescribed by the rude maritime law of that day. Upon Netherland commerce England was especially severe, for the Dutch had more merchant shipping than any other people on the Continent, with a weak navy to protect it. England forbade the Dutch to send timber to France, as it would probably be used in building ships of war. On the 30th of December, 1779, seventeen Dutch vessels, laden with tar and hemp, and other materials useful in shipyards, were sailing through the English Channel, escorted by five ships-of-the-line under Count Bylandt, when toward nightfall they were overtaken and hailed by a British squadron of sixteen ships-of-the-line under Admiral Fielding. A lively parley ensued. Bylandt swore that his ships should not be searched, and Fielding threatened violence. While this was going on, twelve of the Dutch ships got away under cover of darkness, and reached in safety the French ports to which they were bound. Early in the morning, Bylandt fired upon the boat which was bringing a party of British officers to search the merchantmen that remained. Upon this, three British ships instantly poured their broadsides into the Dutch flagship, which returned the compliment, and then hauled down its flag, as resistance was useless. Nobody was killed, but Fielding seized the five merchantmen, and took them in to Portsmouth. The States-General of the Netherlands complained of the outrage to Lord Stormont, the new foreign secretary, and demanded the restitution of the prizes. The matter was referred to the British court of admiralty, and the singular doctrine was there laid down that the Dutch vessels were virtually blockade-runners, and as such were lawfully captured! "Great Britain," said the judge, "by her insular position, blocks naturally all the ports of Spain and France, and she has a right to avail herself of this position as a gift of Providence." But the States-General did not accept this inter-

Affair of Fielding and Bylandt.

pretation of the law and theology of the matter, and they appealed to the Empress of Russia.

Just at this moment events occurred which compelled Catherine to take some decided stand on the question of neutral rights. Through fear of adding her to the list of their enemies, the British ministry had issued the most stringent orders that no Russian vessels should be searched or molested, under any circumstances. The Dutch and Danish flags might be insulted at pleasure, but that of Russia must be respected; and so well were these orders obeyed that Catherine had no grounds for complaint against England on this score. Spain, on the other hand, was less cautious. In the winter of 1779–80, her cruisers captured two Russian vessels laden with wheat, in the mistaken belief that their cargoes were destined for Gibraltar. The ships were taken into Cadiz, their cargoes were sold at auction, and their penniless crews were outrageously treated by the people, and came little short of starving. Catherine was wild with rage, and instantly ordered out fifteen ships-of-the-line and five frigates for the protection of Russian commerce. For a moment war between Spain and Russia seemed imminent. But Panin moved with cautious shrewdness, and consulted the King of Prussia, who persuaded Florida Blanca to restore the captured ships, with compensation to the owners of the cargoes, and an ample apology for the blunder. The empress was satisfied, and Panin assured her that now the time had come for her to act with magnanimity and power, laying down an impartial code for the pro-

Spanish cruisers capture Russian vessels.

tection of maritime commerce, and thus establishing a claim to the gratitude of mankind through all future ages. On the 8th of March, 1780, Catherine issued a proclamation, setting forth the principles of maritime law which she was henceforth resolved to defend by force, if necessary. Henceforth neutral ships were to sail unmolested from port to port, even on the coasts of countries at war. They were to be free to carry into such ports any goods or merchandise whatsoever, except arms and ammunition, and the right of search was to be tolerated as regarded such contraband articles, and for no other purpose. Hereafter no port was to be considered blockaded unless the enemy's ships of war should be near enough to make it dangerous to enter.

Catherine's proclamation, March 8, 1780.

These principles were immediately adopted by Spain, France, and the United States, the three powers actually at war with England. At the same time, Denmark and Sweden entered into an arrangement with Russia for the mutual protection of their commerce. It was announced that for every Danish, Swedish, or Russian ship searched or seized by the cruisers of any belligerent power, a strict retaliation would be made by the allied navies of these three countries. This covenant, known as the Armed Neutrality, was practically a threat aimed at England, and through her unwillingness to alienate Russia it proved a very effective threat. We can now understand the interest shown by Denmark and Russia in the victory of Paul Jones, and we can also appreciate the prodigious moral effect of that

The Armed Neutrality.

victory. So overwhelming was England's naval superiority that the capture of a single one of her war ships was a memorable event. To the lesser maritime powers it seemed to bring the United States at once into the front rank of belligerents. The British ministry was too well instructed to be brought under this spell; but in view of the great hostile combination now formed against it, for the moment it was at its wits' end. "An ambiguous and trimming answer was given," says Sir James Harris; "we seemed equally afraid to accept or dismiss the new-fangled doctrines. I was instructed secretly to oppose, but avowedly to acquiesce in them." In England, the wrath and disgust extended to all parties. Shelburne and Camden joined with North and Thurlow in denouncing Catherine's proclamation as an impudent attempt, on the part of an upstart power, hardly known on the sea till quite lately, to dictate maritime law to the greatest maritime power the world had ever seen. It was contended that the right to search neutral vessels and take an enemy's goods from them was a cardinal principle of international law; and jurists, of course, found the whole body of precedents on the side of this opinion. But in spite of all protests these " new-fangled doctrines," subversive of all precedent, were almost immediately adopted throughout Europe. In December, 1780, the Netherlands joined the Armed Neutrality, under circumstances presently to be related. In May, 1781, it was joined by Prussia; in October, 1781, by the Empire; in July, 1782, by Portugal; in September, 1782, by the Turk; in February, 1783, by the Kingdom of Naples. Though England's maritime strength exceeded that all the members of the league taken together, she could not afford to run the risk of war with all the world at once; and thus the doctrine that free ships make free goods acquired a firm foothold. In the chaos of the Napoleonic wars, indeed, paper blockades and illegal seizures abounded, and it fared ill with neutral commerce on the high seas. But the principles laid down by Catherine survived that terrible crisis, and at last they were formally adopted by England at the close of the Crimean War, in 1856.

This successful assertion of the rights of neutrals was one of the greatest and most beneficent revolutions in the whole history of human warfare. It was the most emphatic declaration that had ever been made of the principle that the interests of peace are paramount and permanent, while those of war are subordinate and temporary. In the interest of commerce it put a mighty curb upon warfare, and announced that for the future the business of the producer is entitled to higher consideration than that of the destroyer. Few things have ever done so much to confine the area of warfare and limit its destructive power. If the old doctrine were in force at the present day, when commerce has expanded to such enormous dimensions, and every sea is populous with merchant ships, it would be well-nigh impossible for any two maritime powers to go to war without dragging all the rest of the world into the struggle. For the speedy accom-

Vast importance of the principles laid down by Catherine.

plishment of this great reform we have chiefly to thank the Empress Catherine, whose action at the critical moment was so prompt and decisive. It is curious to consider that an act which so distinctly subordinated military to industrial interests should have emanated from that country of Europe which had least outgrown the militant stage of civilization, and should have been chiefly opposed by that country which had advanced the farthest into the industrial stage. It is a brilliant instance of what may be achieved by an enlightened despot when circumstances are entirely favourable. Among the many acts of Catherine which, in spite of her horrible vices, have won the admiration of mankind, this is doubtless the most memorable; and as time goes on we shall realize its importance more and more.

The immediate effect of the Armed Neutrality was to deprive England of one of her principal weapons of offence. To add to her embarrassment, there now came war with Holland. While there was strong sympathy between the British and Dutch governments, there was great jealousy between the peoples which had so long been rivals in the colonial world. Hence there were two parties in the Netherlands, — the party of the Stadtholder, Relations between Great Britain and Holland. which was subservient to the policy of the British government, and the popular party, which looked with favour upon the American cause. The popular party was far the more numerous, including all the merchants of the most mercantile of countries, and it was especially strong in the city of Amsterdam. A brisk trade

— illicit from the British point of view — was carried on between Holland and the United States,
chiefly through the little Dutch island of St. Eustatius, in the West Indies.   An equally lively trade
went on between Holland and France, and against
this England felt that she had an especial right to
make complaint.   Her relations with Holland were
regulated not simply by the ordinary law of nations, but by careful and elaborate treaties, made
in the days when the two peoples were leagued in
sympathy against the aggressive policy of Louis
XIV.   In 1678, it had been agreed that if either
England or Holland should be attacked by France,
both powers should make common cause against
their common enemy ; and in 1716 this agreement
had been renewed in such wise as to include the
contingency of an attack by Spain, since a younger
branch of the House of Bourbon had succeeded to
the Spanish throne.   When, in 1779, Spain declared war against England, the latter power accordingly called upon the Netherlands for aid ; but
no aid was given, for the Dutch felt that they had
an especial right to complain of the conduct of
England.   By that same treaty which in 1674 had
finally given New York to the English, it had been
provided that in case either England or Holland
should ever go to war with any other country, the
ordinary rules of maritime law should not be enforced as between these two friendly commercial
powers.   It was agreed that either power might
freely trade with the enemies of the other ; and
such a treaty was at that time greatly to the credit
of both nations.   It was made in a moment when

an honourable spirit of commercial equity pre-vailed. But it was one of the chief symptoms of the utter demoralization of the British government in 1778, after the untimely death of Lord Chat-ham, that these treaty obligations were completely ignored; and in the general plunder of merchant shipping which went on at that time, no nation suffered like the Dutch. George III. now felt that he had got everything into his own hands, and when the Dutch complained he gave them to un-derstand that, treaty or no treaty, he should do as he pleased. Under such circumstances, it was rather cool for England to ask aid against Spain, and the Dutch very naturally turned a deaf ear to the demand.

It was thus a very pretty quarrel as it stood at the end of 1779, when Fielding fired upon the flag-ship of Count Bylandt, and Paul Jones was al-lowed to stay with his prizes ten weeks in a Dutch harbour. Each party was thus furnished with an " outrage." The righteous anger of the Dutch over the high-handed conduct of Fielding was matched by the British chagrin over the victory of Jones. The Stadtholder's weak efforts to keep the peace were quite overwhelmed in the storm of wrath that arose. After much altercation, Eng-land notified Holland that all treaties between the two countries must be considered as abrogated, owing to the faithless behaviour of the Dutch in refusing aid against Spain, in trading with France and America, in resisting the right of search, and in sheltering Paul Jones. Having thus got rid of the treaties, England proceeded to act as if there

were no such thing as international law where
Dutchmen were concerned.   During the summer
of 1780, the wholesale robbery on the high seas
grew worse than ever, and, with a
baseness that seems almost incredible, Holland joins
the British ambassador at the Hague the Armed
Neutrality.
was instructed to act as a spy, and gather information concerning the voyages of Dutch merchants, so that British cruisers might know just
where to pounce upon the richest prizes.   Thus
goaded beyond human endurance, Holland at last
joined the Armed Neutrality, hoping thereby to enlist in her behalf the formidable power of Russia.

But the policy of England, though bold in the
extreme, was so far well considered as to have
provided against such an emergency.   She was
determined to make war on Holland, to punish
her for joining the Armed Neutrality ; but if she
were to avow this reason, it would at once entail
war with Russia also, so that it was necessary to
find some other reason.   The requisite bone of
contention was furnished by a curiously opportune
accident.   In October, 1780, an American packet
was captured off the banks of Newfoundland, and
among the prisoners was Henry Laurens, lately
president of Congress, now on his way Capture of
to the Hague to negotiate a loan.   He Henry Laurens and his
threw his papers overboard, but a papers.
quick-witted tar jumped after them, and caught
them in the water.   Among them was found a
project for a future treaty of commerce between
the Netherlands and the United States, which had
been secretly concerted two years before between

Jean de Neufville, an Amsterdam merchant, and William Lee, an American commissioner to Berlin. It was signed also by Van Berckel, the chief magistrate of Amsterdam; but as it had been neither authorized nor sanctioned by the States-General or by Congress, it had no validity whatever. Quite naturally, however, the discovery of such a document caused much irritation in England,. and it furnished just the sort of excuse for going to war which the ministry wanted. To impose upon the imagination of the common people, Laurens was escorted through the streets of London by a regiment of soldiers, and shut up in the Tower, where he was denied pen and paper, and no one was allowed to enter his room. A demand was made upon Holland to disavow the act of Van Berckel, and to inflict condign punishment upon him and his accomplices, " as disturbers of the public peace and violators of the rights of nations." In making this demand, it was foreseen that the States-General would disavow the act of Van Berckel, but would nevertheless decline to regard him as a fit subject for punishment. The message was sent to the British ambassador at the Hague on the 3d of November. It was then known in England that Holland contemplated joining the Northern league, but the decisive step had not yet been actually taken by the States-General. The ambassador was secretly instructed by Lord Stormont not to present the demand for the disavowal and punishment of Van Berckel unless it should become absolutely certain that Holland had

Great Britain declares war against Holland, Dec. 20, 1780.

joined the league. At their meeting in November, the States-General voted to join the league, and the demand was accordingly presented. Everything happened according to the programme. The States-General freely condemned and disavowed the Amsterdam affair, and offered to make reparation; but with regard to the punishment of Van Berckel, they decided that an inquiry must first be made as to the precise nature of his offence and the court most fit for trying him. England replied by a peremptory demand for the immediate punishment of Van Berckel, and, without waiting for an answer, proceeded to declare war against Holland on the 20th of December. Four days before this, the swiftest ship that could be found was sent to Admiral Rodney, who was then at Barbadoes, ordering him to seize upon St. Eustatius without a moment's delay.

Whatever other qualities may have been lacking in the British ministry at this time, they certainly were not wanting in pluck. England had now to fight single-handed against four nations, three of which were, after herself, the chief naval powers of the world. According to the Malmesbury Diaries, "this bold conduct made a great and useful impression upon the Empress" of Russia. It was partly with a view to this moral effect that the ministry were so ready to declare war. It was just at this time that they were proposing, by the offer of Minorca, to tempt Catherine into an alliance with England; and they did not wish to have her interpret their eagerness to secure her aid as a confession

Catherine decides not to interfere.

of weakness or discouragement. By making war on Holland, they sought to show themselves as full of the spirit of fight as ever. To strengthen the impression, Harris blustered and bragged. The Dutch, said he, "are ungrateful, dirty, senseless boors, and, since they will be ruined, must submit .to their fate." But in all this the British government was sailing very near the wind. Prince Galitzin, the Russian ambassador at the Hague, correctly reported that the accession of Holland to the Armed Neutrality was the real cause of the war, and that the Amsterdam affair was only a pretext. Upon this ground, the Dutch requested armed assistance from Catherine, as chief of the league. The Empress hesitated; she knew the true state of the case as well as any one, but it was open to her to accept the British story or not, as might seem best. Dispatches from Berlin announced that Frederick was very angry. When he first heard the news, he exclaimed, "Well! since the English want a war with the whole world, they shall have it." Catherine then sat down and wrote with her own hand a secret letter to Frederick, asking him if he would join her in making war upon England. On second thoughts, the King of Prussia concluded there was no good reason for taking part in the affair, and he advised Catherine also to keep her hands free. This decided the empress. She did not care to make war upon England, except with such overwhelming force as to be sure of extorting very important concessions. She accordingly chose to believe the British story, and she refused to aid the Dutch, on the ground that their quarrel with England grew out of a matter with which the Armed Neutrality had nothing to do. At the same time, after dallying for a while with the offer of Minorca, she refused that also, and decided to preserve to the end the impartial attitude which she had maintained from the beginning.

Meanwhile, on the 3d of February, 1781, a powerful fleet under Rodney, with the force of 5,000 men which had been detached in November, 1779, from Clinton's army in New York, appeared before the island of St. Eustatius, and summoned it to surrender. The Dutch governor, ignorant of the fact that war had begun, had only fifty-five soldiers on the island. He had no choice but to surrender, and the place was given up without a blow. The British had an especial spleen against this wealthy little island, which had come to be the centre of an enormous trade between France and Holland and the United States. Rodney called it a nest of thieves, and declared that " this rock, only six miles in length and three in breadth, had done England more harm than all the arms of her most potent enemies, and alone supported the infamous American rebellion." His colleague, General Vaughan, who commanded the land force, regarded it as a feeder for the American " colonies," of which the summary extinction would go far toward ending the war. With such feelings, they made up their minds to do their work thoroughly ; and accordingly they confiscated to the Crown not only all the public stores, but all the private property of the inhabitants.

Capture of St. Eustatius, Feb. 3, 1781.

Their orders were carried out with great brutality. The goods in the warehouses were seized and laden upon ships, to be carried away and sold at auction in the neighbouring islands. Every kind of private and personal property was laid hold of, and the beggared inhabitants were turned out-of-doors and ordered to quit the island. The total value of the booty amounted to more than twenty million dollars. Among the victims of this robbery were many British merchants, who were no better treated than the rest. Rodney tore up their remonstrance without reading it, and exclaimed, "This island is Dutch, and everything in it is Dutch, and as Dutch you shall all be treated." The proceedings were fitly crowned by an act of treachery. The Dutch flag was kept flying as a decoy, and in the course of the next seven weeks more than fifty American ships, ignorant of the fate of the island, were captured by the aid of this dirty stratagem.

Shameful proceedings.

The conduct of the government in declaring war against Holland was denounced by the Whigs as criminal, and the true character of the shameful affair of St. Eustatius was shown up by Burke in two powerful speeches. But the government capped the climax when it deliberately approved the conduct of Rodney, and praised him for it. Many of the British victims, however, brought their cases before the courts, and obtained judgments which condemned as illegal the seizure of private property so far as they were concerned. On the continent of Europe, the outrage awakened general indignation, as an infraction of the laws and usages

of civilized warfare, the like of which had not been
seen for many years; and it served to alienate
from Great Britain the little sympathy that remained for her.

The position of England at this time was alarming, as well as ignominious. She had contrived to
league against herself, in various degrees of hostility, nearly the whole of the civilized world, and
the most distressing part of the situation, to all
liberal-minded Englishmen, was the undeniable
fact that this hostility was well deserved. To the
historian who appreciates the glorious part which
England has played in history, the proceedings
here recorded are painful to contemplate; and to
no one should they be more painful than to the
American, whose forefathers climbed with Wolfe
the rugged bank of the St. Lawrence; or a century earlier, from their homes in New England
forests heard with delight of Naseby and Marston
Moor; or back yet another hundred years, in Lin-
colnshire villages defied the tyranny of Gardiner
and Bonner; or at yet a more remote period did
yeoman's service in the army of glorious Earl
Simon, or stood, perhaps, beside great Edward on
the hallowed fields of Palestine. The pride with
which one recalls such memories as these explains
and justifies the sorrow and disgust with which
one contemplates the spectacle of a truculent
George Germain, an unscrupulous Stormont, or
a frivolous North; or hears the dismal stories of
Indian massacres, of defenceless villages laid in
ashes, of the slaughter of unarmed citizens, of le-

galized robbery on the ocean highway, or of colossal buccaneering, such as that which was witnessed at St. Eustatius. The earlier part of the reign of George III. is that period of English history of which an enlightened Englishman must feel most ashamed, as an enlightened Frenchman must feel ashamed of the reigns of Louis XIV. and the two Bonapartes. All these were periods of wholesale political corruption, of oppression at home and unrighteous warfare abroad, and all invited swift retribution in the shape of diminished empire and temporary lowering of the national prestige. It was not until after the downfall of the personal government of George III. that England began to resume her natural place in the foremost rank of liberal and progressive powers. Toward that happy result, the renewal and purification of English political life, the sturdy fight sustained by the Americans in defence of their liberties did much to contribute. The winning of independence by the Americans was the winning of a higher political standpoint for England and for the world.

CHAPTER XIII.

A YEAR OF DISASTERS.

AFTER the surrender of Burgoyne, the military attitude of the British in the northern states became, as we have seen, purely defensive. Their efforts were almost exclusively directed toward maintaining their foothold, at first in the islands of New York and Rhode Island, afterward in New York alone, whence their ships could ascend the Hudson as far as the frowning crags which sentinel the entrance of the Highlands. Their offensive operations were restricted to a few plundering expeditions along the coast, well calculated to remind the worthy Connecticut farmers of the ubiquitousness of British power, and the vanity of hopes that might have been built upon the expectation of naval aid from France. But while the war thus languished at the centre, while at the same time it sent forth waves of disturbance that reverberated all the way from the Mississippi river to the Baltic Sea, on the other hand the southernmost American states were the scene of continuous and vigorous fighting. Upon the reduction of the Carolinas and Georgia the king and Lord George Germain had set their hearts. If the rebellion could not be broken at the centre, it was hoped that it might at least be frayed away at the edges;

and should fortune so far smile upon the royal armies as to give them Virginia also, perhaps the campaigns against the wearied North might be renewed at some later time and under better auspices.

In this view there was much that was plausible. Events had shown that the ministry had clearly erred in striking the rebellion at its strongest point; it now seemed worth while to aim a blow where it was weakest. The people of New England were almost unanimous in their opposition to

State of things in the Far South.

the king, and up to this time the states of Massachusetts and Connecticut in particular had done more to sustain the war than all the others put together. Georgia and the Carolinas, a thousand miles distant, might be regarded as beyond the reach of reinforcements from New England; and it might well be doubted whether they possessed the ability to defend themselves against a well-planned attack. Georgia was the weakest of the thirteen states, and bordered upon the British territory of Florida. In South Carolina the character of the population made it difficult to organize resistance. The citizens of Charleston, and the rich planters of English or Huguenot descent inhabiting the lowlands, were mostly ardent patriots, but they were outnumbered by their negro slaves; and the peculiar features of slavery in South Carolina made this a very embarrassing circumstance. The relations between master and slave were not friendly there, as they were in Virginia; and while the state had kept up a militia during the whole colonial period, this militia found plenty of employment in patrolling the slave quarters, in searching for hidden weapons, and in hunting fugitives. It was now correctly surmised that on the approach of an invading army the dread of negro insurrection, with all its nameless horrors, would paralyze the arm of the state militia. While the patriotic South Carolinians were thus handicapped in entering upon the contest, there were in the white population of the state many discordant elements. There were many Quakers and men of German ancestry who took little interest in politics, and were only too ready to submit to any authority that would protect them in their ordinary pursuits. A strong contrast to the political apathy of these worthy men was to be found in the rugged population of the upland counties. Here the small farmers of Scotch-Irish descent were, every man of them, Whigs, burning with a patriotic ardour that partook of the nature of religious fanaticism ; while, on the other hand, the Scotchmen who had come over since Culloden were mostly Tories, and had by no means as yet cast off that half-savage type of Highland character which we find so vividly portrayed in the Waverley novels. It was not strange that the firebrands of war, thrown among such combustible material, should have flamed forth with a glare of unwonted cruelty ; nor was it strange that a commonwealth containing such incongruous elements, so imperfectly blended, should have been speedily, though but for a moment, overcome. The fit ground for wonder is that, in spite of such adverse circumstances, the state of South Carolina should have shown as much elastic strength as she did under the severest military stress which any American state was called upon to withstand during the Revolutionary War.

Since the defeat of the British fleet before Charleston, in June, 1776, the southern states had been left unmolested until the autumn of 1778, when there was more or less frontier skirmishing between Georgia and Florida, — a slight premonitory symptom of the storm that was coming. The American forces in the southern department were then commanded by General Robert Howe, who was one of the most distinguished patriots of North Carolina, but whose military capacity seems to have been slender. In the autumn of 1778 he had his headquarters at Savannah, for there was war on the frontier. Guerrilla parties, made up chiefly of vindictive loyalist refugees, but aided by a few British regulars from General Augustine Prevost's force in Florida, invaded the rice plantations of Georgia, burning and murdering, and carrying off negroes, — not to set them free, but to sell them for their own benefit. As a counter-irritant, General Howe planned an expedition against St. Augustine, and advanced as far as St. Mary's river; but so many men were swept away by fever that he was obliged to retreat to Savannah. He had scarcely arrived there when 3,500 British regulars from New York, under Colonel Campbell, landed in the neighbourhood, and offered him battle. Though his own force numbered only 1,200, of whom half were militia, Howe accepted the challenge, relying upon

Georgia overrun by the British.

the protection of a great swamp which covered his
flanks. But a path through the swamp was pointed
out to the enemy by a negro, and the Americans,
attacked in front and behind, were instantly routed.
Some 500 prisoners were taken, and Savannah
surrendered, with all its guns and stores ; and this
achievement cost the British but 24 men. A few
days afterward, General Prevost advanced from
Florida and captured Sunbury, with all its garrison, while Colonel Campbell captured Augusta.
A proclamation was issued, offering protection to
such of the inhabitants as would take up arms in
behalf of the king's government, while all others
were by implication outlawed. The ferocious temper of Lord George Germain was plainly visible
in this proclamation and in the proceedings that
followed. A shameless and promiscuous plunder
was begun. The captive soldiers were packed into
prison-ships and treated with barbarity. The more
timid people sought to save their property by taking sides with the enemy, while the bolder spirits
took refuge in the mountains ; and thus General
Prevost was enabled to write home that the state
of Georgia was conquered.

At the request of the southern delegates in Congress, General Howe had already been superseded
by General Benjamin Lincoln, who had won distinction through his management of the New England militia in the Saratoga campaign. When
Lincoln arrived in Charleston, in December, 1778, an attempt was made to Arrival of
General Lin-
call out the lowland militia of South coln.
Carolina, but the dread of the slaves kept them

from obeying the summons. North Carolina, however, sent 2,000 men under Samuel Ashe, one of the most eminent of the southern patriots; and with this force and 600 Continentals the new general watched the Savannah river and waited his chances. But North Carolina sent foes as well as friends to take part in the contest. A party of 700 loyalists from that state were marching across South Carolina to join the British garrison at Augusta, when they were suddenly attacked by Colonel Andrew Pickens with a small force of upland militia. In a sharp fight the Tories were routed, and half their number were taken prisoners. Indictments for treason were brought against many of these prisoners, and, after trial before a civil court, some seventy were found guilty, and five of them were hanged. The rashness of this step soon became apparent. The British had put in command of Augusta one Colonel Thomas Browne, a Tory, who had been tarred and feathered by his neighbours at the beginning of the war. As soon as Browne heard of these executions for treason, he forthwith hanged some of his Whig prisoners; and thus was begun a long series of stupid and cruel reprisals, which, as time went on, bore bitter fruit.

Barbarous reprisals.

While these things were going on in the back country, the British on the coast attempted to capture Port Royal, but were defeated, with heavy loss, by General Moultrie. Lincoln now felt able to assume the offensive, and he sent General Ashe with 1,500 men to threaten Augusta. At his approach the British abandoned the town, and retreated toward Savannah. Ashe pursued closely, but at Briar Creek, on the 3d of March, 1779, the British turned upon him and routed him. The Americans lost 400 in killed and wounded, besides seven Americans routed at Briar Creek, March 3, 1779. pieces of artillery and more than 1,000 stand of arms. Less than 500 succeeded in making their way back to Lincoln's camp ; and this victory cost the British but five men killed and eleven wounded. Augusta was at once retaken ; the royal governor, Sir James Wright, was reinstated in office ; and, in general, the machinery of government which had been in operation previous to 1776 was restored. Lincoln, however, was far from accepting the defeat as final. With the energetic coöperation of Governor Rutledge, to whom extraordinary powers were granted for the occasion, enough militia were got together to repair the losses suffered at Briar Creek ; and in April, leaving Moultrie with 1,000 men to guard the lower Savannah, Lincoln marched upon Augusta with the rest of his army, hoping to capture it, and give the legislature of Georgia a chance to assemble there, and destroy the moral effect of this apparent restoration of the royal government. But as soon as Lincoln had got out of the way, General Prevost crossed the Savannah with 3,000 men and advanced upon Charleston, laying waste the country and driving Moultrie before him. It was a moment of terror and confusion. In General Prevost there was at last found a man after Lord George Germain's own heart. His march was Prevost's vandalism. a scene of wanton vandalism. The houses of the wealthy planters were mercilessly sacked; their treasures of silver plate were loaded on carts and carried off; their mirrors and china were smashed, their family portraits cut to pieces, their gardens trampled out, their shade trees girdled and ruined; and as Prevost had a band of Cherokees with him, the horrors of the tomahawk and scalping-knife in some instances crowned the shameful work. The cabins of the slaves were burned. Cattle, horses, dogs, and poultry, when not carried away, were slaughtered wholesale, and the destruction of food was so great that something like famine set in. More than a thousand negroes are said to have died of starvation.

In such wise did Prevost leisurely make his way toward Charleston; and reaching it on the 11th of May, he sent in a summons to surrender. A strangely interesting scene ensued. Events had occurred which had sorely perturbed the minds of the members of the state council. Pondering upon the best means of making the state militia available, Henry Laurens had hit upon the bold expedient of arming the most stalwart and courageous negroes, and marching them off to camp under the lead of white officers. Such a policy might be expected to improve the relations between whites and blacks by uniting them against a common danger, while the plantations would be to some extent relieved of an abiding source of dread. The plan was warmly approved by Laurens's son, who was an officer on Washington's staff, as well as by Alexander Hamilton, who further suggested that the blacks thus enrolled as

Plan for arming negroes.

militia should at the same time be given their freedom. Washington, on the other hand, feared that
if the South Carolinians were to adopt such a
policy the British would forestall them by offering
better arms and equipments to the negroes, and
thus muster them against their masters. It was
a game, he felt, at which two could play. The
matter was earnestly discussed, and at last was
brought before Congress, which approved of Laurens's plan, and recommended it to the consideration of the people of South Carolina ; and it was
just before the arrival of Prevost and his army
that the younger Laurens reached Charleston with
this message from Congress.

The advice was received in anything but a
grateful spirit. For a century the state had maintained an armed patrol to go about among the
negro quarters and confiscate every pistol, gun, or
knife that could be found, and now it was proposed
that three or four thousand slaves should actually
be furnished with muskets by the state ! People
were startled at the thought, and there might well
be a great diversity of opinion as to the
feasibleness of so bold a measure at so Indignation in
South Caro-
critical a moment. To most persons it lina.
seemed like jumping out of the frying-pan into the
fire. Coming, too, at a moment when the state
was in such desperate need of armed assistance
from Congress, this advice was very irritating.
The people naturally could not make due allow-
ance for the difficulties under which Congress laboured, and their wrath waxed hot. South Carolina seemed to be left in the lurch. Was it to

join such a league as this that she had cast off
allegiance to Great Britain ? She had joined in
the Declaration of Independence reluctantly, and
from an honourable feeling of the desirableness of
united action among the states. On that momentous day, of which it was not yet clear whether the
result was to be the salvation or the ruin of America, her delegates had, with wise courtesy, changed
their vote in deference to the opinions of the other
states, in order that the American people might
seem to be acting as a unit in so solemn a matter.
And now that the state was invaded, her people
Action of the council. robbed and insulted, and her chief city
threatened, she was virtually bidden to
shift for herself ! Under the influence of such feelings as these, after a hot debate, the council, by a
bare majority, decided to send a flag of truce to
General Prevost, and to suggest that South Carolina should remain neutral until the end of the war,
when it should be decided by treaty whether she
should cast in her lot with Great Britain or with
the United States.   What might have come of this
singular suggestion had it been seriously discussed
we shall never know, for Prevost took no notice of
it whatever. He refused to exchange question and
answer with a branch of the rebel government of
South Carolina, but to Moultrie, as military commandant, he announced that his only terms were
unconditional surrender. We can imagine how the
gallant heart of Moultrie must have sunk within
him at what he could not but call the dastardly
action of the council, and how it must have leaped
with honest joy at the British general's ultimatum.

" Very good," said he simply ; " we 'll fight it out, then."

In citing this incident for its real historic interest, we must avoid the error of making too much of it. At this moment of sudden peril, indignation at the fancied neglect of Congress was joined to the natural unwillingness, on the part of the council, to incur the risk of giving up the property of their fellow-citizens to the tender mercies of such a buccaneer as Prevost had shown himself to be. But there is no sufficient reason for supposing that, had the matter gone farther, the suggestion of the council would have been adopted by the legislature or acquiesced in by the people of South Carolina.

On this occasion the danger vanished as suddenly as it came. Count Pulaski, with his legion, arrived from the northern army, and Lincoln, as soon as he learned what was going on, retraced his steps, and presently attacked General Prevost. After an indecisive skirmish, End of the campaign. the latter, judging his force inadequate for the work he had undertaken, retreated into Georgia, and nothing more was done till autumn. The military honours of the campaign, however, remained with the British ; for by his march upon Charleston Prevost had prevented Lincoln from disturbing the British supremacy in Georgia, and besides this he had gained a foothold in South Carolina ; when he retreated he left a garrison in Beaufort which Lincoln was unable to dislodge.

The French alliance, which thus far had been of so little direct military value, now appears

again upon the scene.   During the year which had
elapsed since the futile Rhode Island campaign,
the French fleet had been busy in the West Indies.   Honours were easy, on the whole, between
the two great maritime antagonists, but the French
had so far the advantage that in August, 1779,
Estaing was able once more to give some attention
to his American friends.   On the first day of September he appeared off the coast of Georgia with
a powerful fleet of twenty-two ships-of-the-line and
eleven frigates.   Great hopes were now
conceived by the Americans, and a plan
was laid for the recapture of Savannah.

Attempt to
recapture Sa-
vannah.

By the 23d of the month the place was invested by
the combined forces of Lincoln and Estaing, and
for three weeks the seige was vigorously carried on
by a regular system of approaches, while the works
were diligently bombarded by the fleet.   At length
Estaing grew impatient.   There was not sufficient
harbourage for his great ships, and the captains
feared that they might be overtaken by the dangerous autumnal gales for which that coast is
noted.   To reduce the town by a regular siege
would perhaps take several weeks more, and it was
accordingly thought best to try to carry it by
storm.   On the 9th of October a terrific assault
was made in full force.   Some of the outworks
were carried, and for a moment the stars and
stripes and the fleurs-de-lis were planted on the
redoubts ; but British endurance and the strength
of the position at last prevailed.   The assailants
were totally defeated, losing more than 1,000 men,
while the British, in their sheltered position, lost

but 55. The gallant Pulaski was among the slain, and Estaing received two severe wounds. The French, who had borne the brunt of the fight, now embarked and stood out to sea, but not in time to escape the October gale which they had been dreading. After weathering with difficulty a terrible storm, their fleet was divided; and while part returned to the West Indies, Estaing himself, with the remainder, crossed to France. Thus the second attempt at concerted action between French and Americans had met with much more disastrous failure than the first.

While these things were going on, Washington had hoped, and Clinton had feared, that Estaing might presently reach New York in such force as to turn the scale there against the British. As soon as he learned that the French fleet was out of the way, Sir Henry Clinton proceeded to carry out a plan which he had long had in contemplation. A year had now elapsed since the beginning of active operations in the south, and, although the British arms had been crowned with success, it was desirable to strike a still heavier blow. The capture of the chief southern city was not only the next step in the plan of the campaign, but it was an object of especial desire to Sir Henry Clinton personally, for he had not forgotten the humiliating defeat at Fort Moultrie in 1776. He accordingly made things as snug as possible at the north, by finally withdrawing the garrisons from Rhode Island and the advanced posts on the Hudson. In this way, while leaving Knyphausen with a strong force in command of New York, he was enabled to embark 8,000 men on transports, under convoy of five ships-of-the-line; and on the day after Christmas, 1779, he set sail for Savannah, taking Lord Cornwallis with him.

The voyage was a rough one. Some of the transports foundered, and some were captured by American privateers. Yet when Clinton arrived in Georgia, and united his forces to those of Prevost, the total amounted to more than 10,000 men. He ventured, however, to weaken the garrison of New York still more, and sent back at once for 3,000 men under command of the young Lord Rawdon, of the famous family of Hastings, — better known in after-years as Earl of Moira and Marquis of Hastings, and destined, like Cornwallis, to serve with great distinction as governor-general of India. The event fully justified Clinton's sagacity in taking this step. New York was quite safe for the present; for so urgent was the need for troops in South Carolina, and so great the difficulty of raising them, that Washington was obliged to detach from his army all the Virginia and North Carolina troops, and send them down to aid General Lincoln. With his army thus weakened, it was out of the question for Washington to attack New York.

Lincoln, on the other hand, after his reinforcements arrived, had an army of 7,000 men with which to defend the threatened state of South Carolina. It was an inadequate force, and its commander, a thoroughly brave and estimable man, was far from possessing the rare sagacity which

Washington displayed in baffling the schemes of the enemy. The government of South Carolina deemed the preservation of Charleston to be of the first importance, just as, in 1776, Congress had insisted upon the importance of keeping the city of New York. But we have seen how Washington, in that trying time, though he could not keep the city, never allowed himself to get his army into a position from which he could not withdraw it, and at last, through his sleepless vigilance, won all the honours of the campaign. In the defence of Charleston no such high sagacity was shown. Clinton advanced slowly overland, until on the 26th of February, 1780, he came in sight of the town. It had by that time become so apparent that his overwhelming superiority of force would enable him to encompass it on every side, that Lincoln should have evacuated the place without a moment's delay; and such was Washington's opinion as soon as he learned the facts. The loss of Charleston, however serious a blow, could in no case be so disastrous as the loss of the army. But Lincoln went on strengthening the fortifications, and gathering into the trap all the men and all the military resources he could find. For some weeks the connections with the country north of the Cooper river were kept open by two regiments of cavalry; but on the 14th of April these regiments were cut to pieces by Colonel Banastre Tarleton, the cavalry commander, who now first appeared on the scene upon which he was soon to become so famous. Five days later, the reinforcement under Lord

The British advance upon Charleston.

Rawdon, arriving from New York, completed the investment of the doomed city. The ships entering the harbour did not attempt to batter down Fort Moultrie, but ran past it; and on the 6th of May this fortress, menaced by troops in the rear, surrendered.

The British army now held Charleston engirdled with a cordon of works on every side, and were ready to begin an assault which, with the disparity of forces in the case, could have but one possible issue. On the 12th of May, to avoid a wanton waste of life, the city was surrendered, and Lincoln and his whole army became prisoners of war.

The Continental troops, some 3,000 in number, were to be held as prisoners till regularly exchanged. The militia were allowed to return home on parole, and all the male citizens were reckoned as militia, and paroled likewise. The victorious Clinton at once sent expeditions to take possession of Camden and other strategic points in the interior of the state. One regiment of the Virginia line, under Colonel Buford, had not reached Charleston, and on hearing of the great catastrophe it retreated northward with all possible speed. But Tarleton gave chase as far as Waxhaws, near the North Carolina border, and there, overtaking Buford, cut his force to pieces, slaying 113 and capturing the rest. Not a vestige of an American army was left in all South Carolina.

"We look on America as at our feet," said Horace Walpole; and doubtless, after the capture of Fort Washington, this capture of Lincoln's army

Surrender of
Charleston,
May 12, 1780.

at Charleston was the most considerable disaster which befell the American arms during the whole course of the war. It was of less critical importance than the affair of Fort Washington, as it occurred at what every one must admit to have been a less critical moment. The loss of Fort Washington, taken in connection with the misconduct of Charles Lee, came within a hair's-breadth of wrecking the cause of American independence at the outset; and it put matters into so bad a shape that nothing short of Washington's genius could have wrought victory out of them. The loss of South Carolina, in May, 1780, serious as it was, did not so obviously imperil the whole American cause. The blow did not come at quite so critical a time, or in quite so critical a place. South Carolina overrun by the British. The loss of South Carolina would not have dismembered the confederacy of states, and in course of time, with the American cause elsewhere successful, she might have been recovered. The blow was nevertheless very serious indeed, and, if all the consequences which Clinton contemplated had been achieved, it might have proved fatal. To crush a limb may sometimes be as dangerous as to stab the heart. For its temporary completeness, the overthrow may well have seemed greater than that of Fort Washington. The detachments which Clinton sent into the interior met with no resistance. Many of the inhabitants took the oath of allegiance to the Crown; others gave their parole not to serve against the British during the remainder of the war. Clinton issued a circular, inviting all well-disposed people to assemble

and organize a loyal militia for the purpose of sup-
pressing any future attempts at rebellion. All
who should again venture to take up arms against
the king were to be dealt with as traitors, and
their estates were to be confiscated; but to all who
should now return to their allegiance
Clinton re-
turns to New a free pardon was offered for past of-
York.
fences, except in the case of such people
as had taken part in the hanging of Tories. Having struck this great blow, Sir Henry Clinton returned, in June, to New York, taking back with
him the larger part of his force, but leaving Cornwallis with 5,000 men to maintain and extend the
conquests already made.

Just before starting, however, Sir Henry, in a
too hopeful moment, issued another proclamation,
which went far toward destroying the effect of his
previous measures. This new proclamation required all the people of South Carolina to take an
An injudicious active part in reëstablishing the royal
proclamation. government, under penalty of being
dealt with as rebels and traitors. At the same
time, all paroles were discharged except in the
case of prisoners captured in ordinary warfare,
and thus everybody was compelled to declare himself as favourable or hostile to the cause of the
invaders. The British commander could hardly
have taken a more injudicious step. Under the
first proclamation, many of the people were led to
comply with the British demands because they
wished to avoid fighting altogether; under the
second, a neutral attitude became impossible, and
these lovers of peace and quiet, when they found

themselves constrained to take an active part on one side or the other, naturally preferred to help their friends rather than their enemies. Thus the country soon showed itself restless under British rule, and this feeling was strengthened by the cruelties which, after Clinton's departure, Cornwallis found himself quite unable to prevent. Officers endowed with civil and military powers combined were sent about the country in all directions, to make full lists of the inhabitants for the purpose of enrolling a loyalist militia. In the course of these unwelcome circuits many affrays occurred, and instances were not rare in which people were murdered in cold blood. Debtors took occasion to accuse their creditors of want of loyalty, and the creditor was obliged to take the oath of allegiance before he could collect his dues. Many estates were confiscated, and the houses of such patriots as had sought refuge in the mountains were burned. Bands of armed men, whose aim was revenge or plunder, volunteered their services in preserving order, and, getting commissions, went about making disorder more hideous, and wreaking their evil will without let or hindrance. The loyalists, indeed, asserted that they behaved no worse than the Whigs when the latter got the upper hand, and in this there was much truth. Cornwallis, who was the most conscientious of men and very careful in his statements of fact, speaks, somewhat later, of "the shocking tortures and inhuman murders which are every day committed by the enemy, not only on those who have taken part with us, but on many

Disorders in South Carolina.

who refuse to join them." There can be no doubt that Whigs and Tories were alike guilty of cruelty and injustice. But on the present occasion all this served to throw discredit on the British, as the party which controlled the country, and must be held responsible accordingly.

Organized resistance was impossible. The chief strategic points on the coast were Charleston, The strategic Beaufort, and Savannah; in the interior, Augusta was the gateway of Georgia, and the communications between this point and the wild mountains of North Carolina were dominated by a village known as "Ninety-Six," because it was just that number of miles distant from Keowee, the principal town of the Cherokees. Eighty miles to the northeast of Ninety-Six lay the still more important post of Camden, in which centred all the principal inland roads by which South Carolina could be reached from the North. All these strategic points were held in force by the British, and save by help from without there seemed to be no hope of releasing the state from their iron grasp. Among the patriotic Whigs, however, there were still some stout hearts that Partisan com- did not despair. Retiring to the dense manders. woods, the tangled swamps, or the steep mountain defiles, these sagacious and resolute men kept up a romantic partisan warfare, full of midnight marches, sudden surprises, and desperate hand-to-hand combats. Foremost among these partisan commanders, for enterprise and skill, were James Williams, Andrew Pickens, Thomas Sumter, and Francis Marion.

Of all the picturesque characters of our Revolutionary period, there is perhaps no one who, in the memory of the people, is so closely associated with romantic adventure as Francis Marion. He belonged to that gallant race of men of whose services France had been forever deprived when Louis XIV. revoked the edict of Nantes. His father had been a planter near Georgetown, Francis Marion. on the coast, and the son, while following the same occupation, had been called off to the western frontier by the Cherokee war of 1759, in the course of which he had made himself an adept in woodland strategy. He was now forty-seven years old, a man of few words and modest demeanour, small in stature and slight in frame, delicately organized, but endowed with wonderful nervous energy and sleepless intelligence. Like a woman in quickness of sympathy, he was a knight in courtesy, truthfulness, and courage. The brightness of his fame was never sullied by an act of cruelty. "Never shall a house be burned by one of my people," said he; "to distress poor women and children is what I detest." To distress the enemy in legitimate warfare was, on the other hand, a business in which few partisan commanders have excelled him. For swiftness and secrecy he was unequalled, and the boldness of his exploits seemed almost incredible, when compared with the meagreness of his resources. His force sometimes consisted of less than twenty men, and seldom exceeded seventy. To arm them, he was obliged to take the saws from sawmills and have them wrought into rude swords at the country

forge, while pewter mugs and spoons were cast
into bullets. With such equipment he would attack and overwhelm parties of more than two
hundred Tories; or he would even swoop upon a
column of British regulars on their march, throw
them into disorder, set free their prisoners, slay
and disarm a score or two, and plunge out of sight
in the darkling forest as swiftly and mysteriously
as he had come.

Second to Marion alone in this wild warfare
was Thomas Sumter, a tall and powerful man, stern in countenance and
haughty in demeanour. Born in Virginia in 1734,
he was present at Braddock's defeat in 1755, and
after prolonged military service on the frontier
found his way to South Carolina before the beginning of the Revolutionary War. He lived nearly
a hundred years; sat in the Senate of the United
States during the War of 1812, served as minister
to Brazil, and witnessed the nullification acts of
his adopted state under the stormy presidency of
Jackson. During the summer of 1780, he kept
up so brisk a guerrilla warfare in the upland regions north of Ninety-Six that Cornwallis called
him "the greatest plague in the country." "But
for Sumter and Marion," said the British commander, "South Carolina would be at peace."
The first advantage of any sort gained over the
enemy since Clinton's landing was the destruction
of a company of dragoons by Sumter, on the 12th
of July. Three weeks later, he made a desperate
attack on the British at Rocky Mount, but was repulsed. On the 6th of August, he surprised the

*Thomas Sum-
ter.*

enemy's post at Hanging Rock, and destroyed a whole regiment. It was on this oc- casion that Andrew Jackson made his First appearance of Andrew Jackson. first appearance in history, an orphan boy of thirteen, staunch in the fight as any of his comrades.

But South Carolina was too important to be left dependent upon the skill and bravery of its partisan commanders alone. Already, before the fall of Charleston, it had been felt that further reinforcements were needed there, and Washington had sent down some 2,000 Maryland and Delaware troops under Baron Kalb, an Advance of Kalb. excellent officer. It was a long march, and the 20th of June had arrived when Kalb halted at Hillsborough, in North Carolina, to rest his men and seek the coöperation of General Caswell, who commanded the militia of that state. By this time the news of the capture of Lincoln's army had reached the north, and the emergency was felt to be a desperate one. Fresh calls for militia were made upon all the states south of Pennsylvania. That resources obtained with such difficulty should not be wasted, it was above all desirable that a competent general should be chosen to succeed the unfortunate Lincoln. The opinions of the commander-in-chief with reference to this matter were well known. Washington wished to have Greene appointed, as the ablest general in the army. But the glamour which enveloped the circumstances of the great victory at Saratoga was not yet dispelled. Since the downfall of the Conway Cabal, Gates had never recovered the extraor-

dinary place which he had held in public esteem at
the beginning of 1778, but there were few as yet
who seriously questioned the reputation he had so
lightly won for generalship. Many people now
called for Gates, who had for the moment retired
from active service and was living on his plantation in Virginia, and the suggestion found favour
with Congress. On the 13th of June Gates was
appointed to the chief command of the

*Gates ap-
pointed to the
chief com-
mand in the
South.*

southern department, and eagerly accepted the position. The good wishes
of the people went with him. Richard
Peters, secretary of the Board of War, wrote him
a very cordial letter, saying, " Our affairs to the
southward look blue : so they did when you took
command before the *Burgoynade.* I can only
now say, *Go and do likewise* — God bless you."
Charles Lee, who was then living in disgrace on
his Virginia estate, sent a very different sort of
greeting. Lee and Gates had always been friends,
— linked together, perhaps, by pettiness of spirit
and a common hatred for the commander-in-chief,
whose virtues were a perpetual rebuke to them.
But the cynical Lee knew his friend too well to
share in the prevailing delusion as to his military
capacity, and he bade him good-by with the ominous warning, " Take care that your northern
laurels do not change to southern willows ! "

With this word of ill omen, which doubtless he
little heeded, the " hero of Saratoga " made his
way to Hillsborough, where he arrived on the 19th
of July, and relieved Kalb of the burden of anx-
iety that had been thrust upon him. Gates found

things in a most deplorable state : lack of arms,
lack of tents, lack of food, lack of medicines, and,
above all, lack of money.   The all-pervading need-
iness which in those days beset the American people, through their want of an efficient government,
was never more thoroughly exemplified.   It required a very different man from Gates to mend
matters.   Want of judgment and want of decision
were faults which he had not outgrown, and all his
movements were marked by weakness and rashness.   He was adventurous where caution was
needed, and timid when he should have been bold.
The objective point of his campaign was the town
of Camden.   Once in possession of this important
point, he could force the British from their other
inland positions and throw them upon the defensive
at Charleston.   It was not likely that so great an
object would be attained without a battle, but
there was a choice of ways by which the
strategic point might be approached.   Choice of
roads to Cam-
Two roads led from Hillsborough to den.
Camden.   The westerly route passed through Salisbury and Charlotte, in a long arc of a circle,
coming down upon Camden from the northwest.
The country through which it passed was fertile,
and the inhabitants were mostly Scotch-Irish
Whigs.   By following this road, the danger of a
sudden attack by the enemy would be slight, wholesome food would be obtained in abundance, and in
case of defeat it afforded a safe line of retreat.
The easterly route formed the chord of this long
arc, passing from Hillsborough to Camden almost
in a straight line 160 miles in length.   It was 50

miles shorter than the other route, but it lay through a desolate region of pine barrens, where farmhouses and cultivated fields were very few and far between, and owned by Tories. This line of march was subject to flank attacks, it would yield no food for the army, and a retreat through it, on the morrow of an unsuccessful battle, would simply mean destruction. The only advantage of this route was its directness. The British forces were more or less scattered about the country. Lord Rawdon held Camden with a comparatively small force, and Gates was anxious to attack and overwhelm him before Cornwallis could come up from Charleston.

Gates accordingly chose the shorter route, with all its disadvantages, in spite of the warnings of Kalb and other officers, and on the 27th of July he put his army in motion. On the 3d of August, having entered South Carolina and crossed the Pedee river, he was joined by Colonel Porterfield with a small force of Virginia regulars, which had been hovering on the border since the fall of Charleston. On the 7th he effected a junction with General Caswell and his North Carolina militia, and on the 10th his army, thus reinforced, reached Little Lynch's Creek, about fifteen miles northeast of Camden, and confronted the greatly inferior force of Lord Rawdon. The two weeks' march had been accomplished at the rate of about eleven miles a day, with no end of fatigue and suffering. The few lean kine slaughtered by the roadside had proved quite insufficient

Gates chooses the wrong road.

Distress of the troops.

to feed the army, and for want of any better diet
the half-starved men had eaten voraciously of un-
ripe corn, green apples, and peaches. All were
enfeebled, and many were dying of dysentery and
cholera morbus, so that the American camp presented a truly distressing scene.

Rawdon's force stood across the road, blocking
the way to Camden, and the chance was offered
for Gates to strike the sudden blow for the sake
of which he had chosen to come by this bad road.
There was still, however, a choice of methods.
The two roads, converging toward their point of
intersection at Camden, were now very near together. Gates might either cross the creek in
front, and trust to his superior numbers to overwhelm the enemy, or, by a forced march of ten
miles to the right, he might turn Rawdon's flank
and gain Camden before him. A good general
would have done either the one of these things or
the other, and Kalb recommended the immediate
attack. But now at the supreme mo-   Gates loses the
ment Gates was as irresolute as he had   moment for
been impatient when 160 miles away.   striking;
He let the opportunity slip, waited two days where
he was, and on the 13th marched slowly to the
right and took up his position at Clermont, on the
westerly road; thus abandoning the whole purpose
for the sake of which he had refused to advance
by that road in the first place. On the 14th he
was joined by General Stevens with 700 Virginia
militia; but on the same day Lord Cornwallis
reached Camden with his regulars, and the golden
moment for crushing the British in detachments
was gone forever.

The American army now numbered 3,052 men, but only 1,400 were regulars, chiefly of the Maryland line. The rest were mostly raw militia. The united force under Cornwallis amounted to only 2,000 men, but they were all thoroughly trained soldiers. It was rash for the Americans to hazard an attack under such circumstances, especially in their forlorn condition, faint as they were with hunger and illness, and many of them hardly fit to march or take the field. But, strange as it may seem, a day and a night passed by, and **and weakens his army on the eve of battle;** Gates had not yet learned that Cornwallis had arrived, but still supposed he had only Rawdon to deal with. It was no time for him to detach troops on distant expeditions, but on the 14th he sent 400 of his best Maryland regulars on a long march southward, to coöperate with Sumter in cutting off the enemy's supplies on the road between Charleston and Camden. At ten o'clock on the night of the 15th, Gates moved his army down the road from Clermont to Camden, intending to surprise Lord Rawdon before daybreak. The distance was ten miles through the woods, by a rough road, hemmed in on either side, now by hills, and now by impassable swamps. At the very same hour, Cornwallis started up the road, with the similar purpose of surprising General Gates. A little before three in the morning, the British and American advance guards of light infantry encountered each other on the road, five miles north of Camden, and a brisk skirmish ensued, in which the Americans were routed and the gallant Colonel Porterfield was slain. Both armies, however, having failed in their scheme of surprising each other, lay on their arms and waited for daylight. Some prisoners who fell into the hands of the Americans now brought the news that the army opposed to them was commanded by Cornwallis himself, and they overstated its numbers at 3,000 men. The astonished Gates called together his officers, and asked what and is surprised by Cornwallis. was to be done. No one spoke for a few moments, until General Stevens exclaimed, "Well, gentlemen, is it not too late *now* to do anything but fight?" Kalb's opinion was in favour of retreating to Clermont and taking a strong position there; but his advice had so often been unheeded that he no longer urged it, and it was decided to open the battle by an attack on the British right.

The rising sun presently showed the two armies close together. Huge swamps, at a short distance from the road, on either side, covered both flanks of both armies. On the west side of the road the British left was commanded by Lord Rawdon, on the east side their right was led by Colonel James Webster, while Tarleton and his cavalry hovered a little in the rear. The American right wing, opposed to Rawdon, was commanded by Kalb, and consisted of the Delaware regiment and the second Maryland brigade in front, supported by the first Maryland brigade at some distance in the rear. The American left wing, op- Battle of Camden, Aug. 16, 1780. posed to Webster, consisted of the militia from Virginia and North Carolina, under Generals Stevens and Caswell. Such an arrangement of troops invited disaster. The battle was to begin with an attack on the British right, an attack upon disciplined soldiers; and the lead in this attack was entrusted to raw militia who had hardly ever been under fire, and did not even understand the use of the bayonet! This work should have been given to those splendid Maryland troops that had gone to help Sumter. The militia, skilled in woodcraft, should have been sent on that expedition, and the regulars should have been retained for the battle. The militia did not even know how to advance properly, but became tangled up; and while they were straightening their lines, Colonel Webster came down upon them in a furious charge. The shock of the British column was resistless. The Virginia militia threw down their guns and fled without firing a shot. The North Carolina militia did likewise, and within fifteen minutes the whole American left became a mob of struggling men, smitten with mortal panic, and huddling like sheep in their wild flight, while Tarleton's cavalry gave chase and cut them down by scores. Leaving Tarleton to deal with them, Webster turned upon the first Maryland brigade, and slowly pushed it off the field, after an obstinate resistance. The second Maryland brigade, on the other hand, after twice repelling the assault of Lord Rawdon, broke through his left with a spirited bayonet charge, and remained victorious upon that part of the field, until the rest of the fight was ended; when being attacked in flank by Webster, these stalwart troops retreated westerly by a narrow road between swamp and hillside, and made

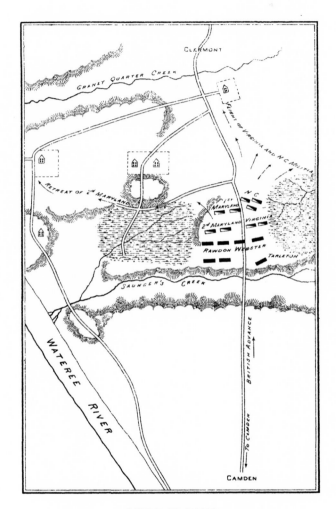

CLERMONT

GRANEY QUARTER CREEK

FLIGHT OF VIRGINIA AND N C MILITIA

RETREAT OF 2ND MARYLAND

N C

1ST MARYLAND

2D MARYLAND VIRGINIA

RAWDON WEBSTER TARLETON

SAUNDER'S CREEK

WATEREE RIVER

BRITISH ADVANCE

TO CAMDEN

CAMDEN

BATTLE OF CAMDEN

AUGUST 16, 1780

their escape in good order. Long after the battle was lost in every other quarter, the gigantic form of Kalb, unhorsed and fighting on foot, was seen directing the movements of his brave Maryland and Delaware troops, till he fell dying from eleven wounds. Gates, caught in the throng of fugitives at the beginning of the action, was borne in headlong flight as far as Clermont, where, taking a fresh horse, he made the distance of nearly two hundred miles to Hillsborough in less than four days. The laurels of Saratoga had indeed changed into willows. It was the most disastrous defeat ever inflicted upon an American army, and ignominious withal, since it was incurred through a series of the grossest blunders. The Maryland troops lost half their number, the Delaware regiment was almost entirely destroyed, and all the rest of the army was dispersed. The number of killed and wounded has never been fully ascertained, but it can hardly have been less than 1,000, while more than 1,000 prisoners were taken, with seven pieces of artillery and 2,000 muskets. The British loss in killed and wounded was 324.

Total and ignominious defeat of Gates.

The reputation of General Gates never recovered from this sudden overthrow, and his swift flight to Hillsborough was made the theme of unsparing ridicule. Yet, if duly considered, that was the one part of his conduct for which he cannot fairly be blamed. The best of generals may be caught in a rush of panic-stricken fugitives and hurried off the battlefield: the flight of Frederick the Great at Mollwitz was

His campaign was a series of blunders.

much more ignominious than that of Gates at Camden. When once, moreover, the full extent of the disaster had become apparent, it was certainly desirable that Gates should reach Hillsborough as soon as possible, since it was the point from which the state organization of North Carolina was controlled, and accordingly the point at which a new army might soonest be collected. Gates's flight was a singularly dramatic and appropriate end to his silly career, but our censure should be directed to the wretched generalship by which the catastrophe was prepared : to the wrong choice of roads, the fatal hesitation at the critical moment, the weakening of the army on the eve of battle ; and, above all, to the rashness in fighting at all after the true state of affairs had become known. The campaign was an epitome of the kind of errors which Washington always avoided ; and it admirably illustrated the inanity of John Adams's toast, " A short and violent war," against an enemy of superior strength.

If the 400 Maryland regulars who had been sent to help General Sumter had remained with the main army and been entrusted with the assault on the British right, the result of this battle would doubtless have been very different. It might not have been a victory, but it surely would not have been a rout. On the day before the battle, Sumter had attacked the British supply train on its way from Charleston, and captured all the stores, with more than 100 prisoners. But the defeat at Camden deprived this exploit of its value. Sumter retreated up the Wateree river to Fishing

Creek, but on the 18th Tarleton for once caught him napping, and routed him ; taking 300 prisoners, setting free the captured British, and recovering all the booty. The same day witnessed an American success in another quarter. _{Partisan opera-} At Musgrove's Mills, in the western _{tions.} part of the state, Colonel James Williams defeated a force of 500 British and Tories, killing and wounding nearly one third of their number. Two days later, Marion performed one of his characteristic exploits. A detachment of the British army was approaching Nelson's Ferry, where the Santee river crosses the road from Camden to Charleston, when Marion, with a handful of men, suddenly darting upon these troops, captured 26 of their number, set free 150 Maryland prisoners whom they were taking down to the coast, and got away without losing a man.

Such deeds showed that the life of South Carolina was not quite extinct, but they could not go far toward relieving the gloom which overspread the country after the defeat of Camden. For a second time within three months the American army in the south had been swept out of existence. Gates could barely get together 1,000 men at Hillsborough, and Washington could not well spare any more from his already depleted force. To muster and train a fresh army of regulars would be slow and difficult work, and it was as certain as anything could be that Cornwallis would immediately proceed to attempt the conquest of North Carolina.

Never was the adage that the darkest time comes just before day more aptly illustrated than in the general aspect of American affairs during the summer and fall of 1780. The popular feeling had not so much the character of panic as in those " times which tried men's souls," when the broad Delaware river screened Washington's fast dwindling army from destruction. It was not now a feeling of quick alarm so much as of

Weariness and depression of the people.

utter weariness and depression. More than four years had passed since the Declaration of Independence, and although the enemy had as yet gained no firm foothold in the northern states except in the city of New York, it still seemed impossible to dislodge them from that point, while Cornwallis, flushed with victory, boasted that he would soon conquer all the country south of the Susquehanna. For the moment it began to look as if Lord George Germain's policy of tiring the Americans out might prove successful, after all. The country was still without anything fit to be called a general government. After three years' discussion, the Articles of Confederation, establishing a " league of friendship " between the thirteen states, had not yet been adopted. The Continental Congress had continued to decline in reputation and capacity. From this state of things, rather than from any real poverty of the country, there had ensued a general administrative paralysis, which went on increasing even after the war was ended, until it was brought to a close by the adoption of the Federal Constitution. It was not because the thirteen states were lacking in mate-

rial resources or in patriotism that the conduct of
the war languished as it did. The resources were
sufficient, had there been any means of concentrat-
ing and utilizing them. The relations of the states
to each other were not defined ; and while there
were thirteen powers which could plan and criti-
cise, there was no single power which could act
efficiently. Hence the energies of the people were
frittered away.

The disease was most plainly visible in those
money matters which form the basis of all human
activity. The condition of American finance in
1780 was simply horrible. The "greenback" delusion possessed people's minds even
more strongly then than in the days fol- Evils wrought
by the paper
lowing our Civil War. Pelatiah Web- currency.
ster, the ablest political economist in America at
that time, a thinker far in advance of his age, was
almost alone in insisting upon taxation. The popular feeling was expressed by a delegate in Congress who asked, with unspeakable scorn, why he
should vote to tax the people, when à Philadelphia
printing-press could turn out money by the bushel.
But indeed, without an amendment, Congress had
no power to lay any tax, save through requisitions
upon the state governments. There seemed to
be no alternative but to go on issuing this money,
which many people glorified as the "safest possible currency," because "nobody could take it out
of the country." As Webster truly said, the country had suffered more from this cause than from
the arms of the enemy. "The people of the states
at that time," said he, "had been worried and

fretted, disappointed and put out of humour, by so
many tender acts, limitations of prices, and other
compulsory methods to force value into paper
money, and compel the circulation of it, and by
so many vain funding schemes and declarations
and promises, all which issued from Congress, but
died under the most zealous efforts to put them
into operation, that their patience was exhausted.
These irritations and disappointments had so destroyed the courage and confidence of the people
that they appeared heartless and almost stupid
when their attention was called to any new proposal." During the summer of 1780 this wretched
" Continental ", currency fell into contempt. As
Washington said, it took a wagon-load of money
to buy a wagon-load of provisions. At the end
of the year 1778, the paper dollar was worth sixteen cents in the northern states and twelve cents
in the south. Early in 1780 its value had fallen
to two cents, and before the end of the year it
took ten paper dollars to make a cent. In October, Indian corn sold wholesale in Boston for
$150 a bushel, butter was $12 a pound, tea $90,
sugar $10, beef $8, coffee $12, and a barrel of
flour cost $1,575. Samuel Adams paid $2,000 for
a hat and suit of clothes. The money soon ceased
to circulate, debts could not be collected, and there
"Not worth a was a general prostration of credit. To
Continental." say that a thing was " not worth a Continental " became the strongest possible expression
of contempt. A barber in Philadelphia papered
his shop with bills, and a dog was led up and
down the streets, smeared with tar, with this un-

happy money sticking all over him, — a sorry sub-
stitute for the golden-fleeced sheep of the old Norse
legend. Save for the scanty pittance of gold which
came in from the French alliance, from the little
foreign commerce that was left, and from trade ·
with the British army itself, the country was without any circulating medium. In making its requisitions upon the states, Congress resorted to a
measure which reminds one of the barbaric ages
of barter. Instead of asking for money, it requested the states to send in their "specific supplies" of beef and pork, flour and rice, salt and
hay, tobacco and rum. The finances of what was
so soon to become the richest of nations were thus
managed on the principle whereby the meagre sal-
aries of country clergymen in New England used
to be eked out. It might have been called a continental system of "donation parties."

Under these circumstances, it became almost
impossible to feed and clothe the army. The commissaries, without either money or credit, could
do but little ; and Washington, sorely against his
will, was obliged to levy contributions on the
country surrounding his camp. It was done as
gently as possible. The county magistrates were
called on for a specified quantity of flour and meat;
the supplies brought in were duly appraised, and
certificates were given in exchange for them by
the commissaries. Such certificates were received
at their nominal value in payment of taxes. But
this measure, which simply introduced a new kind
of paper money, served only to add to the general confusion. These difficulties, enhanced by

the feeling that the war was dragged out to an

Difficulty of keeping the army together. interminable length, made it impossible to keep the army properly recruited. When four months' pay of a private ·soldier would not buy a single bushel of wheat for his family, and when he could not collect even this pittance, while most of the time he went barefoot and half-famished, it was not strange that he should sometimes feel mutinous. The desertions to the British lines at this time averaged more than a hundred a month. Ternay, the French admiral, wrote to Vergennes that the fate of North America was as yet very uncertain, and the Revolution by no means so far advanced as people in Europe supposed. The accumulated evils of the time had greatly increased the number of persons who, to save the remnant of their fortunes, were ready to see peace purchased at any price. In August, before he had heard of the disaster at Camden, Washington wrote to President Huntington, reminding him that the term of service of half the army would expire at the end of the year. "The shadow of an army that will remain," said Washington, "will have every motive except mere patriotism to abandon the service, without the hope, which has hitherto supported them, of a change for the better. This is almost extinguished now, and certainly will not outlive the campaign unless it finds something more substantial to rest upon. To me it will appear miraculous if our affairs can maintain themselves much longer in their present train. If either the temper or the resources of the country will not admit of an alteration, we may expect soon to be reduced to the humiliating condition of seeing the cause of America in America upheld by foreign arms."

To appreciate the full force of this, we must remember that, except in South Carolina, there had been no fighting worthy of mention during the year. The southern campaign absorbed the energies of the British to such an extent that they did nothing whatever in the north but make an unsuccessful attempt at invading New Jersey in June. While this fact shows how severely the strength of England was taxed by the coalition that had been formed against her, it shows even more forcibly how the vitality of America had been sapped by causes that lay deeper down than the mere presence of war. It was, indeed, becoming painfully apparent that little was to be hoped save through the aid of France. The alliance had The French thus far achieved but little that was im- alliance. mediately obvious to the American people, but it had really been of enormous indirect benefit to us. Both in itself and in the European complications to which it had led, the action of France had very seriously crippled the efficient military power of England. It locked up and neutralized much British energy that would otherwise have been directed against the Americans. The French government had also furnished Congress with large sums of money. But as for any direct share in military enterprises on American soil or in American waters, France had as yet done almost nothing. An evil star had presided over both the joint expeditions for the recovery of Newport and Savannah, and no French army had been landed on our shores to cast in its lot with Washington's brave Continentals in a great and decisive campaign.

It had long been clear that France could in no way more effectively further the interests which she shared with the United States than by sending a strong force of trained soldiers to act under Washington's command. Nothing could be more obvious than the inference that such a general, once provided with an adequate force, might drive the British from New York, and thus deal a blow which would go far toward ending the war. This had long been Washington's most cherished scheme. In February, 1779, Lafayette had returned to France to visit his family, and to urge that aid of this sort might be granted. To chide him for his

Lafayette's visit to France. naughtiness in running away to America in defiance of the royal mandate, the king ordered him to be confined for a week at his father-in-law's house in Paris. Then he received him quite graciously at court, while the queen begged him to " tell us good news of our dearly beloved Americans." The good Lafayette, to whom, in the dreadful years that were to come, this dull king and his bright, unhappy queen were to look for compassionate protection, now ventured to give them some sensible words of advice. " The money that you spend on one of your old court balls," he said, " would go far toward sending a serviceable army to America, and dealing England a blow where she would most feel it." For several months he persisted in urging Vergennes to send over at least 12,000 men, with a good general, and to put them distinctly under Washington's command, so that there might be no disastrous wrangling about precedence, and no repetition of such misunderstandings as had ruined the Newport campaign. When Estaing arrived in Paris, early in 1780, after his defeat at Savannah, he gave similar advice. The idea commended itself to Vergennes, and when, in April, 1780, Lafayette returned to the United States, he was authorized to inform Washington that France would soon send the desired reinforcement.

On the 10th of July, Admiral Ternay, with seven *July 10, 1780* ships-of-the-line and three frigates, arrived at Newport, bringing with him a force of 6,000 men, commanded by a good general, Count Rochambeau. This was the first installment of an army of which the remainder was to be sent as soon as adequate means of transport could be furnished. On the important question of military etiquette, Lafayette's advice had been strictly heeded.

Arrival of part of the French auxiliary force under Rochambeau.

Rochambeau was told to put himself under Washington's command, and to consider his troops as part of the American army, while American officers were to take precedence of French officers of equal rank. This French army was excellent in discipline and equipment, and among its officers were some, such as the Duke de Lauzun-Biron and the Marquis de Chastellux, who had won high distinction. Rochambeau wrote to Vergennes that on his arrival he found the people of Rhode Island sad and discouraged. Everybody thought the country was going to the dogs. But when it was understood that this was but the advance guard of a considerable army and that France was this time in deadly earnest, their spirits rose, and the streets of Newport were noisy with hurrahs and brilliant with fireworks.

The hearts of the people, however, were still further to be sickened with hope deferred. Several British ships-of-the-line, arriving at New York, gave the enemy such a preponderance upon the water that Clinton resolved to take the offensive, and started down the Sound with 6,000 men to attack the French at Newport. Washington foiled this scheme by a sudden movement against New York, which obliged the British commander to fall back hastily for its defence ; but the French fleet was nevertheless blockaded in Narragansett Bay by a powerful British squadron, and Rochambeau felt it necessary to keep his troops in Rhode Island to aid the admiral in case of such contingencies as might arise. The second installment of the French army, on which their hopes had been built, never came, for a British fleet of thirty-two sail held it blockaded in the harbour of Brest.

The remainder is detained in France by a British fleet.

The maritime supremacy of England thus continued to stand in the way of any great enterprise ; and for a whole year the gallant army of Rochambeau was kept idle in Rhode Island, impatient and chafing under the restraint. The splendid work it was destined to perform under Washington's leadership lay hidden in the darkness of the future, and for the moment the gloom which had overspread the country was only deepened. Three years had passed since the victory of Saratoga, but the vast consequences which were already flowing from that event had not yet disclosed their meaning. Looking only at the surface of things, it might well be asked — and many did ask — whether that great victory had General despondency. really done anything more than to prolong a struggle which was essentially vain and hopeless. Such themes formed the burden of discourse at gentlemen's dinner-tables and in the back parlours of country inns, where stout yeomen reviewed the situation of affairs through clouds of tobacco smoke; and never, perhaps, were the Tories more jubilant or the Whigs more crestfallen than at the close of this doleful summer.

It was just at this moment that the country was startled by the sudden disclosure of a scheme of blackest treason. For the proper explanation of this affair, a whole chapter will be required.

CHAPTER XIV.

BENEDICT ARNOLD.

To understand the proximate causes of Arnold's treason, we must start from the summer of 1778, when Philadelphia was evacuated by the British.

Arnold put in command of Philadelphia, June 18, 1778.

On that occasion, as General Arnold was incapacitated for active service by the wound he had received at Saratoga, Washington placed him in command of Philadelphia. This step brought Arnold into direct contact with Congress, toward which he bore a fierce grudge for the slights it had put upon him; and, moreover, the command was in itself a difficult one. The authority vested in the commandant was not clearly demarcated from that which belonged to the state government, so that occasions for dispute were sure to be forthcoming. While the British had held the city many of the inhabitants had given them active aid and encouragement, and there was now more or less property to be confiscated. By a resolve of Congress, all public stores belonging to the enemy were to be appropriated for the use of the army, and the commander-in-chief was directed to suspend the sale or transfer of goods until the general question of ownership should have been determined by a joint committee of Congress and of the Executive Council of Pennsylvania. It became Arnold's duty to carry out this order, which not only wrought serious disturbance to business, but made the city a hornet's nest of bickerings and complaints. The qualities needed for dealing successfully with such an affair as this were very different from the qualities which had distinguished Arnold in the field. The utmost delicacy of tact was required, and Arnold was blunt, and self-willed, and deficient in tact. He was accordingly soon at loggerheads with the state government, and lost, besides, much of the personal popularity with which he started. Stories were whispered about to his discredit. It was charged against Arnold that the extravagance of his style of living was an offence against republican simplicity, and a scandal in view of the distressed condition of the country; that in order to obtain the means of meeting his heavy expenses he resorted to peculation and extortion; and that he showed too much favour to the Tories. These charges were doubtless not without some foundation. This era of paper money and failing credit was an era of ostentatious expenditure, not altogether unlike that which, in later days, preceded the financial break-down of 1873. People in the towns lived extravagantly, and in no other town was this more conspicuous than in Philadelphia; while perhaps no one in Philadelphia kept a finer stable of horses or gave more costly dinners than General Arnold. He ran in debt, and engaged in commercial speculations to remedy the evil; and, in view of the light afterward thrown upon his character, it is not unlikely that he may

have sometimes availed himself of his high position to aid these speculations.

The charge of favouring the Tories may find
its explanation in a circumstance which possibly
throws a side-light upon his lavish use of money.
Miss Margaret Shippen, daughter of a gentleman
Miss Margaret of moderate Tory sympathies, who some
Shippen.   years afterward became chief justice of
Pennsylvania, was one of the most beautiful and
fascinating women in America, and at that time
the reigning belle of Philadelphia; and no sooner
had the new commandant arrived at his post than
he was taken captive. The lady was scarcely
twenty years old, while Arnold was a widower of
thirty-five, with three sons; but his handsome
face, his gallant bearing, and his splendid career
outweighed these disadvantages, and in the autumn
of 1778 he was betrothed to Miss Shippen, and
thus entered into close relations with a prominent
Tory family. In the moderate section of the
Tory party, to which the Shippens belonged, there
were many people who, while strongly opposed to
the Declaration of Independence, would nevertheless have deemed it dishonourable to lend active
aid to the enemy. In 1778, such people thought
Views of the   that Congress did wrong in making an
moderate To-   alliance with France instead of accept-
ries.   ing the liberal proposals of Lord North.
The Declaration of Independence, they argued,
would never have been made had it been supposed
that the constitutional liberties of the American
people could any otherwise be securely protected.
Even Samuel Adams admitted this. In the war

which had been undertaken in defence of these
liberties, the victory of Saratoga had driven the
British government to pledge itself to concede
them once and forever. Then why not be magnanimous in the hour of triumph? Why not consider the victory of Saratoga as final, instead of
subjecting the resources of the country to a terrible strain in the doubtful attempt to secure a result which, only three years before, even Washington himself had regarded as undesirable? Was
it not unwise and unpatriotic to reject the overtures of our kinsmen, and cast in our lot with that
Catholic and despotic power which had ever been
our deadliest foe?

Such were the arguments to which Arnold must
have listened again and again, during the summer
and autumn of 1778. How far he may have been
predisposed toward such views it would be impossible to say. He always declared himself disgusted
with the French alliance,[1] and in this there is
nothing improbable. But that, under the circumstances, he should gradually have drifted into the
Tory position was, in a man of his temperament,
almost inevitable. His nature was warm, impulsive, and easily impressible, while he
was deficient in breadth of intelligence Arnold's drift
toward Tory-
and in rigorous moral conviction; and ism.
his opinions on public matters took their hue
largely from his personal feelings. It was not
surprising that such a man, in giving splendid
entertainments, should invite to them the Tory

[1] The story of his attempt to enter the service of Luzerne, the
French minister, rests upon insufficient authority.

friends of the lady whose favour he was courting. His course excited the wrath of the Whigs. General Reed wrote indignantly to General Greene that Arnold had actually given a party at which " not only common Tory ladies, but the wives and daughters of persons proscribed by the state, and now with the enemy at New York," were present in considerable numbers. When twitted with such things, Arnold used to reply that it was the part of a true soldier to fight his enemies in the open field, but not to proscribe or persecute their wives and daughters in private life. But such an explanation naturally satisfied no one. His quarrels with the Executive Council, sharpened by such incidents as these, grew more and more violent, until when, in December, his most active enemy, Joseph Reed, became president of the Council, he suddenly made up his mind to resign his post and leave the army altogether. He would

He makes up his mind to leave the army.

quit the turmoil of public affairs, obtain a grant of land in western New York, settle it with his old soldiers, with whom he had always been a favourite, and lead henceforth a life of Arcadian simplicity. In this mood he wrote to Schuyler, in words which to-day seem strange and sad, that his ambition was not so much to " shine in history " as to be " a good citizen ; " and about the 1st of January, 1779, he set out for Albany to consult with the New York legislature about the desired land.

His scheme was approved by John Jay and others, and in all likelihood would have succeeded ; but as he stopped for a day at Morristown, to visit

Washington, a letter overtook him, with the information that as soon as his back had been turned upon Philadelphia he had been publicly attacked by President Reed and the Council. Formal charges were brought against him : 1, Charges are brought against him, Jan., 1779. of having improperly granted a pass for a ship to come into port ; 2, of having once used some public wagons for the transportation of private property ; 3, of having usurped the privilege of the Council in allowing people to enter the enemy's lines ; 4, of having illegally bought up a lawsuit over a prize vessel ; 5, of having " imposed menial offices upon the sons of freemen" serving in the militia ; and 6, of having made purchases for his private benefit at the time when, by his own order, all shops were shut. These charges were promulgated in a most extraordinary fashion. Not only were they laid before Congress, but copies of them were sent to the governors of all the states, accompanied by a circular letter from President Reed requesting the governors to communicate them to their respective legislatures. Arnold was naturally enraged at such an elaborate attempt to prepossess the public mind against him, but his first concern was for the possible effect it might have upon Miss Shippen. He instantly returned to Philadelphia, and demanded an investigation. He had obtained Washington's permission to resign his command, but deferred acting He is acquitted by a committee of Congress in March. upon it till the inquiry should have ended. The charges were investigated by a committee of Congress, and about the middle of March this committee brought in a report stating that all the accusations were ground-less, save the two which related to the use of the wagons and the irregular granting of a pass ; and since in these instances there was no evidence of wrong intent, the committee recommended an un-qualified verdict of acquittal. Arnold thereupon, considering himself vindicated, resigned his com-mand. But Reed now represented to Congress that further testimony was forthcoming, and urged that the case should be reconsidered. Accord-ingly, instead of acting upon the report of its com-mittee, Congress referred the matter anew to a joint committee of Congress and the Assembly and Council of Pennsylvania. This joint com-

The case is re-ferred to a court-martial, April 3, 1779. mittee shirked the matter by recom-mending that the case be referred to a court-martial, and this recommendation was adopted by Congress on the 3d of April. The vials of Arnold's wrath were now full to overflow-ing ; but he had no cause to complain of Miss Shippen, for their marriage took place in less than a week after this action of Congress. Washing-ton, who sympathized with Arnold's impatience, appointed the court-martial for the 1st of May, but the Council of Pennsylvania begged for more time to collect evidence. And thus, in one way and another, the summer and autumn were frit-tered away, so that the trial did not begin until the 19th of December. All this time Arnold kept clamouring for a speedy trial, and Washington did his best to soothe him while paying due heed to the representations of the Council.

In the excitement of this fierce controversy the

Arcadian project seems to have been forgotten. Up to this point Arnold's anger had been chiefly directed toward the authorities of Pennsylvania; but when Congress refused to act upon the report of its committee exonerating him from blame, he became incensed against the whole party which, as he said, had so ill requited his services. It is supposed to have been about that time, in April, 1779, that he wrote a letter to Sir Henry Clinton, in disguised handwriting and under the signature of "Gustavus," describing himself as an American officer of high rank, who, through disgust at the French alliance and *other recent proceedings of Congress*, might perhaps be persuaded to go over to the British, provided he could be indemnified for any losses he might incur by so doing. The beginning of this correspondence — if this was really the time — coincided cu- First correspondence with Clinton. riously with the date of Arnold's marriage, but it is in the highest degree probable that down to the final catastrophe Mrs. Arnold knew nothing whatever of what was going on.[1] The correspondence was kept up at intervals, Sir Henry's replies being written by Major John André, his adjutant-general, over the signature of "John Anderson." Nothing seems to have been thought of at first beyond the personal desertion of Arnold to the enemy; the betrayal of a fortress was a later development of infamy. For the pres-

---

[1] The charge against Mrs. Arnold, in Parton's *Life of Burr*, i. 126, is conclusively refuted by Sabine, in his *Loyalists of the American Revolution*, i. 172–178. I think there can be no doubt that Burr lied.

ent, too, we may suppose that Arnold was merely playing with fire, while he awaited the result of the court-martial.

The summer was not a happy one. His debts went on increasing, while his accounts with Congress remained unsettled, and he found it impossible to collect large sums that were due him. At last the court-martial met, and sat for five weeks.

On the 26th of January, 1780, the verdict was rendered, and in substance it agreed exactly with that of the committee of Congress ten months before. Arnold was fully acquitted of all the charges which alleged dishonourable dealings. The pass which he had granted was irregular, and public wagons, which were standing idle, had once been used to remove private property that was in imminent danger from the enemy. The court exonerated Arnold of all intentional wrong, even in these venial matters, which it characterized as "imprudent;" but, as a sort of lame concession to the Council of Pennsylvania, it directed that he should receive a public reprimand from the commander-in-chief for his imprudence in the use of wagons, and for hurriedly giving a pass in which all due forms were not attended to. The decision of the court-martial was promptly confirmed by Congress, and Washington had no alternative but to issue the reprimand, which he couched in words as delicate and gracious as possible.[1]

The court-martial acquits Arnold of all serious charges, but directs Washington to reprimand him for two very trivial ones, Jan. 26, 1780.

---

[1] The version of the reprimand given by Marbois, however, is somewhat apocryphal.

It was too late, however. The damage was
done. Arnold had long felt persecuted and in-.
sulted. He had already dallied with temptation,
and the poison was now working in his veins. His
sense of public duty was utterly distorted by the
keener sense of his private injuries. We may
imagine him brooding over some memorable incidents in the careers of Monk, of the great Mon-
trose and the greater Marlborough, until he persuaded himself that to change sides in a civil war
was not so heinous a crime after all. Especially
the example of Monk, which had al- Arnold
ready led Charles Lee to disgrace, seems thirsts for revenge upon
to have riveted the attention of Arnold, Congress.
although only the most shallow scrutiny could discover any resemblance between what the great
English general had done and what Arnold pur-
posed to do. There was not a more scrupulously
honourable soldier in his day than George Monk.
Arnold's thoughts may have run somewhat as follows. He would not become an ordinary deserter,
a villain on a small scale. He would not sell himself cheaply to the devil; but he would play as
signal a part in his new career as he had played in
the old one. He would overwhelm this blundering
Congress, and triumphantly carry the country
back to its old allegiance. To play such a part,
however, would require the blackest treachery.
Fancy George Monk, "honest old George," asking for the command of a fortress in order to betray it to the enemy!

When once Arnold had committed himself to
this evil course, his story becomes a sickening one,

lacking no element of horror, whether in its foul beginnings or in its wretched end. To play his new part properly, he must obtain an important command, and the place which obviously suggested itself was West Point.

Since Burgoyne's overthrow, Washington had built a chain of strong fortresses there, for he did not intend that the possession of the Hudson river should ever again be put in question, so far as fortifications could go. Could this cardinal position be delivered up to Clinton, the prize would be worth tenfold the recent triumphs at Charleston and Camden. It would be giving the British what Burgoyne had tried in vain to get; and now it was the hero of Saratoga who plotted to undo his own good work at the dictates of perverted ambition and unhallowed revenge.

Significance of West Point.

To get possession of this stronghold, it was necessary to take advantage of the confidence with which his great commander had always honoured him. From Washington, in July, 1780, Arnold sought the command of West Point, alleging that his wounded leg still kept him unfit for service in the field; and Washington immediately put him in charge of this all-important post, thus giving him the strongest proof of unabated confidence and esteem which it was in his power to give; and among all the dark shades in Arnold's treason, perhaps none seems darker than this personal treachery toward the man who had always trusted and defended him. What must the traitor's feelings have been when

Arnold put in command of West Point, July, 1780.

he read the affectionate letters which Schuyler wrote him at this very time? In better days he had shown much generosity of nature. Can it be that this is the same man who on the field of Sara- toga saved the life of the poor soldier who in hon- est fight had shot him and broken his leg? Such are the strange contrasts that we sometimes see in characters that are governed by impulse, and not by principle. Their virtue may be real enough while it lasts, but it does not weather the storm; and when once wrecked, the very same emotional nature by which alone it was supported often prompts to deeds of incredible wickedness.

After taking command of West Point, the cor- respondence with André, carefully couched in such terms as to make it seem to refer to some commer- cial enterprise, was vigorously kept up; and hints were let drop which convinced Sir Henry Clinton that the writer was Arnold, and the betrayal of the highland stronghold his purpose. Troops were accordingly embarked on the Hudson, and the flo- tilla was put in command of Admiral Rodney, who had looked in at New York on his way to the West Indies. To disguise the purpose of the embarka- tion, a rumour was industriously circulated that a force was to be sent southward to the Chesapeake. To arrange some important details of the affair it seemed desirable that the two correspondents, "Gustavus" and "John Anderson," should meet, and talk over matters which could not safely be com- mitted to paper. On the 18th of September, Washington, accompanied by Lafayette and Ham-

Secret inter- view between Arnold and André, Sept. 22.

ilton, set out for Hartford, for an interview with Rochambeau ; and advantage was taken of his absence to arrange a meeting between the plotters. On the 20th André was taken up the river on the Vulture, sloop-of-war, and on the night of the 21st Arnold sent out a boat which brought him ashore about four miles below Stony Point. There in a thicket of fir-trees, under the veil of blackest midnight, the scheme was matured ; but as gray dawn came on before all the details had been arranged, the boatmen became alarmed, and refused to take André back to the ship, and he was accordingly persuaded, though against his will, to accompany Arnold within the American lines. The two conspirators walked up the bank a couple of miles to the house of one Joshua Smith, a man of doubtful allegiance, who does not seem to have understood the nature and extent of the plot, or to have known who Arnold's visitor was. It was thought that they might spend the day discussing their enterprise, and when it should have grown dark André could be rowed back to the Vulture.

But now a quite unforeseen accident occurred. Colonel Livingston, commanding the works on the opposite side of the river, was provoked by the sight of a British ship standing so near ; and he opened such a lively fire upon the Vulture that she was obliged to withdraw from the scene. As the conspirators were waiting in Smith's house for breakfast to be served, they heard the booming of the guns, and André, rushing to the window, beheld with dismay the ship on whose presence so much depended dropping out of sight down the stream. On second thoughts, however, it was clear that she would not go far, as her commander had orders not to return to New York without André, and it was still thought that he might regain her. After breakfast he went to an upper chamber with Arnold, and several hours were spent in perfecting their plans. Immediately upon André's return to New York, the force under Clinton and Rodney was to ascend the river. To obstruct the approach of a hostile flotilla, an enormous chain lay stretched across the river, guarded by water-batteries. Under pretence of repairs, one link was to be taken out for a few days, and supplied by a rope which a slight blow would tear away. The approach of the British was to be announced by a concerted system of signals, and the American forces were to be so distributed that they could be surrounded and captured in detail, until at the proper moment Arnold, taking advantage of the apparent defeat, was to surrender the works, with all the troops — 3,000 in number — under his command. It was not unreasonably supposed that such a catastrophe, coming on the heels of Charleston and Camden and general bankruptcy, would put a stop to the war and lead to negotiations, in which Arnold, in view of such decisive service, might hope to play a leading part.

The plot for surrendering West Point.

When André set out on this perilous undertaking, Sir Henry Clinton specially warned him not to adopt any disguise or to carry any papers which might compromise his safety. But André disregarded the advice, and took from Arnold six pa-

pers, all but one of them in the traitor's own handwriting, containing descriptions of the fortresses
and information as to the disposition of the troops.

André takes
compromising
documents; Much risk might have been avoided by
putting this information into cipher, or
into a memorandum which would have
been meaningless save to the parties concerned.
But André may perhaps have doubted Arnold's
fidelity, and feared lest under a false pretence of
treason he might be drawing the British away into
a snare. The documents which he took, being in
Arnold's handwriting and unmistakable in their
purport, were such as to put him in Clinton's
power, and compel him, for the sake of his own
safety, to perform his part of the contract. André
intended, before getting into the boat, to tie up
these papers in a bundle loaded with a stone, to
be dropped into the water in case of a sudden
challenge ; but in the mean time he put them where
they could not so easily be got rid of, between his
stockings and the soles of his feet. Arnold furnished the requisite passes for Smith and André to
go either by boat or by land, and, having thus apparently provided for all contingencies, took leave
before noon, and returned in his barge to his headquarters, ten miles up the stream. As evening approached, Smith, who seems to have been a man
of unsteady nerves, refused to take André out to
the Vulture. He had been alarmed by the firing in
the morning, and feared there would be more risk
in trying to reach the ship than in travelling down
to the British lines by land, and he promised to
ride all night with André if he would go that way.

The young officer reluctantly consented, and partially disguised himself in some of Smith's clothes. At sundown the two crossed the river at King's Ferry, and pursued their journey on horseback toward White Plains.

and is reluctantly persuaded to return to New York by land, Sept. 22.

The roads east of the Hudson, between the British and the American lines, were at this time infested by robbers, who committed their depredations under pretence of keeping up a partisan warfare. There were two sets of these scapegraces,— the " Cowboys," or cattle-thieves, and the " Skinners," who took everything they could find. These epithets, however, referred to the political complexion they chose to assume, rather than to any difference in their evil practices. The Skinners professed to be Whigs, and the Cowboys called themselves Tories ;

The roads infested by robbers.

but in point of fact the two parties were alike political enemies to any farmer or wayfarer whose unprotected situation offered a prospect of booty ; and though murder was not often committed, nobody's property was safe. It was a striking instance of the demoralization wrought in a highly civilized part of the country through its having so long continued to be the actual seat of war. Rumours that the Cowboys were out in force made Smith afraid to continue the journey by night, and the impatient André was thus obliged to stop at a farmhouse with his timid companion. Rising before dawn, they kept on until they reached the Croton river, which marked the upper boundary of the neutral ground between the British and the

American lines. Smith's instructions had been, in case of adopting the land route, not to leave his charge before reaching White Plains; but he now became uneasy to return, and André, who was beginning to consider himself out of danger, was perhaps not unwilling to part with a comrade who annoyed him by his loquacious and inquisitive disposition. So Smith made his way back to headquarters, and informed Arnold that he had escorted " Mr. Anderson " within a few miles of the British lines, which he must doubtless by this time have reached in safety.

Meanwhile, André, left to himself, struck into the road which led through Tarrytown, expecting to meet no worse enemies than Cowboys, who would either respect a British officer, or, if bent on plunder, might be satisfied by his money and watch. But it happened that morning that a party of seven young men had come out to intercept some Cowboys who were expected up the road; and about nine o'clock, as André was approaching the creek above Tarrytown, a short distance from the farfamed Sleepy Hollow, he was suddenly confronted by three of this party, who sprang from the bushes and, with levelled muskets, ordered him to halt. These men had let several persons, with whose Arrest of André, Sept. 23. faces they were familiar, pass unquestioned; and if Smith, who was known to almost every one in that neighbourhood, had been with André, they too would doubtless have been allowed to pass. André was stopped because he was a stranger. One of these men happened to have on the coat of a Hessian soldier. Held

by the belief that they must be Cowboys, or
members of what was sometimes euphemistically
termed the " lower party," André expressed a hope
that such was the case ; and on being assured that
it was so, his caution deserted him, and, with that
sudden sense of relief which is apt to come after
unwonted and prolonged constraint, he avowed himself a British officer, travelling on business of great
importance. To his dismay, he now learned his
mistake. John Paulding, the man in the Hessian
coat, informed him that they were Americans, and
ordered him to dismount. When he now showed
them Arnold's pass they disregarded it, and insisted
upon searching him, until presently the six papers
were discovered where he had hidden them. " By
God, he is a spy!" exclaimed Paulding, as he
looked over the papers. Threats and promises
were of no avail. The young men, who were not
to be bought or cajoled, took their prisoner twelve
miles up the river, and delivered him into the hands
of Colonel John Jameson, a Virginian officer, who
commanded a cavalry outpost at North Castle.
When Jameson looked over the papers, they
seemed to him very extraordinary documents to
be travelling toward New York in the stockings of
a stranger who could give no satisfactory account
of himself. But so far from his suspecting Arnold
of any complicity in the matter, he could think of
nothing better than to send the prisoner straightway to Arnold himself, together with a
brief letter in which he related what Colonel Jame-
had happened. To the honest Jameson son's perplex-
it seemed that this must be some foul ruse of the

enemy, some device for stirring up suspicion in the camp, — something, at any rate, which could not too quickly be brought to his general's notice. But the documents themselves he prudently sent by an express-rider to Washington, accompanying them with a similar letter of explanation. André, in charge of a military guard, had already proceeded some distance toward West Point when Jameson's second in command, Major Benjamin Tallmadge, came in from some errand on which he had been engaged. On hearing what had happened, Tallmadge suspected that all was not right with Arnold, and insisted that André and the letter should be recalled. After a hurried discussion, Jameson sent out a party which brought André back; but he still thought it his duty to inform Arnold, and so the letter which saved the traitor's life was allowed to proceed on its way.

Now, if Washington had returned from Hartford by the route which it was supposed he would take, through Danbury and Peekskill, Arnold would not even thus have been saved. For some reason Washington returned two or three days sooner than had been expected; and, moreover, he chose a more northerly route, through Farmington and Litchfield, so that the messenger failed to meet him. It was on the evening of Saturday, the 23d, that Jameson's two letters started. On Sunday afternoon Washington arrived at Fish-

Washington returns from Hartford sooner than expected.

kill, eighteen miles above West Point, and was just starting down the river road when he met Luzerne, the French minister, who was on his way to consult with Ro-

chambeau. Wishing to have a talk with this gentleman, Washington turned back to the nearest inn,
where they sat down to supper and chatted, all
unconsciously, with the very Joshua Smith from
whom André had parted at the Croton river on
the morning of the day before. Word was sent to
Arnold to expect the commander-in-chief and his
suite to breakfast the next morning, and before
daybreak of Monday they were galloping down the
wooded road. As they approached the Robinson
House, where Arnold had his headquarters, opposite West Point, Washington turned his horse
down toward the river, whereat Lafayette reminded
him that they were late already, and ought not to
keep Mrs. Arnold waiting. " Ah, marquis," said
Washington, laughing, " I know you young men
are all in love with Mrs. Arnold : go and get your
breakfast, and tell her not to wait for me." Lafayette did not adopt the suggestion. He accompanied Washington and Knox while they rode
down to examine some redoubts. Hamilton and
the rest of the party kept on to the house, and sat
down to breakfast in its cheerful wainscoted din-
ing-room, with Arnold and his wife and several of
his officers.

As they sat at table, a courier entered, and
handed to Arnold the letter in which Colonel Jameson informed him that one John Anderson had
been taken with compromising documents in his
possession, which had been forwarded to the
commander-in-chief. With astonishing Flight of Ar-
presence of mind, he folded the letter nold, Sept. 25.
and put it in his pocket, finished the remark

which had been on his lips when the courier entered, and then, rising, said that he was suddenly called across the river to West Point, but would return to meet Washington without delay ; and he ordered his barge to be manned. None of the officers observed anything unusual in his manner, but the quick eye of his wife detected something wrong, and as he left the room she excused herself and hurried after him. Going up to their bedroom, he told her that he was a ruined man and must fly for his life ; and as she screamed and fainted in his arms, he laid her upon the bed, called in the maid to attend her, stooped to kiss his baby boy who was sleeping in the cradle, rushed down to the yard, leaped on a horse that was standing there, and galloped down a by-path to his barge. It had promptly occurred to his quick mind that the Vulture would still be waiting for André some miles down stream, and he told the oarsmen to row him thither without delay, as he must get back soon to meet Washington. A brisk row of eighteen miles brought them to the Vulture, whose commander was still wondering why André did not come back. From the cabin of the Vulture Arnold sent a letter to Washington, assuring him of Mrs. Arnold's innocence, and begging that she might be allowed to return to her family in Philadelphia, or come to her husband, as she might choose. Then the ill-omened ship weighed anchor, and reached New York next morning.

Meanwhile, about noonday Washington came in for his breakfast, and, hearing that Arnold had crossed the river to West Point, soon hurried off to meet him there, followed by all his suite except Hamilton. As they were ferried across, no salute of cannon greeted them, and on landing they learned with astonishment that Arnold had not been there that morning ; but no one as yet had a glimmer of suspicion. When they returned to the Robinson House, about two o'clock, they found Hamilton walking up and down before the door in great excitement. Jameson's courier had arrived, with the letters for Washington, which the aide had just opened and read. The commander and his aide went alone into the house, and examined the papers, which, taken in connection with the traitor's flight, but too plainly told the story. From Mrs. Arnold, who was in hysterics, Washington could learn nothing. He privately sent Hamilton and another aide in pursuit of the fugitive; and coming out to meet Lafayette and Knox, his voice choking and tears rolling down his cheeks, he exclaimed, " Arnold is a traitor, and has fled to the British ! Whom can we trust now ? " In a moment, however, he had regained his wonted composure. It was no time for giving way to emotion. It was as yet impossible to tell how far the scheme might have extended. Even now the enemy's fleet might be ascending the river (as but for André's capture it doubtless would have been doing that day), and an attack might be made before the morrow. Riding anxiously about the works, Washington soon detected the treacherous arrangements that had been made, and by seven in the evening he had done much to correct them and to make ready for

Discovery of the treasonable plot.

an attack. As he was taking supper in the room which Arnold had so hastily quitted in the morning, the traitor's letter from the Vulture was handed him. " Go to Mrs. Arnold," said he quietly to one of his officers, " and tell her that though my duty required no means should be neglected to arrest General Arnold, I have great pleasure in acquainting *her* that he is now safe on board a British vessel."

But while the principal criminal was safe it was far otherwise with the agent who had been employed in this perilous business. On Sunday, from his room in Jameson's quarters, André had written a letter to Washington, pathetic in its frank simplicity, setting forth his high position in the British army, and telling his story without any attempt at evasion. From the first there could be no doubt as to the nature of his case, yet André for the moment did not fully comprehend it. On Thursday, the 28th, he was taken across the river to Tappan, where the main army was encamped. His escort, Major Tallmadge, was a graduate of Yale College and a classmate of Nathan Hale, whom General Howe had hanged as a spy four years before. Tallmadge had begun to feel a warm interest in André, and as they rode their horses side by side into Tappan, when his prisoner asked how his case would probably be regarded, Tallmadge's countenance fell, and it was not until the question had been twice repeated that he replied by a gentle allusion to the fate of his lamented classmate. " But surely," said poor André, " you do not consider his case

André taken
to Tappan,
Sept. 28.

and mine alike ! " " They are precisely similar," answered Tallmadge gravely, " and similar will be your fate."

Next day a military commission of fourteen generals was assembled, with Greene presiding, to sit in judgment on the unfortunate young officer. " It is impossible to save him," said the kindly Steuben, who was one of the judges. " Would to God the wretch who has drawn him to his death might be made to suffer in his stead ! " The opinion of the court was unanimous that André had acted as a spy, and incurred the penalty of death. Washington allowed a brief respite, that Sir Henry Clinton's views might be considered. The British commander, in his sore distress over the danger of his young friend, could find no better grounds to allege in his defence than that he had, presumably, gone ashore under a flag of truce, and that when taken he certainly was travelling under the protection of a pass which Arnold, in the ordinary exercise of his authority, had a right to grant. But clearly these safeguards were vitiated by the treasonable purpose of the commander who granted them, and in availing himself of them André, who was privy to this treasonable purpose, took his life in his hands as completely as any ordinary spy would do. André himself had already candidly admitted before the court " that it was impossible for him to suppose that he came ashore under the sanction of a flag ; " and Washington struck to the root of the matter, as he invariably did, in his letter to Clinton, where he said that André " was

André's trial and sentence, Sept. 29.

employed in the execution of measures very foreign to the objects of flags of truce, and such as they were never meant to authorize or countenance in the most distant degree." The argument was conclusive, but it was not strange that the British general should have been slow to admit its force. He begged that the question might be submitted to an impartial committee, consisting of Knyphausen from the one army and Rochambeau from the other; but as no question had arisen which the military commission was not thoroughly competent to decide, Washington very properly refused to permit such an unusual proceeding. Lastly, Clinton asked that André might be exchanged for Christopher Gadsden, who had been taken in the capture of Charleston, and was then imprisoned at St. Augustine. At the same time, a letter from Arnold to Washington, with characteristic want of tact, hinting at retaliation upon the persons of sundry South Carolinian prisoners, was received with silent contempt.

There was a general feeling in the American army that if Arnold himself could be surrendered to justice, it might perhaps be well to set free the less guilty victim by an act of executive clemency; and Greene gave expression to this feeling in an interview with Lieutenant-General Robertson, whom Clinton sent up on Sunday, the 1st of October, to plead for André's life. No such suggestion could be made in the form of an official proposal. Under no circumstances could Clinton be expected to betray the man from whose crime he had sought to profit, and who had now thrown himself upon him for protection. Nevertheless, in a roundabout way' the suggestion was made. On Saturday, Captain Ogden, with an escort of twenty-five men and a flag of truce, was sent down to Paulus Hook with letters for Clinton, and he contrived to whisper to the commandant there that if in any way Arnold might be suffered to slip into the hands of the Americans André would be set free. It was Lafayette who had authorized Ogden to offer the suggestion, and so, apparently, Washington must have connived at it; but Clinton, naturally, refused to entertain the idea for a moment. The conference between Greene and Robertson led to nothing. A petition from André, in which he begged to be shot rather than hanged, was duly considered and rejected; and, accordingly, on Monday, the 2d of October, the ninth day after his capture by the yeomen at Tarrytown, the adjutant-general of the British army was led to the gallows. His remains were buried near the spot where he suffered, but in 1821 they were disinterred and removed to Westminster Abbey.

The fate of this gallant young officer has always called forth tender commiseration, due partly to his high position and his engaging personal qualities, but chiefly, no doubt, to the fact that, while he suffered the penalty of the law, the chief conspirator escaped. One does not easily get rid of a vague sense of injustice in this, but the injustice was not of man's contriving. But for the remarkable series of accidents — if it be philosophical to call them so — resulting in André's capture, the

Captain Ogden's mesage, Sept. 30.

Execution of André, Oct. 2.

treason would very likely have been successful, and the cause of American independence might have been for the moment ruined.   But for an equally remarkable series of accidents Arnold would not have received warning in time to escape.   If both had been captured, both would probably have been hanged.   Certainly both alike had incurred the penalty of death.   It was not the fault of Washington or of the court-martial that the chief offender went unpunished, and in no wise was André made a scapegoat for Arnold.   It is right that we should feel pity for the fate of André ; but it is unfortunate that pity should be permitted to cloud the judgment of the historian, as in the case of Lord Stanhope, who stands almost alone among competent writers in impugning the justice of André's sentence.   One remark of Lord Stanhope's I am tempted to quote, as an amusing instance of that certain air of " condescension " which Mr. Lowell

Lord Stanhope's unconscious impudence.

has observed in our British cousins.   He seeks to throw discredit upon the military commission by gravely assuming that the American generals must, of course, have been ignorant men, " who had probably never so much as heard the names of Vattel or Puffendorf," and, accordingly, " could be no fit judges on any nice or doubtful point " of military law.   Now, of the twelve American generals who sat in judgment on André, at least seven were men of excellent education, two of them having taken degrees at Harvard, and two at English universities.   Greene, the president, a self-educated man, who used, in leisure moments, to read Latin poets by

the light of his camp-fire, had paid especial attention to military law, and had carefully read and
copiously annotated his copy of Vattel. The judgment of these twelve men agreed with that of Steuben (formerly a staff officer of Frederick the
Great) and Lafayette, who sat with them on the
commission ; and, moreover, no nice or intricate
questions were raised. It was natural enough that
André's friends should make the most of the fact
that when captured he was travelling under a pass
granted by the commander of West Point ; but to
ask the court to accept such a plea was not introducing any nice or doubtful question ; it was simply
contending that " the wilful abuse of a privilege
is entitled to the same respect as its legitimate exercise." Accordingly, historians on both sides of
the Atlantic have generally admitted the justice of
André's sentence, though sometimes its rigorous
execution has been censured as an act of unnecessary severity. Yet if we withdraw our attention
for a moment from the irrelevant fact   There is no
that the British adjutant-general was an   reason in the
                                           world why An-
amiable and interesting young man, and   dré should
concentrate it upon the essential fact   have been
                                           spared.
that he had come within our lines to aid a treacherous commander in betraying his post, we cannot
fail to see that there is no principle of military policy upon which ordinary spies are rigorously put
to death which does not apply with tenfold force
to the case of André. Moreover, while it is an
undoubted fact that military morality permits, and
sometimes applauds, such enterprises as that in
which André lost his life, I cannot but feel that

the flavour of treachery which clings about it must somewhat weaken the sympathy we should otherwise freely accord; and I find myself agreeing with the British historian, Mr. Massey, when he doubts " whether services of this character entitle his memory to the honours of Westminster Abbey."

As for Arnold, his fall had been as terrible as that of Milton's rebellious archangel, and we may well believe his state of mind to have been desperate. It was said that on hearing of Captain Ogden's suggestion as to the only possible means of saving André, Arnold went to Clinton and offered to surrender himself as a ransom for his fellow-conspirator. This story was published in the *Captain Battersby's story.* London "Morning Herald" in February, 1782, by Captain Battersby, of the 29th regiment, — one of the " Sam Adams" regiments. Battersby was in New York in September, 1780, and was on terms of intimacy with members of Clinton's staff. In the absence of further evidence, one must beware of attaching too much weight to such a story. Yet it is not inconsistent with what we know of Arnold's impulsive nature. In the agony of his sudden overthrow it may well have seemed that there was nothing left to live for, and a death thus savouring of romantic self-sacrifice might serve to lighten the burden of his shame as nothing else could. Like many men of weak integrity, Arnold was over-sensitive to public opinion, and his treason, as he had planned it, though equally indefensible in point of morality, was something very different from what it seemed now that it was frustrated. It was not for this that he had bartered his soul to Satan. He had aimed at an end so vast that, when once attained, it Arnold's terrible downfall. might be hoped that the nefarious means employed would be overlooked, and that in Arnold, the brilliant general who had restored America to her old allegiance, posterity would see the counterpart of that other general who, for bringing back Charles Stuart to his father's throne, was rewarded with the dukedom of Albemarle. Now he had lost everything, and got nothing in exchange but £6,000 sterling and a brigadiership in the British army. He had sold himself cheap, after all, and incurred such hatred and contempt that for a long time, by a righteous retribution, even his past services were forgotten. Even such weak creatures as Gates could now point the finger of scorn at him, while Washington, his steadfast friend, could never speak of him again without a shudder. From men less reticent than Washington strong words were heard. "What do you think of the damnable doings of that diabolical dog?" wrote Colonel Otho Williams to Arnold's old friend and fellow in the victory of Saratoga, Daniel Morgan. "Curse on his folly and perfidy," said Greene, "how mortifying to think that he is a New Englander!" These were the men who could best appreciate the hard treatment Arnold had received from Congress. But in the frightful abyss of his crime all such considerations were instantly swallowed up and lost. No amount of personal wrong could for a moment excuse or even palliate such a false step as he had taken.

Within three months from the time when his

treason was discovered, Arnold was sent by Sir
Henry Clinton on a marauding expedition into
Virginia, and in the course of one of his raids an
American captain was taken prisoner. "What do
you suppose my fate would be," Arnold is said to
have inquired, "if my misguided countrymen were
to take me prisoner?" The captain's
Anecdotes. reply was prompt and frank: "They
would cut off the leg that was wounded at Quebec
and Saratoga and bury it with the honours of war,
and the rest of you they would hang on a gibbet."
After the close of the war, when Arnold, accompanied by his wife, made England his home, it is
said that he sometimes had to encounter similar
expressions of contempt. The Earl of Surrey
once, seeing him in the gallery of the House of
Commons, asked the Speaker to have him put out,
that the House might not be contaminated by the
presence of such a traitor. The story is not well
authenticated; but it is certain that in 1792 the
Earl of Lauderdale used such language about him
in the House of Lords as to lead to a bloodless
duel between Arnold and the noble earl. It does
not appear, however, that Arnold was universally
despised in England. Influenced by the political
passions of the day, many persons were ready to
condone his crime; and his generous and affectionate nature won him many friends. It is said that
so high-minded a man as Lord Cornwallis became
attached to him, and always treated him with respect.

Mrs. Arnold proved herself a devoted wife and
mother; and the record of her four sons, during

long years of service in the British army, was
highly honourable. The second son, Lieutenant-
General Sir James Robertson Arnold, served with
distinction in the wars against Napoleon. A
grandson who was killed in the Crimean war was
especially mentioned by Lord Raglan for valour and
skill. Another grandson, the Rev. Ed- Arnold's fam-
ward Arnold, is now rector of Great ily.
Massingham, in Norfolk. The family has inter-
married with the peerage, and has secured for itself an honourable place among the landed gentry
of England. But the disgrace of their ancestor
has always been keenly felt by them. At Surinam
in 1804, James Robertson Arnold, then a lieutenant, begged the privilege of leading a desperate
forlorn hope, that he might redeem the family
name from the odium which attached to it; and
he acquitted himself in a way that was worthy of
his father in the days of Quebec and Saratoga.
All the family tradition goes to show that the last
years of Benedict Arnold in London were years of
bitter remorse and self-reproach. The great name
which he had so gallantly won and so wretchedly
lost left him no repose by night or day. The iron
frame, which had withstood the fatigue of so many
trying battlefields and still more trying marches
through the wilderness, broke down at last under
the slow torture of lost friendships and merited
disgrace. In the last sad days in London, in June,
1801, the family tradition says that Arnold's mind
kept reverting to his old friendship with Washington. He had always carefully preserved the
American uniform which he wore on the day when

he made his escape to the Vulture; and now as, broken in spirit and weary of life, he felt the last

His remorse and death, June 14, 1801. moments coming, he called for this uniform and put it on, and decorated himself with the epaulettes and sword-knot which Washington had given him after the victory of Saratoga. " Let me die," said he, " in this old uniform in which I fought my battles. May God forgive me for ever putting on any other ! "

As we thus reach the end of one of the saddest episodes in American history, our sympathy cannot fail for the moment to go out toward the sufferer, nor can we help contrasting these passionate dying words with the last cynical scoff of that other traitor, Charles Lee, when he begged that he might not be buried within a mile of any church, as he did not wish to keep bad company after death. From beginning to end the story of Lee is little more than a vulgar melodrama; but into the story of Arnold there enters that element of awe and pity which, as Aristotle pointed out, is an essential part of real tragedy. That Arnold had been very shabbily treated, long before any thought of treason entered his mind, is not to be denied. That he may honestly have come to consider the American cause hopeless, that he may really have lost his interest in it because of the French alliance, — all this is quite possible. Such considerations might have justified him in resigning his commission ; or even, had he openly and frankly gone over to the enemy, much as we should have deplored such a step, some persons would always have been found to judge him leniently, and accord him the credit of acting upon principle. But the dark and crooked course which he did choose left open no alternative but that of unqualified condemnation. If we feel less of contempt and more of sorrow in the case of Arnold than in the case of such a weakling as Charles Lee, our verdict is not the less unmitigated. Arnold's fall was by far the more terrible, as he fell from a greater height, and into a depth than which none could be lower. It is only fair that we should recall his services to the cause of American independence, which were unquestionably greater than those of any other man in the Continental army except Washington and Greene. But it is part of the natural penalty that attaches to backsliding such as his, that when we hear the name of Benedict Arnold these are not the things which it suggests to our minds, but the name stands, and will always stand, as a symbol of unfaithfulness to trust.

The enormity of Arnold's conduct stands out in all the stronger relief when we contrast with it the behaviour of the common soldiers whose mutiny furnished the next serious obstacle with which Washington had to contend at this period of the war.

In the autumn of 1780, owing to the financial and administrative chaos which had overtaken the country, the army was in a truly pitiable condition. The soldiers were clothed in rags and nearly starved, and many of them had not seen a dollar of pay since the beginning of the year. As the winter frosts came on there was much discontent, and the irritation was greatest among the soldiers of the Pennsylvania line who were encamped on the heights of Morristown. Many of these men had enlisted at the beginning of 1778, to serve "for three years or during the war;" but at that bright and hopeful period, just after the victory of Saratoga, nobody supposed that the war could last for three years more, and the alternative was inserted only to insure them against being kept in service for the full term of three years in spite of the cessation of hostilities. Now the three years had passed, the war was not ended, and the prospect seemed less hopeful than in 1778. The men felt that their contract was fulfilled and asked to be discharged. But the officers, unwilling to lose such disciplined troops, the veterans of Monmouth and Stony Point, insisted that the contract provided for three years' service or more, in case the war should last longer; and they refused the

Mutiny of Pennsylvania troops, Jan. 1, 1781. requested discharge. On New Year's Day, 1781, after an extra ration of grog, 1,300 Pennsylvania troops marched out of camp, in excellent order, under command of their sergeants, and seizing six field-pieces, set out for Philadelphia, with declared intent to frighten Congress and obtain redress for their wrongs. Their commander, General Wayne, for whom they entertained great respect and affection, was unable to stop them, and after an affray in which one man was killed and a dozen were wounded, they were perforce allowed to go on their way. Alarm guns were fired, couriers were sent to forewarn

Congress and to notify Washington, and Wayne, attended by two colonels, galloped after the mutineers, to keep an eye upon them, and restrain their passions so far as possible. Washington could not come to attend to the affair in person, for the Hudson was not yet frozen and the enemy's fleet was in readiness to ascend to West Point the instant he should leave his post. Congress sent out a committee from Philadelphia, accompanied by President Reed, to parley with the insurgents, who had halted at Princeton and were behaving themselves decorously, doing no harm to the people in person or property. They allowed Wayne and his colonels to come into their camp, but gave them to understand that they would take no orders from them. A sergeant - major acted as chief-commander, and his orders were implicitly obeyed. When Lafayette, with St. Clair and Laurens, came to them from Washington's headquarters, they were politely but firmly told to go about their business. And so matters went on for a week. President Reed came as far as Trenton, and wrote to Wayne requesting an interview outside of Princeton, as he did not wish to come to the camp himself and run the risk of such indignity as that with which Washington's officers had just been treated. As the troops assembled on parade Wayne read them this letter. Such a rebuke from the president of their native state touched these poor fellows in a sensitive point. Tears rolled down many a bronzed and haggard cheek. They stood about in little groups, talking and pondering and not half liking the business which they had undertaken.

At this moment it was discovered that two emissaries from Sir Henry Clinton were·in the camp, seeking to tamper with the sergeant-major, and promising high pay, with bounties and pensions, if they would come over to Paulus Hook or Staten Island and cast in their lot with the British. In
Fate of Clinton's emissaries. a fury of wrath the tempters were seized and carried to Wayne to be dealt with as spies. " We will have General Clinton understand," said the men, " that we are not Benedict Arnolds ! " Encouraged by this incident, President Reed came to the camp next day, and was received with all due respect. He proposed at once to discharge all those who had enlisted for three years or the war, to furnish them at once with such clothing as they most needed, and to give paper certificates for the arrears of their pay, to be redeemed as soon as possible. These terms, which granted unconditionally all the demands of the insurgents, were instantly accepted. All those not included in the terms received six weeks' furlough, and thus the whole force was dissolved. The two spies were tried by court-martial and promptly hanged.

The quickness with which the demands of these men were granted was an index to the alarm which their defection had excited ; and Washington feared that their example would be followed by
Further mutiny suppressed. the soldiers of other states. On the 20th of January, indeed, a part of the New Jersey troops mutinied at Pompton, and declared their intention to do like the men of Pennsylvania. The case was becoming se-

rious ; it threatened the very existence of the army ; and a sudden blow was needed. Washington sent from West Point a brigade of Massachusetts troops, which marched quickly to Pompton, surprised the mutineers before daybreak, and compelled them to lay down their arms without a struggle. Two of the ringleaders were summarily shot, and so the insurrection was quelled.

Thus the disastrous year which had begun when Clinton sailed against Charleston, the year which had witnessed the annihilation of two American armies and the bankruptcy of Congress, came at length to an end amid treason and mutiny. It had been the most dismal year of the war, and it was not strange that many Americans despaired of their country. Yet, as we have already seen, the resources of Great Britain, attacked as she was by the united fleets of France, Spain, and Holland, were scarcely less exhausted than those of the United States. The moment had come when a decided military success must turn the scale irrevocably the one way or the other ; and events had already occurred at the South which were soon to show that all the disasters of 1780 were but the darkness that heralds the dawn.

CHAPTER XV.

In the invasion of the South by Cornwallis, as in the invasion of the North by Burgoyne, the first serious blow which the enemy received was dealt by the militia. After his great victory over Gates, Cornwallis remained nearly a month at Camden resting his troops, who found the August heat intolerable.

By the middle of September, 1780, he had started on his march to North Carolina, of which he expected to make an easy conquest. But his reception in that state was anything but hospitable. Advancing as far as Charlotte, he found himself in the midst of that famous Mecklenburg County which had issued its "declaration of independence" immediately on receiving the news of the battle of Lexington. These rebels, he said, were the most obstinate he had found in America, and he called their country a "hornet's nest." Bands of yeomanry lurking about every woodland road cut off his foraging parties, slew his couriers, and captured his dispatches. It was difficult for him to get any information; but bad news proverbially travels fast, and it was not long before he received intelligence of dire disaster.

Cornwallis invades North Carolina, Sept., 1780.

Before leaving South Carolina Cornwallis had detached Major Ferguson — whom, next to Tarleton, he considered his best partisan officer — to scour the highlands and enlist as large a force of Tory auxiliaries as possible, after which he was to join the main army at Charlotte. Ferguson took with him 200 British light infantry and 1,000 Tories, whom he had drilled until they had become excellent troops. It was not supposed that he would meet with serious opposition, but in case of any unforeseen danger he was to retreat with all possible speed and join the main army. Now the enterprising Ferguson undertook to entrap and capture a small force of American partisans ; and while pursuing this bait, he pushed into the wilderness as far as Gilbert Town, in the heart of what is now the county of Rutherford, when all at once he became aware that enemies were swarming about him on every side. The approach of a hostile force and the rumour of Indian war had aroused the hardy backwoodsmen who dwelt in these wild and romantic glens. Accustomed to Indian raids, these quick and resolute men were always ready to assemble at a moment's warning ; and now they came pouring from all directions, through the defiles of the Alleghanies, a picturesque and motley crowd, in fringed and tasselled hunting-shirts, with sprigs of hemlock in their hats, and armed with long knives and rifles that seldom missed their aim. From the south came James Williams, of Ninety-Six, with his 400 men ; from the north, William Campbell, of Virginia, Benja-

Ferguson's expedition.

Rising of the backwoodsmen.

min Cleveland and Charles McDowell, of North Carolina, with 560 followers ; from the west, Isaac Shelby and John Sevier, whose names were to become so famous in the early history of Kentucky and Tennessee. By the 30th of September 3,000 of these " dirty mongrels," as Ferguson called them, — men in whose veins flowed the blood of Scottish Covenanters and French Huguenots and English sea rovers, — had gathered in such threatening proximity that the British commander started in all haste on his retreat toward the main army at Charlotte, sending messengers ahead, who were duly waylaid and shot down before they could reach Cornwallis and inform him of the danger. The pursuit was vigorously pressed, and on the night of the 6th of October, finding escape impossible without a fight, Ferguson planted himself on the top of King's Mountain, a ridge about half a mile in length and 1,700 feet above sea level, situated just on the border line between the two Carolinas. The crest is approached on three sides by rising ground, above which the steep summit towers for a hundred feet; on the north side it is an unbroken precipice. The mountain was covered with tall pine-trees, beneath which the ground, though little cumbered with underbrush, was obstructed on every side by huge moss-grown boulders. Perched with 1,125 staunch men on this natural stronghold, as the bright autumn sun came up on the morning of the 7th, Ferguson looked about him exultingly, and cried, " Well, boys, here is a place from which all the rebels outside of hell cannot drive us ! "

He was dealing, however, with men who were used to climbing hills. About three o'clock in the afternoon, the advanced party of Americans, 1,000 picked men, arrived in the ravine below the mountain, and, tying their horses to the trees, prepared to storm the position. The precipice on the north was too steep for the enemy to descend, and thus effectually cut off their retreat. Divided into three equal parties, the Americans ascended the other three sides simultaneously. Campbell and Shelby pushed up in front until near the crest, when Ferguson opened fire on them. They then fell apart behind trees, returning the fire most effectively, but suffering little themselves, while slowly they crept up nearer the crest. As the British then charged down upon them with bayonets, they fell back, until the British ranks were suddenly shaken by a deadly flank fire from the division of Sevier and McDowell on the right. Turning furiously to meet these new assailants, the British received a volley in their backs from the left division, under Cleveland and Williams, while the centre division promptly rallied, and attacked them on what was now their flank. Thus dreadfully entrapped, the British fired wildly and with little effect, while the trees and boulders prevented the compactness needful for a bayonet charge. The Americans, on the other hand, sure of their prey, crept on steadily toward the summit, losing scarcely a man, and firing with great deliberateness and precision, while hardly a word was spoken. As they closed in upon the ridge a rifleball pierced the brave Fer-

Battle of King's Mountain, Oct. 7, 1780.

guson's heart, and he fell from his white horse, which sprang wildly down the mountain side. All further resistance being hopeless, a white flag was raised, and the firing was stopped. Of Ferguson's 1,125 men, 389 were killed or wounded and 20 were missing, and the remaining 716 now surrendered themselves prisoners of war, with 1,500 stand of arms. The total American loss was 28 killed and 60 wounded ; but among the killed was the famous partisan commander James Williams, whose loss might be regarded as offsetting that of Major Ferguson.

This brilliant victory at King's Mountain resembled the victory at Bennington in its suddenness and completeness, as well as in having been gained by militia. It was also the harbinger of greater victories at the South, as Bennington had been the harbinger of greater victories at the North. The Effect of the blow. backwoodsmen who had dealt such a blow did not, indeed, follow it up, and hover about the flanks of Cornwallis, as the Green Mountain boys had hovered about the flanks of Burgoyne. Had there been an organized army opposed to Cornwallis, to serve as a nucleus for them, perhaps they might have done so. As it was, they soon dispersed and returned to their homes, after having sullied their triumph by hanging a dozen prisoners, in revenge for some of their own party who had been massacred at Augusta. They had, nevertheless, warded off for the moment the threatened invasion of North Carolina. Thoroughly alarmed by this blow, Cornwallis lost no time in falling back upon Winnsborough, there to wait for reinforcements, for he was in no condition to afford the loss of 1,100 men. General Leslie had been sent by Sir Henry Clinton to Virginia with 3,000 men, and Cornwallis ordered this force to join him without delay.

Hope began now to return to the patriots of South Carolina, and during the months of October and November their activity was greatly increased. Marion in the northeastern part of the state, and Sumter in the northwest, redoubled their energies, and it was more than even Tarleton could do to look after them both. On the 20th of November Tarleton was defeated by Sumter in a sharp action at Blackstock Hill, and the disgrace of the 18th of August was thus wiped out. On the retreat of Cornwallis, the remnants of the American regular army, which Gates had been slowly collecting at Hillsborough, advanced and occupied Charlotte. There were scarcely 1,400 of them, all told, and their condition was forlorn enough. But reinforcements from the North were at hand ; and first of all came Daniel Morgan, always a host in himself. Morgan, like Arnold, had been ill-treated by Congress. His services at Quebec and Saratoga had been hardly inferior to Arnold's, yet, in 1779, he had seen junior officers promoted over his head, and had resigned his commission, and retired to his home in Virginia. When Gates took command of the southern army, Morgan was urged to enter the service again ; but, as it was not proposed to restore him to his relative rank, he refused. After Camden, however, he declared that it was no time

Arrival of Daniel Morgan.

to let personal considerations have any weight, and he straightway came down and joined Gates at Hillsborough in September. At last, on the 13th of October, Congress had the good sense to give him the rank to which he was entitled; and it was not long, as we shall see, before it had reason to congratulate itself upon this act of justice.

But, more than anything else, the army which it was now sought to restore needed a new commander-in-chief. It was well known that Washington had wished to have Greene appointed to that position, in the first place. Congress had persisted in appointing its own favourite instead, and had lost an army in consequence. It could now hardly do better, though late in the day, than take Washington's advice. It would not do to run the risk of another Camden. In every campaign since the beginning of the war Greene had been Washington's right arm; and for indefatigable industry, for strength and breadth of intelligence, and for unselfish devotion to the public service, he was scarcely inferior to the commander-in-chief. Yet he too had been repeatedly insulted and abused by men who liked to strike at Washington through his favourite officers. As quartermaster-general, since the spring of 1778, Greene had been malevolently persecuted by a party in Congress, until, in July, 1780, his patience gave way, and he resigned in disgust. His enemies seized the occasion to urge his dismissal from the army, and but for his own keen sense of public duty and Washington's unfailing tact his services might have been

Greene appointed to the chief command at the South.

lost to the country at a most critical moment. On the 5th of October Congress called upon Washington to name a successor to Gates, and he immediately appointed Greene, who arrived at Charlotte and took command on the 2d of December. Steuben accompanied Greene as far as Virginia, and was placed in command in that state, charged with the duty of collecting and forwarding supplies and reinforcements to Greene, and of warding off the forces which Sir Henry Clinton sent to the Chesapeake to make diversions in aid of Cornwallis. The first force of this sort, under General Leslie, had just been obliged to proceed by sea to South Carolina, to make good the loss inflicted upon Cornwallis by the battle of King's Mountain ; and to replace Leslie in Virginia, Sir Henry Clinton, in December, sent the traitor Arnold, fresh from the scene of his treason, with 1,600 men, mostly New York loyalists. Steuben's duty was to guard Virginia against Arnold, and to keep open Greene's communications with the North. At the same time, Washington sent down with Greene the engineer Kosciusko and Henry Lee with his admirable legion of cavalry. Another superb cavalry commander now appears for the first time upon the scene in the person of Lieutenant-Colonel William Washington, of Virginia, a distant cousin of the commander-in-chief.

The southern army, though weak in numbers, was thus extraordinarily strong in the talent of its officers. They were men who knew how to accomplish great results with small means, and Greene understood how far he might rely upon them. No

sooner had he taken command than he began a
series of movements which, though daring in the
extreme, were as far as possible from partaking of
the unreasoned rashness which had characterized
the advance of Gates. That unintelligent commander had sneered at cavalry as useless, but
Greene largely based his plan of operations upon
what could be done by such swift blows as Washington and Lee knew how to deal. Gates had despised the aid of partisan chiefs, but
Greene saw at once the importance of
utilizing such men as Sumter and Marion. His army as a solid whole was
too weak to cope with that of Cornwallis. By a
bold and happy thought, he divided it, for the moment, into two great partisan bodies. The larger
body, 1,100 strong, he led in person to Cheraw Hill,
on the Pedee river, where he coöperated with Marion. From this point Marion and Lee kept up a
series of rapid movements which threatened Cornwallis's communications with the coast. On one
occasion, they actually galloped into Georgetown
and captured the commander of that post. Cornwallis was thus gravely annoyed, but he was unable to advance upon these provoking antagonists
without risking the loss of Augusta and Ninety-
Six; for Greene had thrown the other part of his
little army, 900 strong, under Morgan, to the westward, so as to threaten those important inland
posts and to coöperate with the mountain militia.
With Morgan's force went William Washington,
who accomplished a most brilliant raid, penetrating the enemy's lines, and destroying a party of
250 men at a single blow.

Greene's dar-
ing strategy;
he threatens
Cornwallis on
both flanks.

Thus worried and menaced upon both his flanks, Cornwallis hardly knew which way to turn. He did not underrate his adversaries. He had himself seen what sort of man Greene was, at Princeton and Brandywine and Germantown, while Morgan's abilities were equally well known. He could not leave Morgan and attack Greene without losing his hold upon the interior; but if he were to advance in full force upon Morgan, the wily Greene would be sure to pounce upon Charleston and cut him off from the coast. In this dilemma, Cornwallis at last decided to divide his own forces. With his main body, 2,000 strong, he advanced into North Carolina, hoping to draw Greene after him; while he sent Tarleton with the rest of his army, 1,100 strong, to take care of Morgan. By this division the superiority of the British force was to some extent neutralized. Both commanders were playing a skilful but hazardous game, in which much depended on the sagacity of their lieutenants; and now the brave but over-confident Tarleton was outmarched and outfought. On his approach, Morgan retreated to a grazing ground known as the Cowpens, a few miles from King's Mountain, where he could fight on ground of his own choosing. His choice was indeed a peculiar one, for he had a broad river in his rear, which cut off retreat; but this, he said, was just what he wanted, for his militia would know that there was no use in running away. It was cheaper than stationing regulars in the rear, to shoot down the cowards. Morgan's daring was justified by the

Cornwallis retorts by sending Tarleton to deal with Morgan.

result. The ground, a long rising slope, commanded the enemy's approach for a great distance.

Morgan's position at the Cowpens. On the morning of January 17, 1781, as Tarleton's advance was descried, Morgan formed his men in order of battle. First he arranged his Carolinian and Georgian militia in a line about three hundred yards in length, and exhorted them not to give way until they should have delivered at least two volleys "at killing distance." One hundred and fifty yards in the rear of this line, and along the brow of the gentle hill, he stationed the splendid Maryland brigade which Kalb had led at Camden, and supported it by some excellent Virginia troops. Still one hundred and fifty yards farther back, upon a second rising ground, he placed Colonel Washington with his cavalry. Arranged in this wise, the army awaited the British attack.

Tarleton's men had been toiling half the night over muddy roads and wading through swollen brooks, but nothing could restrain his eagerness to strike a sudden blow, and just about sunrise he charged upon the first American line. The militia, who were commanded by the redoubtable Pickens, behaved very well, and delivered, not two, but many deadly volleys at close range, causing the British lines to waver for a moment. As the

Battle of the Cowpens, Jan. 17, 1781. British recovered themselves and pressed on, the militia retired behind the line of Continentals; while the British line, in pursuing, became so extended as to threaten the flanks of the Continental line. To avoid being overlapped, the Continentals refused their right

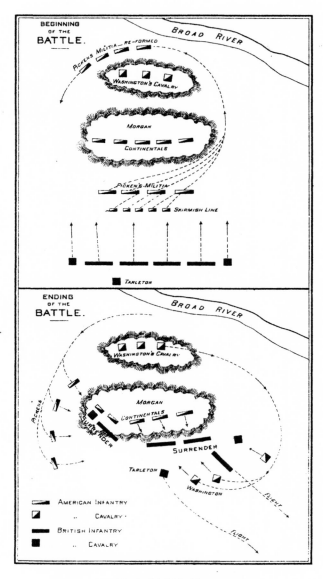

BATTLE OF THE COWPENS

JANUARY 17, 1781

wing and fell back a little; the British following
them hastily and in some confusion, having become too confident of victory. At this moment,
Colonel Washington, having swept down from his
hill in a semicircle, charged the British right flank
with fatal effect; Pickens's militia, who had re-
formed in the rear and marched around the hill,
advanced upon their left flank; while the Continentals, in front, broke their ranks with a deadly
fire at thirty yards, and instantly rushed upon
them with the bayonet. The greater part of the
British army thereupon threw down their arms
and surrendered, while the rest were scattered in
flight. It was a complete rout. The
British lost 230 in killed and wounded, Destruction of Tarleton's force.
600 prisoners, two field-pieces, and 1,000
stand of arms. Their loss was about equal to the
whole American force engaged. Only 270 escaped
from the field, among them Tarleton, who barely
saved himself in a furious single combat with
Washington. The American loss, in this astonishing battle, was 12 killed and 61 wounded. In
point of tactics, it was the most brilliant battle of
the War for Independence.

Having struck this crushing blow, which deprived Cornwallis of one third of his force, Morgan did not rest for a moment. The only direct
road by which he could rejoin Greene lay to the
northward, across the fords of the Catawba river,
and Cornwallis was at this instant nearer than
himself to these fords. By a superb march, Morgan reached the river first, and, crossing it, kept
on northeastward into North Carolina, with Corn-

wallis following closely upon his heels. On the
24th of January, one week after the
battle of the Cowpens, the news of it
reached Greene in his camp on the Pedee, and he learned the nature of Morgan's movements after the battle. Now was the time for putting into execution a brilliant scheme. If he could
draw the British general far enough to the northward, he might compel him to join battle under
disadvantageous circumstances and at a great distance from his base of operations. Accordingly,
Greene put his main army in motion ûnder General Huger, telling him to push steadily to the
northward ; while he himself, taking only a sergeant's guard of dragoons, rode with all possible
speed a hundred and fifty miles across the country,
and on the morning of the 30th reached the valley
of the Catawba, and put himself at the head of
Morgan's force, which Cornwallis was still pursuing. Now the gallant earl realized the deadly
nature of the blows which at King's Mountain and
the Cowpens had swept away nearly all his light
troops. In his eagerness and mortification, he
was led to destroy the heavy baggage which encumbered his headlong march. He was falling
into the trap. A most exciting game
of strategy was kept up for the next ten
days ; Greene steadily pushing northeastward on a line converging toward
that taken by his main army, Cornwallis vainly
trying to get near enough to compel him to fight.
The weather had been rainy, and an interesting
feature of the retreat was the swelling of the

*Brilliant
movements of
Morgan and
Greene.*

*Greene leads
Cornwallis a
chase across
North Caro-
lina.*

YORKTOWN. 257

rivers, which rendered them unfordable. Greene took advantage of this circumstance, having, with admirable forethought, provided himself with boats, which were dragged overland on light wheels and speedily launched as they came to a river; carrying as part of their freight the wheels upon which they were again to be mounted so soon as they should have crossed. On the 9th of February Greene reached Guilford Court-House, in the northern part of North Carolina, only thirty miles from the Virginia border; and there he effected a junction with the main army, which Huger had brought up from the camp on the Pedee. On the next day, the gallant Morgan, broken down by illness, was obliged to give up his command.

It had not been a part of Greene's plan to retreat any farther. He had intended to offer battle at this point, and had sent word to Steuben to forward reinforcements from Virginia for this purpose. But Arnold's invasion of Virginia had so far taxed the good baron's resources that he had not yet been able to send on the reinforcements; and as Greene's force was still inferior to the enemy's, he decided to continue his retreat. After five days of fencing, he placed his army on the north side of the Dan, a broad and rapid stream, which Cornwallis had no means of crossing. Thus baulked of his prey, the earl proceeded to Hills- _{Further ma-} borough, and issued a proclamation an- _{nœuvres.} nouncing that he had conquered North Carolina, and inviting the loyalists to rally around his standard. A few Tories came out and enlisted, but these proceedings were soon checked by the news that the American general had recrossed the river, and was advancing in a threatening manner. Greene had intended to await his reinforcements on the Virginia side of the river, but he soon saw that it would not do to encourage the Tories by the belief that he had abandoned North Carolina. On the 23d he recrossed the Dan, and led Cornwallis a will-o'-the-wisp chase, marching and countermarching, and foiling every attempt to bring him to bay, until, on the 14th of March, having at last been reinforced till his army numbered 4,404 men, he suddenly pulled up at Guilford Court-House, and offered his adversary the long-coveted battle. Cornwallis had only 2,213 men, but they were all veterans, and a battle had come to be for him an absolute military necessity. He had risked everything in this long march, and could not maintain himself in an exposed position, so far from support, without inflicting a crushing defeat upon his opponent. To Greene a battle was now almost equally desirable, but it need not necessarily be an out-and-out victory : it was enough that he should seriously weaken and damage the enemy.

On the morning of March 15th Greene drew up his army in three lines. The first, con-sisting of North Carolina militia, was placed in front of an open cornfield. It was expected that these men would give way before the onset of the British regulars; but it was thought that they could be depended upon to fire two or three volleys first, and, as they were excellent marksmen, this would make gaps in the

Battle of
Guilford,
March 15.

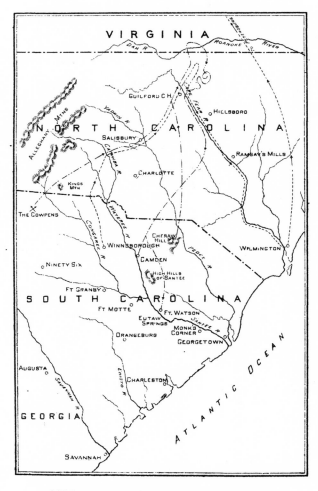

GREENE AND CORNWALLIS IN THE CAROLINAS

JANUARY–APRIL, 1781

British line. In a wood three hundred yards behind stood the second line, consisting of Virginia
militia, whose fire was expected still further to im-
pede the enemy's advance. On a hill four hundred yards in the rear of these were stationed the
regulars of Maryland and Virginia. The flanks
were guarded by Campbell's riflemen and the cavalry under Washington and Lee. Early in the
afternoon the British opened the battle by a charge
upon the North Carolina militia, who were soon
driven from the field in confusion. The Virginia
line, however, stood its ground bravely, and it was
only after a desperate struggle that the enemy
slowly pushed it back. The attack upon the third
American line met with varied fortunes. On the
right the Maryland troops prevailed, and drove
the British at the point of the bayonet; but on
the left the other Maryland brigade was overpow-
ered and forced back, with the loss of two cannon.
A charge by Colonel Washington's cavalry restored the day, the cannon were retaken, and for
a while the victory seemed secured for the Americans. Cornwallis was thrown upon the defensive,
but after two hours of hard fighting he succeeded
in restoring order among his men and concentra-
ting them upon the hill near the court-house, where
all attempts to break their line proved futile. As
evening came on, Greene retired, with a loss of
more than 400 men, leaving the enemy in possession of the field, but too badly crippled to move.
The British fighting was magnificent, — worthy to
be compared with that of Thomas and his men at
Chickamauga. In the course of five hours they

had lost about 600 men, more than one fourth of their number. This damage was irretrievable. The little army, thus cut down to a total of scarcely 1,600 men, could not afford to risk another battle. Greene's audacious scheme had been crowned with success. He had lured Cornwallis far into a hostile country, more than two hundred miles distant from his base of operations. The earl now saw too late that he had been out-

Retreat of Cornwallis.

generaled. To march back to South Carolina was more than he dared to venture, and he could not stay where he was. Accordingly, on the third day after the battle of Guilford, abandoning his wounded, Cornwallis started in all haste for Wilmington, the nearest point on the coast at which he could look for aid from the fleet.

By this movement Lord Cornwallis virtually gave up the game. The battle of Guilford, though tactically a defeat for the Americans, was strategically a decisive victory, and the most important one since the capture of Burgoyne. Its full significance was soon made apparent. When Cornwallis, on the 7th of April, arrived at Wilmington, what was he to do next? To transport his army by sea to Charleston, and thus begin his work over again, would be an open confession of defeat. The most practicable course appeared to be to shift the scene altogether, and march into Virginia, where a fresh opportunity seemed to present itself. Sir Henry Clinton had just sent General Phillips down to Virginia, with a force which, if combined with that of Cornwallis, would amount to more

than 5,000 men ; and with this army it might prove
possible to strike a heavy blow in Vir- He abandons
ginia, and afterward invade the Caroli- the Carolinas, and marches
nas from the north. Influenced by such into Virginia.
considerations, Cornwallis started from Wilmington on the 25th of April, and arrived on the 20th
of May at Petersburg, in Virginia, where he effected a junction with the forces of Arnold and
Phillips. This important movement was made by
Cornwallis on his own responsibility. It was never
sanctioned by Sir Henry Clinton, and in after
years it became the occasion of a bitter controversy
between the two generals ; but the earl was at this
time a favourite with Lord George Germaine, and
the commander-in-chief was obliged to modify his
own plans in order to support a movement of which
he disapproved.

But while Cornwallis was carrying out this extensive change of programme, what was his adversary doing ? Greene pursued the retreating enemy
about fifty miles, from Guilford Court-House to
Ramsay's Mills, a little above the fork of the
Cape Fear river, and then suddenly left him to
himself, and faced about for South Carolina.
Should Cornwallis decide to follow him, at least
the state of North Carolina would be relieved ;
but Greene had builded even better than he knew.
He had really eliminated Cornwallis from the
game, had thrown him out on the mar- Greene's mas-
gin of the chessboard ; and now he could ter-stroke ; he returns to
go to work with his hands free and re- South Caroli-
deem South Carolina. The strategic na, April 6–18;
points there were still held by the enemy ; Camden,

Ninety-Six, and Augusta were still in their possession. Camden, the most important of all, was held
by Lord Rawdon with 900 men ; and toward Camden, a hundred and sixty miles distant, Greene
turned on the 6th of April, leaving Cornwallis to
make his way unmolested to the seaboard. Greene
kept his counsel so well that his own officers failed
to understand the drift of his profound and daring
strategy. The movement which he now made had
not been taken into account by Cornwallis, who
had expected by his own movements at least to de-
tain his adversary. That Greene should actually
ignore him was an idea which he had not yet taken
in, and by the time he fully comprehended the situation he was already on his way to Virginia, and
committed to his new programme. The patriots
in South Carolina had also failed to understand
Greene's sweeping movements, and his long absence
had cast down their hopes ; but on his return without Cornwallis, there was a revulsion of feeling.
People began to look for victory.

On the 18th of April the American army approached Camden, while Lee was detached to co-
operate with Marion in reducing Fort Watson.
This stronghold, standing midway between Camden and Charleston, commanded Lord Rawdon's
line of communications with the coast. The execution of this cardinal movement was marked by a
picturesque incident. Fort Watson was built on
an Indian mound, rising forty feet sheer above
the champaign country in which it stood, and had
no doubt witnessed many a wild siege before ever
the white man came to Carolina. It was garrisoned

by 120 good soldiers, but neither they nor the be-
siegers had any cannon. It was to be an
affair of rifles. Lee looked with disgust
on the low land about him. Oh for a
hill which might command this fortress
even as Ticonderoga was overlooked on
that memorable day when Phillips dragged his
guns up Mount Defiance! A happy thought now
flashed upon Major Mayham, one of Marion's officers. Why not make a hill? There grew near
by a forest of superb yellow pine, heavy and hard
as stone. For five days and nights the men
worked like beavers in the depths of the wood,
quite screened from the sight of the garrison. Forest trees were felled, and saws, chisels, and adzes
worked them into shape. Great beams were fitted
with mortise and tenon; and at last, in a single
night, they were dragged out before the fortress
and put together, as in an old-fashioned New England " house-raising." At daybreak of April 23,
the British found themselves overlooked by an
enormous wooden tower, surmounted by a platform
crowded with marksmen, ready to pick off the garrison at their leisure ; while its base was protected
by a breastwork of logs, behind which lurked a
hundred deadly rifles. Before the sun was an hour
high, a white flag was hung out, and Fort Watson
was surrendered at discretion.

While these things were going on Greene
reached Camden, and, finding his force insufficient
either to assault or to invest it, took up a strong
position at Hobkirk's Hill, about two miles to the
north. On the 25th of April Lord Rawdon ad-

Marginal note: and, by taking Fort Watson, cuts Lord Rawdon's communications, April 23.

vanced, to drive him from this position, and a battle ensued, in which the victory, nearly won, slipped through Greene's fingers.

Rawdon defeats Greene at Hobkirk's Hill, April 25 ;

The famous Maryland brigade, which in all these southern campaigns had stood forth preëminent, like Cæsar's tenth legion, — which had been the last to leave the disastrous field of Camden, which had overwhelmed Tarleton at the Cowpens, and had so nearly won the day at Guilford, — now behaved badly, and, falling into confusion through a misunderstanding of orders, deranged Greene's masterly plan of battle. He was driven from his position, and three days later retreated ten miles to Clermont; but, just as at Guilford, his plan of campaign was so good that he proceeded forthwith to reap all the fruits of victory. The fall of Fort Watson, breaking Rawdon's communication with the coast, made it impossible for him to stay where he was.

but is none the less obliged to give up Camden and save his army, May 10.

On the 10th of May the British general retreated rapidly, until he reached Monk's Corner, within thirty miles of Charleston; and the all-important post of Camden, the first great prize of the campaign, fell into Greene's hands.

Victories followed now in quick succession. Within three weeks Lee and Marion had taken Fort Motte and Fort Granby, Sumter had taken Orangeburg, and on the 5th of June, after an obstinate defence, Augusta surrendered to Lee, thus throwing open the state of Georgia. Nothing was left to the British but Ninety-Six, which was strongly garrisoned, and now withstood a vigorous siege of twenty-

eight days. Determined not to lose this last hold
upon the interior, and anxious to crush
his adversary in battle, if possible, Lord
Rawdon collected all the force he could,
well - nigh stripping Charleston of its
defenders, and thus, with 2,000 men, came up in
all haste to raise the siege of Ninety-Six. His
bold movement was successful for the moment.
Greene, too prudent to risk a battle, withdrew, and
the frontier fortress was relieved. It was impossible, however, for Rawdon to hold it and keep his
army there, so far from the seaboard, after all the
other inland posts had fallen, and on the 29th of
June he evacuated the place, and retreated upon
Orangeburg ; while Greene, following him, took
up a strong position on the High Hills of Santee.
Thus, within three months after Greene's return
from Guilford, the upper country of South Carolina had been completely reconquered, and only
one successful battle was now needed to drive the
enemy back upon Charleston. But first it was
necessary to take some rest and recruit the little
army, which had toiled so incessantly since the last
December. The enemy, too, felt the need of rest,
and the heat was intolerable. Both armies, accordingly, lay and watched each other until after the
middle of August.

During this vacation, Lord Rawdon, worn out
and ill from his rough campaigning, embarked for
England, leaving Colonel Stuart in command of
the forces in South Carolina. Greene
busied himself in recruiting his army,
until it numbered 2,600 men, though 1,000 of

All the inland posts taken from the Brit- ish, May- June.

Rawdon goes to England.

these were militia. His position on the High Hills
of Santee was, by an air line, distant only sixteen
miles from the British army. The intervening
space was filled by meadows, through which the
Wateree and Congaree rivers flowed to meet each
other ; and often, as now, when the swift waters,
swollen by rain, overflowed the lowlands, it seemed
like a vast lake, save for the tops of tall pine-trees
that here and there showed themselves in deepest
green, protruding from the mirror-like surface.
Greene understood the value of this meadow land
as a barrier, when he chose the site for his summer
camp. The enemy could reach him only by a cir-
cuitous march of seventy miles. On the 22d of

Greene
marches
against the
British, Aug.
22.

August Greene broke up his camp very
quietly, and started out on the last of
his sagacious campaigns. The noonday
heat was so intense that he marched
only in the morning and evening, in order to keep
his men fresh and active ; while by vigilant scouting parties he so completely cut off the enemy's
means of information that Stuart remained ignorant of his approach until he was close at hand.
The British commander then fell back upon Eutaw
Springs, about fifty miles from Charleston, where
he waited in a strong position.

The battle of Eutaw Springs may be resolved

Battle of Eu-
taw Springs,
Sept. 8.

into two brief actions between sunrise
and noon of the 8th of September, 1781.
In the first action the British line was
broken and driven from the field. In the second
Stuart succeeded in forming a new line, supported
by a brick house and palisaded garden, and from

this position Greene was unable to drive him. It has therefore been set down as a British victory. If so, it was a victory followed the next evening by the hasty retreat of the victors, who were hotly pursued for thirty miles by Marion and Lee. Strategically considered, it was a decisive victory for the Americans. The state government was restored to supremacy, and, though partisan scrimmages were kept up for another year, these were but the dying embers of the fire. The British were cooped up in Charleston till the end of the war, protected by their ships. Less than thirteen months had elapsed since the disaster of Camden had seemed to destroy all hope of saving the state. All this change had been wrought by Greene's magnificent generalship. Coming upon the scene under almost every imaginable disadvantage, he had reorganized the remnant of Gates's broken and dispirited army, he had taken the initiative from the first, and he had held the game in his own hands till the last blow was struck. So consummate had been his strategy that whether victorious or defeated on the field, he had, in every instance, gained the object for which the campaign was made. Under one disadvantage, indeed, he had not laboured : he had excellent officers. Seldom has a more brilliant group been seen than that which comprised Morgan, Campbell, Marion, Sumter, Pickens, Otho Williams, William Washington, and the father of Robert Edward Lee. It is only an able general, however, who knows how to use such admirable instruments. Men of narrow intelligence do not

Greene's superb generalship.

like to have able men about them, and do not
know how to deal with them.   Gates had Kalb
and Otho Williams, and put them in places where
their talent was unavailable and one of them was
uselessly sacrified, while he was too dull to detect
the extraordinary value of Marion.   But genius is
quick to see genius, and knows what to do with it.
Greene knew what each one of his officers would
do, and took it into the account in planning his
sweeping movements.   Unless he had known that
he could depend upon Morgan as certainly as
Napoleon, in after years, relied upon Davoust on
the day of Jena and Auerstadt, it would have been
foolhardy for him to divide his force in the beginning of the campaign, — a move which, though
made in apparent violation of military rules, nevertheless gave him the initiative in his long and
triumphant game.   What Greene might have accomplished on a wider field and with more ample
resources can never be known.   But the intellect-
ual qualities which he showed in his southern campaign were those which have characterized some of
the foremost strategists of modern times.

When Lord Cornwallis heard, from time to time,
what was going on in South Carolina, he was not
cheered by the news.   But he was too far away to
interfere, and it was on the very day of Eutaw
Springs that the toils were drawn about him which
were to compass his downfall.   When he reached
Petersburg, on the 20th of May, the youthful Lafayette, whom Washington had sent down to watch
and check the movements of the traitor Arnold,

was stationed at Richmond, with a little army of
3,000 men, two thirds of them raw militia. To
oppose this small force Cornwallis had Lord Cornwal-
now 5,000 veterans, comprising the men lis arrives at
Petersburg,
whom he had brought away from Guil- May 20, 1781.
ford, together with the forces lately under Arnold
and Phillips. Arnold, after some useless burning
and plundering, had been recalled to New York.
Phillips had died of a fever just before Cornwallis
arrived. The earl entertained great hopes. His
failure in North Carolina rankled in his soul, and
he was eager to make a grand stroke and retrieve
his reputation. Could the powerful state of Virginia be conquered, it seemed as if everything
south of the Susquehanna must fall, in spite of
Greene's successes. With his soul thus full of
chivalrous enterprise, Cornwallis for the moment
saw things in rose colour, and drew wrong conclu-
sions. He expected to find half the people Tories,
and he also expected to find a state of chronic hostility between the slaves and their masters. On
both points he was quite mistaken.

But while Cornwallis underrated the difficulty
of the task, he knew, nevertheless, that 5,000 men
were not enough to conquer so strong a state, and
he tried to persuade Clinton to abandon New York,
if necessary, so that all the available British force
might be concentrated upon Virginia. Clinton
wisely refused. A state like Virginia, which, for
the want of a loyalist party, could be held only by
sheer conquest, was not fit for a basis of operations
against the other states ; while the abandoning of
New York, the recognized strategic centre of the

Atlantic coast, would be interpreted by the whole
world, not as a change of base, but as a confession
of defeat.   Clinton's opinion was thus founded
upon a truer and clearer view of the whole situation than Cornwallis's; nor is it likely that the
latter would ever have urged such a scheme had
he not been, in such a singular and unexpected
way, elbowed out of North Carolina.   Being now
in Virginia, it was incumbent on him to do something, and, with the force at his disposal, it seemed
as if he might easily begin by crushing Lafayette.
" The boy cannot escape me," said Cornwallis ; but
the young Frenchman turned out to be more formidable than was supposed.   Lafayette has never
been counted a great general, and, indeed, though a noble and interesting
character, he was in no wise a man of
original genius ; but he had much good sense and
was quick at learning.   He was now twenty-three
years old, buoyant and kind, full of wholesome enthusiasm, and endowed with no mean sagacity.   A
Fabian policy was all that could be adopted for
the moment.   When Cornwallis advanced from
Petersburg to Richmond, Lafayette began the
skilful retreat which proved him an apt learner in
the school of Washington and Greene.   From Richmond toward Fredericksburg — over the ground
since made doubly famous by the deeds of Lee and
Grant — the youthful general kept up his retreat,
never giving the eager earl a chance to deal him
a blow; for, as with naïve humour he wrote to
Washington, " I am not strong enough even to be
beaten."   On the 4th of June Lafayette crossed

His campaign
against La-
fayette.

the Rapidan at Ely's Ford, and placed himself in a secure position; while Cornwallis, refraining from the pursuit, sent Tarleton on a raid westward to Charlottesville, to break up the legislature, which was in session there, and to capture the governor, Thomas Jefferson. The raid, though conducted with Tarleton's usual vigour, failed of its principal prey; for Jefferson, forewarned in the nick of time, got off to the mountains about twenty minutes before the cavalry surrounded his house at Monticello. It remained for Tarleton to seize the military stores collected at Albemarle; but on the 7th of June Lafayette effected a junction with 1,000 Pennsylvania regulars under Wayne, and thereupon succeeded in placing his whole force between Tarleton and the prize he was striving to reach. Unable to break through this barrier, Tarleton had nothing left him but to rejoin Cornwallis; and as Lafayette's army was reinforced from various sources until it amounted to more than 4,000 men, he became capable of annoying the earl in such wise as to make him think it worth while to get nearer to the sea. Cornwallis, turning southwestward from the North Anna river, had proceeded as far inland as Point of Forks, when Tarleton joined him. On the 15th of June, the British commander, finding that he could not catch " the boy," and was accomplishing nothing by his marches and countermarches in the interior, retreated down the James river to Richmond. In so doing he did not yet put Cornwallis retreats to the coast, himself upon the defensive. Lafayette was still too weak to risk a battle, or to prevent his going wherever he liked. But Cornwallis was too prudent a general to remain at a long distance from his base of operations, among a people whom he had found, to his great disappointment, thoroughly hostile. By retreating to the seaboard, he could make sure of supplies and reinforcements, and might presently resume the work of invasion. Accordingly, on the 20th he continued his retreat from Richmond, crossing the Chickahominy a little above White Oak Swamp, and marching down the York peninsula as far as Williamsburg. Lafayette, having been further reinforced by Steuben, so that his army numbered more than 5,000, pressed closely on the rear of the British all the way down the peninsula ; and on the 6th of July an action was fought between parts of the two armies, at Green Spring, near Williamsburg, in which the Americans were repulsed with a loss of 145 men. The campaign was ended by the first week in August, when Cornwallis occupied Yorktown, adding

and occupies   the garrison of Portsmouth to his army,
Yorktown.   so that it numbered 7,000 men, while Lafayette planted himself on Malvern Hill, and awaited further developments. Throughout this game of strategy, Lafayette had shown commendable skill, proving himself a worthy antagonist for the ablest of the British generals. But a far greater commander than either the Frenchman or the Englishman was now to enter unexpectedly upon the scene. The elements of the catastrophe were prepared, and it only remained for a master hand to strike the blow.

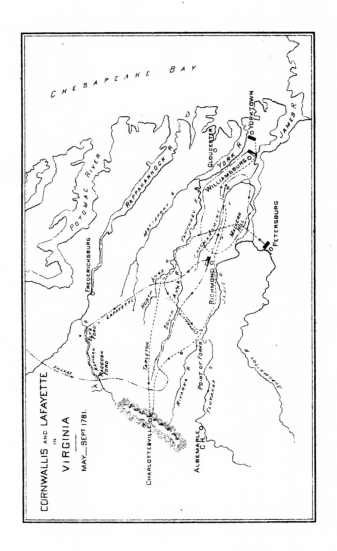

CORNWALLIS AND LAFAYETTE
IN
VIRGINIA
MAY — SEPT 1781.

As early as the 22d of May, just two days before the beginning of this Virginia campaign,
Washington had held a conference with Rochambeau, at Wethersfield, in Connecticut, and it was
there decided that a combined attack should be
made upon New York by the French and American armies. If they should succeed in taking
the city, it would ruin the British cause; and,
at all events, it was hoped that if New
York was seriously threatened Sir Henry
Clinton would take reinforcements from
Cornwallis, and thus relieve the pressure
upon the southern states. In order to undertake
the capture of New York, it would be necessary to
have the aid of a powerful French fleet; and the
time had at last arrived when such assistance was
confidently to be expected. The naval war between France and England in the West Indies had
now raged for two years, with varying fortunes.
The French government had exerted itself to the
utmost, and early in the spring of this year had
sent out a magnificent fleet of twenty-eight ships-
of-the-line and six frigates, carrying 1,700 guns
and 20,000 men, commanded by Count de Grasse,
one of the ablest of the French admirals. It was
designed to take from England the great island of
Jamaica; but as the need for naval coöperation
upon the North American coast had been strongly
urged upon the French ministry, Grasse was ordered to communicate with Washington and Rochambeau, and to seize the earliest opportunity of
acting in concert with them.

The arrival of this fleet would introduce a fea-

Elements of the final catastrophe; arrival of the French fleet.

ture into the war such as had not existed at any
time since hostilities had begun. It would inter-
rupt the British control over the water. The utmost force the British were ready to oppose to it
amounted only to nineteen ships-of-the-line, carrying 1,400 guns and 13,000 men, and this disparity
was too great to be surmounted by anything short
of the genius of a Nelson. The conditions of the
struggle were thus about to be suddenly and deci-
sively altered. The retreat of Cornwallis upon
Yorktown had been based entirely upon the assump-
tion of that British naval supremacy which had
hitherto been uninterrupted. The safety of his
position depended wholly upon the ability of
the British fleet to control the Virginia waters.
Once let the French get the upper hand there, and
the earl, if assailed in front by an overwhelming
land force, would be literally " between the devil
and the deep sea." He would be no better off
than Burgoyne in the forests of northern New
York.

It was not yet certain, however, where Grasse
would find it best to strike the coast. The elements of the situation disclosed themselves but
slowly, and it required the master mind of Washington to combine them. Intelligence travelled at
snail's pace in those days, and operations so vast in
extent were not within the compass of anything
but the highest military genius. It took ten days
for Washington to hear from Lafayette, and it
took a month for him to hear from Greene, while
there was no telling just when definite information
would arrive from Grasse. But so soon as Wash-

ington heard from Greene, in April, how he had manœuvred Cornwallis up into Virginia, he began secretly to consider the possibility of leaving a small force to guard the Hudson, while taking the bulk of his army southward to overwhelm Cornwallis. At the Wethersfield conference, he spoke of this to Rochambeau, but to no one else; and a dispatch to Grasse gave him the choice of sailing either for the Hudson or for the Chesapeake. So matters stood till the middle of August, while Washington, grasping all the elements of the problem, vigilantly watched the whole field, holding himself in readiness for either alternative, — to strike New York close at hand, or to hurl his army to a distance of four hun- News from Grasse and dred miles. On the 14th of August a Lafayette. message came from Grasse that he was just starting from the West Indies for Chesapeake Bay, with his whole fleet, and hoped that whatever the armies had to do might be done quickly, as he should be obliged to return to the West Indies by the middle of October. Washington could now couple with this the information, just received from Lafayette, that Cornwallis had established himself at Yorktown, where he had deep water on three sides of him, and a narrow neck in front.

The supreme moment of Washington's military career had come, — the moment for realizing a conception which had nothing of a Fabian character about it, for it was a conception of the same order as those in which Cæsar and Napoleon dealt. He decided at once to transfer his army to Virginia and overwhelm Cornwallis. He had everything in readiness. The army of Rochambeau had marched through Connecticut, and joined him on the Hudson in July. He could afford to leave West Point with a comparatively small force, for that strong fortress could be taken only by a regular siege, and he had planned his march so as to blind Sir Henry Clinton completely. This was one of the finest points in Washington's scheme, in which the perfection of the details matched the audacious grandeur of the whole. Sir Henry was profoundly unconscious of any such movement as Washington was about to execute; but he was anxiously looking out for an attack upon New York. Now, from the American headquarters near West Point, Washington could take his army more than halfway through New Jersey without arousing any suspicion at all; for the enemy would be sure to interpret such a movement as preliminary to an occupation of Staten Island, as a point from which to assail New York. Sir Henry knew that the French fleet might be expected at any moment; but he had not the clue which Washington held, and his anxious thoughts were concerned with New York harbour, and not with Chesapeake Bay. Besides all this, the sheer audacity of the movement served still further to screen its true meaning. It would take some time for the enemy to comprehend so huge a sweep as that from New York to Virginia, and doubtless Washington could reach Philadelphia before his purpose could be fathomed.

The events justified his foresight. On the 19th

Subtle and audacious scheme of Washington.

of August, five days after receiving the dispatch from Grasse, Washington's army crossed the Hudson at King's Ferry, and began its march. Lord Stirling was left with a small force at Saratoga, and General Heath, with 4,000 men, remained at West Point. Washington took with him southward 2,000 Continentals and 4,000 Frenchmen. It was the only time during the war that French and American land forces marched together, save on the occasion of the disastrous attack upon Savannah. None save Washington and Rochambeau knew whither they were going. So precious was the secret that even the general officers supposed, until New Brunswick was passed, that their destination was Staten Island. So rapid was the movement that, however much the men might have begun to wonder, they had reached Philadelphia before the purpose of the expedition was distinctly understood.

He transfers his army to Virginia, Aug. 19–Sept. 18.

As the army marched through the streets of Philadelphia, there was an outburst of exulting hope. The plan could no longer be concealed. Congress was informed of it, and a fresh light shone upon the people, already elated by the news of Greene's career of triumph. The windows were thronged with fair ladies, who threw sweet flowers on the dusty soldiers as they passed, while the welkin rang with shouts, anticipating the great deliverance that was so soon to come. The column of soldiers, in the loose order adapted to its swift march, was nearly two miles in length. First came the war-worn Americans, clad in rough toggery, which eloquently told the story of the meagre

resources of a country without a government. Then
followed the gallant Frenchmen, clothed in gor-
geous trappings, such as could be provided by a
government which at that time took three fourths
of the earnings of its people in unrighteous taxation. There was some parading of these soldiers
before the president of Congress, but time was precious. Washington, in his eagerness galloping on
to Chester, received and sent back the joyful intelligence that Grasse had arrived in Chesapeake
Bay, and then the glee of the people knew no
bounds. Bands of music played in the streets,
every house hoisted its stars-and-stripes, and all the
roadside taverns shouted success to the bold general. " Long live Washington ! " was the toast of
the day. " He has gone to catch Cornwallis in
his mousetrap ! "

But these things did not stop for a moment the
swift advance of the army. It was on the 1st of
September that they left Trenton behind them,
and by the 5th they had reached the head of Chesapeake Bay, whence they were conveyed in ships,
and reached the scene of action, near Yorktown,
by the 18th.

Meanwhile, all things had been working together
most auspiciously. On the 31st of August the
great French squadron had arrived on the scene,
and the only Englishman capable of defeating it,
under the existing odds, was far away. Admiral
Rodney's fleet had followed close upon its heels
from the West Indies, but Rodney himself was not
in command. He had been taken ill suddenly,
and had sailed for England, and Sir Samuel Hood

WASHINGTON'S MARCH UPON YORKTOWN

AUGUST 19–SEPTEMBER 26, 1781

commanded the fleet. Hood outsailed Grasse, passed him on the ocean without know- Movements of ing it, looked in at the Chesapeake on the fleets. the 25th of August, and, finding no enemy there, sailed on to New York to get instructions from Admiral Graves, who commanded the naval force in the North. This was the first that Graves or Clinton knew of the threatened danger. Not a moment was to be lost. The winds were favourable, and Graves, now chief in command, crowded sail for the Chesapeake, and arrived on the 5th of September, the very day on which Washington's army was embarking at the head of the great bay. Graves found the French fleet blocking the entrance to the bay, and instantly attacked it. A decisive naval victory for the British would at this moment have ruined everything. But after a sharp fight of two hours' duration, in which some 700 men were killed and wounded on the two fleets, Admiral Graves withdrew. Three of his ships were badly damaged, and after manœuvring for four days he returned, baffled and despondent, to New York, leaving Grasse in full possession of the Virginia waters. The toils were thus fast closing around Lord Cornwallis. He knew nothing as yet of Washington's approach, but there was just a chance that he might realize his danger, and, crossing the James river, seek safety in a retreat upon North Carolina. Lafayette forestalled this solitary chance. Immediately upon the arrival of the French squadron, the troops of the Marquis de Saint-Simon, 3,000 in number, had been set on shore and added to Lafayette's army ;

and with this increased force, now amounting to more than 8,000 men, " the boy " came down on the 7th of September, and took his stand across the neck of the peninsula at Williamsburg, cutting off Cornwallis's retreat.

Thus, on the morning of the 8th, the very day on which Greene, in South Carolina, was fighting his last battle at Eutaw Springs, Lord Cornwallis, in Virginia, found himself surrounded. The door of the mousetrap was shut. Still, but for the arrival of Washington, the plan would probably have failed. It was still in Cornwallis's power to burst the door open. His force was nearly equal to Lafayette's in numbers, and better in quality, for Lafayette's contained 3,000 militia. Cornwallis carefully reconnoitred the American
Cornwallis surrounded at Yorktown. lines, and seriously thought of breaking through ; but the risk was considerable, and heavy loss was inevitable. He had not the slightest inkling of Washington's movements, and he believed that Graves would soon return with force enough to drive away Grasse's blockading squadron. So he decided to wait before striking a hazardous blow. It was losing his last chance. On the 14th Washington reached Lafayette's headquarters, and took command. On the 18th the northern army began arriving in detachments, and by the 26th it was all concentrated at Williamsburg, more than 16,000 strong. The problem was solved. The surrender of Cornwallis was only a question of time. It was the great military surprise of the Revolutionary War. Had any one predicted, eight months before, that Washington

on the Hudson and Cornwallis on the Catawba, eight hundred miles apart, would so soon come together and terminate the war on the coast of Virginia, he would have been thought a wild prophet indeed. For thoroughness of elaboration and promptness of execution, the movement, on Washington's part, was as remarkable as the march of Napoleon in the autumn of 1805, when he swooped from the shore of the English Channel into Bavaria, and captured the Austrian army at Ulm.

By the 2d of September, Sir Henry Clinton, learning that the American army had *Clinton's attempt at a counterstroke.* reached the Delaware, and coupling with this the information he had got from Admiral Hood, began to suspect the true nature of Washington's movement, and was at his wit's end. The only thing he could think of was to make a counterstroke on the coast of Connecticut, and he accordingly detached Benedict Arnold with 2,000 men to attack New London.

It was the boast of this sturdy little state that no hostile force had ever slept a night upon her soil. Such blows as her coast towns had received had been dealt by an enemy who retreated as quickly as he had come; and such was again to be the case. The approach to New *Arnold's proceedings at New London, Sept. 6.* London was guarded by two forts on opposite banks of the river Thames, but Arnold's force soon swept up the west bank, bearing down all opposition and capturing the city. In Fort Griswold, on the east bank, 157 militia were gathered, and made a desperate resistance. The fort was attacked by 600 regulars, and after losing 192 men, or 35 more than the entire number of the garrison, they carried it by storm. No quarter was given, and of the little garrison only 26 escaped unhurt. The town of New London was laid in ashes ; minute-men came swarming by hundreds ; the enemy reëmbarked before sunset and returned up the Sound. And thus, on the 6th of September, 1781, with this wanton assault upon the peaceful neighbourhood where the earliest years of his life had been spent, the brilliant and wicked Benedict Arnold disappears from American history.

A thoroughly wanton assault it was, for it did not and could not produce the slightest effect upon the movements of Washington. By the time the news of it had reached Virginia, the combination against Cornwallis had been completed, and day by day the lines were drawn more closely about the doomed army. Yorktown was invested, and on the 6th of October the first parallel was opened by General Lincoln. On the 11th, the second parallel, within three hundred yards of the enemy's works, was opened by Steuben. On the night of the 14th Alexander Hamilton and the Baron de Viomenil carried two of the British redoubts by storm. On the next night the British made a gallant but fruitless sortie. By noon of the 16th their works were fast crumbling to pieces, under the fire of seventy cannon. On the 17th — the fourth anniversary of Burgoyne's surrender — Cornwallis hoisted the white flag. The terms of the surrender were like those of Lincoln's at Charleston. The British army became prisoners of war, subject to the ordinary rules of exchange. The only delicate question related to the American loyalists in the army, whom Cornwallis felt it wrong to leave in the lurch. This point was neatly disposed of by allowing him to send a ship to Sir Henry Clinton, with news of the catastrophe, and to embark in it such troops as he might think proper to send to New York, and no questions asked. On a little matter of etiquette the Americans were more exacting. The practice of playing the enemy's tunes had always been cherished as an inalienable prerogative of British soldiery; and at the surrender of Charleston, in token of humiliation, General Lincoln's army had been expressly forbidden to play any but an American tune. Colonel Laurens, who now conducted the negotiations, directed that Lord Cornwallis's sword should be received by General Lincoln, and that the army, on marching out to lay down its arms, should play a British or a German air. There was no help for it; and on the 19th of October, Cornwallis's army, 7,247 in number, with 840 seamen, marched out with colours furled and cased, while the band played a quaint old English melody, of which the significant title was " The World Turned Upside Down " !

Surrender of Cornwallis, Oct. 19, 1781.

On the very same day that Cornwallis surrendered, Sir Henry Clinton, having received naval reinforcements, sailed from New York with twenty-five ships-of-the-line and ten frigates, and 7,000 of his best troops. Five days brought him to the mouth of the Chesapeake, where he learned that

he was too late, as had been the case four years
before, when he tried to relieve Burgoyne. A
fortnight earlier, this force could hardly have
failed to alter the result, for the fleet was strong
enough to dispute with Grasse the control over
the coast. The French have always taken to
themselves the credit of the victory of Yorktown.

In the palace of Versailles there is a
room the walls of which are covered
with huge paintings depicting the innu-
merable victories of France, from the
days of Chlodwig to those of Napoleon. Near the
end of the long series, the American visitor cannot
fail to notice a scene which is labelled " Bataille de
Yorcktown " (misspelled, as is the Frenchman's
wont in dealing with the words of outer barbarians), in which General Rochambeau occupies the
most commanding position, while General Washington is perforce contented with a subordinate
place. This is not correct history, for the glory of
conceiving and conducting the movement undoubt-
edly belongs to Washington. But it should never
be forgotten, not only that the 4,000 men of Rochambeau and the 3,000 of Saint-Simon were necessary for the successful execution of the plan, but
also that without the formidable fleet of Grasse the
plan could not even have been made. How much
longer the war might have dragged out its tedious
length, or what might have been its final issue,
without this timely assistance, can never be known;
and our debt of gratitude to France for her aid
on this supreme occasion is something which cannot be too heartily acknowledged.

Importance of
the aid ren-
dered by the
French fleet
and army.

Early on a dark morning of the fourth week in October, an honest old German, slowly pacing the streets of Philadelphia on his night watch, began shouting, " Basht dree o'glock, und Gornvallis ish dakendt ! " and light sleepers sprang out of bed and threw up their windows. Washington's courier laid the dispatches before Congress in the forenoon, and after dinner a service of prayer and thanksgiving was held in the Lutheran Church. At New Haven and Cambridge the students sang triumphal hymns, and every village green in the country was ablaze with bonfires. The Duke de Lauzun sailed for France in a swift ship, and on the 27th of November all the houses in Paris were illuminated, and the aisles of Notre Dame resounded with the Te Deum. At noon of November 25, the news was brought to Lord George Germain, at his house in Pall Mall. Getting into a cab, he drove hastily to the Lord Chancellor's house in Great Russell Street, Bloomsbury, and took him in ; and then they drove to Lord North's office in Downing Street. At the staggering news, all the Prime Minister's wonted gayety forsook him. He walked wildly up and down the room, throwing his arms about and crying, " O God ! it is all over ! it is all over ! it is all over ! " A dispatch was sent to the king at Kew, and when Lord George received the answer that evening, at dinner, he observed that his Majesty wrote calmly, but had forgotten to date his letter, — a thing which had never happened before.

Effect of the news in England.

" The tidings," says Wraxall, who narrates these

incidents, " were calculated to diffuse a gloom over
the most convivial society, and opened a wide field
for political speculation." There were many people in England, however, who looked at the matter
differently from Lord North. This crushing defeat was just what the Duke of Richmond, at the
beginning of the war, had publicly declared he
hoped for. Charles Fox always took especial delight in reading about the defeats of invading
armies, from Marathon and Salamis downward;
and over the news of Cornwallis's surrender he
leaped from his chair and clapped his hands. In
a debate in Parliament, four months before, the
youthful William Pitt had denounced the American war as "most accursed, wicked, barbarous,
cruel, unnatural, unjust, and diabolical," which led
Burke to observe, " He is not a chip of the old
block; he is the old block itself ! "

The fall of Lord North's ministry, and with it
the overthrow of the personal government of
George III., was now close at hand. For a long
time the government had been losing favour. In
the summer of 1780, the British victories in South
Carolina had done something to strengthen it ; yet
when, in the autumn of that year, Parliament was
dissolved, although the king complained that his
expenses for purposes of corruption had been twice
as great as ever before, the new Parliament was
scarcely more favourable to the ministry than the
old one. Misfortunes and perplexities

Difficult posi-
tion of Great
Britain.

crowded in the path of Lord North and
his colleagues. The example of Ameri-
can resistance had told upon Ireland, and it was in

the full tide of that agitation which is associated with the names of Flood and Grattan that the news of Cornwallis's surrender was received. For more than a year there had been war in India, where Hyder Ali, for the moment, was carrying everything before him. France, eager to regain her lost foothold upon Hindustan, sent a strong armament thither, and insisted that England must give up all her Indian conquests except Bengal. For a moment England's great Eastern empire tottered, and was saved only by the superhuman exertions of Warren Hastings, aided by the wonderful military genius of Sir Eyre Coote. In May, 1781, the Spaniards had taken Pensacola, thus driving the British from their last position in Florida. In February, 1782, the Spanish fleet captured Minorca, and the siege of Gibraltar, which had been kept up for nearly three years, was pressed with redoubled energy. During the winter the French recaptured St. Eustatius, and handed it over to Holland; and Grasse's great fleet swept away all the British possessions in the West Indies, except Jamaica, Barbadoes, and Antigua. All this time the Northern League kept up its jealous watch upon British cruisers in the narrow seas, and among all the powers of Europe the government of George III. could not find a single friend.

The maritime supremacy of England was, however, impaired but for a moment. Rodney was sent back to the West Indies, and on the 12th of April, 1782, his fleet of thirty-six ships encountered the French near the island of Sainte-Marie-Galante. The battle of eleven hours which en-

sued, and in which 5,000 men were killed or
wounded, was one of the most tremendous contests ever witnessed upon the
ocean before the time of Nelson. The
French were totally defeated, and Grasse was
taken prisoner, — the first French commander-in-
chief, by sea or land, who had fallen into an enemy's hands since Marshal Tallard gave up his
sword to Marlborough, on the terrible day of Blen-
heim. France could do nothing to repair this
crushing disaster. Her naval power was eliminated from the situation at a single blow; and in
the course of the summer the English achieved
another great success by overthrowing the Spaniards at Gibraltar, after a struggle which, for dogged tenacity, is scarcely paralleled in the annals
of modern warfare. By the autumn of 1782, England, defeated in the United States, remained victorious and defiant as regarded the other parties
to the war.

But these great successes came too late to save
the doomed ministry of Lord North. After the
surrender of Cornwallis, no one but the king
thought of pursuing the war in America any further. Even he gave up all hope of subduing the
United States; but he insisted upon retaining the
state of Georgia, with the cities of Charleston and
New York; and he vowed that, rather than acknowledge the independence of the United States,
he would abdicate the throne and retire to Hanover. Lord George Germain was dismissed from
office, Sir Henry Clinton was superseded by Sir
Guy Carleton, and the king began to dream of a

*Rodney's vic-
tory over
Grasse, April
12, 1782.*

new campaign. But his obstinacy was of no avail. During the winter and spring, General Wayne, acting under Greene's orders, drove the British from Georgia, while at home the country squires began to go over to the opposition; and Lord North, utterly discouraged and disgusted, refused any longer to pursue a policy of which he disapproved. The baffled and beaten king, like the fox in the fable, declared that the Americans were a wretched set of knaves, and he was glad to be rid of them. The House of Commons began to talk of a vote of censure Resignation of Lord North, March 20, 1782. on the administration. A motion of Conway's, petitioning the king to stop the war, was lost by only a single vote; and at last, on the 20th of March, 1782, Lord North bowed to the storm, and resigned. The two sections of the Whig party coalesced. Lord Rockingham became Prime Minister, and with him came into office Shelburne, Camden, and Grafton, as well as Fox and Conway, the Duke of Richmond, and Lord John Cavendish, — staunch friends of America, all of them, whose appointment involved the recognition of the independence of the United States.

Lord North observed that he had often been accused of issuing lying bulletins, but he had never told so big a lie as that with which the new ministry announced its entrance into power; for in introducing the name of each of these gentlemen, the official bulletin used the words, " His Majesty has been *pleased* to appoint " ! It was indeed a day of bitter humiliation for George III., and the men who had been his tools. But it was a day of happy omen for the English race, in the Old World as well as in the New. For the advent of Lord Rockingham's ministry meant not merely the independence of the United States; it meant the downfall of the only serious danger with which English liberty has been threatened since the expulsion of the Stuarts. The personal government which George III. had sought to establish, with its wholesale corruption, its shameless violations of public law, and its attacks upon freedom of speech and of the press, became irredeemably discredited, and tottered to its fall; while the great England of William III., of Walpole, of Chatham, of the younger Pitt, of Peel, and of Gladstone was set free to pursue its noble career. Such was the priceless boon which the younger nation, by its sturdy insistence upon the principles of political justice, conferred upon the elder. The decisive battle of freedom in England, as well as in America, and in that vast colonial world for which Chatham prophesied the dominion of the future, had now been fought and won. And foremost in accomplishing this glorious work had been the lofty genius of Washington, and the steadfast valour of the men who suffered with him at Valley Forge, and whom he led to victory at Yorktown.

INDEX.

INDEX.

Declaratory Act, i. 27; suspends New York assembly, i. 32; relation to the colonies, i. 34; colonial representation, i. 34; Whig leaders, i. 42; receives news of the Boston Tea Party, i. 93; passes Lord North's five acts, i. 95; debates on Chatham's bill of 1774, i. 111; and Franklin, i. 113, 114; opposition to hiring German troops, i. 161; act to close American ports, i. 175; on the employment of Indians, i. 276.

Parsons' Cause, and Patrick Henry, i. 18.

Patterson, Colonel, and Washington, i. 203.

Paulding, John, captures André, ii. 223.

Pearson, Captain, of the Serapis, ii. 124, 126.

Penn, Richard, carries a petition to the king, i. 159.

Pennsylvania, advises payment for tea, i. 103; proprietary government opposes independence, i. 185; lukewarm supporter of Declaration of Independence, i. 261; Charles Lee on, i. 302; rivalry of, and Virginia, ii. 95; and Arnold, ii. 212; meeting of troops, ii. 240.

Percy, Lord, at Lexington, i. 124; ordered to storm Dorchester Heights, i. 171; at Harlem Heights, i. 217; sent to Newport, i. 228; in Rhode Island, ii. 73.

Peters, Richard, letter to Gates, ii. 186.

Philadelphia, panic at, i. 228; Charles Lee advises the capture of, i. 302; British enter, i. 317; Arnold in command at, ii. 206, 207.

Phillips, General, takes Ticonderoga, i. 269; death of, ii. 270.

Pickens, Colonel Andrew, hangs Tory prisoners, ii. 168; at the Cowpens, ii. 255.

Pickering, Colonel, at Lexington, i. 125.

Pigott, General, i. 140; supersedes Prescott, ii. 75; tries to storm Butts Hill, ii. 79.

Pitcairn, Major, at Lexington, i. 122; his death, i. 143.

Pitt, William, Earl of Chatham, urges repeal of Stamp Act, i. 26; and passage of Declaratory Act, i. 26; becomes Earl of Chatham, i. 28; urges Townshend's dismissal, i. 29; head of New Whigs, i. 42; and George III., i. 43; Chatham on first Continental Congress, i. 111; withdraws his son from the army, i. 160; hopes for conciliation, ii. 6; the hope of England, ii. 12; probable plans for America, ii. 15; last speech in House of Lords, ii. 16; dies, ii.

17; character of, ii. 18; likened to Charlemagne, ii. 20; Horace Walpole on, ii. 21.

Pittsburgh, the "Gateway of the West," ii. 95.

Point Pleasant, battle of, on Great Kanawha, ii. 100.

Pompton, mutiny at, ii. 242.

Porterfield, Colonel, ii. 188; death of, ii. 190.

Portland, burning of, i. 163; effects upon Congress, i. 164.

Port Royal, British attempt to capture, ii. 168.

Portsmouth and Norfolk sacked, ii. 110.

Potemkin, Prince, ii. 144.

Prerogative, royal, how upheld, i. 3.

Prescott, Colonel, i. 137; at New York, i. 206; withdraws from Governor's Island, i. 212.

Prescott, British general, captured in Rhode Island, ii. 59; at Newport, ii. 74.

Preston, Captain, and the Boston Massacre, i. 67.

Prevost, General Augustine, ii. 166; captures Sunbury, ii. 167; his vandalism, ii. 169; result of campaign, ii. 173.

Princeton, Cornwallis at, i. 231.

Provincial Congress, i. 109.

Pulaski, Count, i. 242; aids General Moultrie, ii. 173; death, ii. 175.

Putnam, Israel, leaves his plough, i. 126; fortifies Bunker Hill, i. 139; character of, i. 151; at Brooklyn Heights, i. 206; quits New York, i. 214.

Quakers, oppose independence, i. 185; hanged for treason, ii. 59.

Quebec, Arnold's assault upon, i. 167.

Quebec Act, i. 97; influence on Canada, i. 169; ii. 101.

Quincy, Josiah, defends soldiers engaged in Boston Massacre, i. 72.

Rahl, Colonel, killed at Trenton i., 230.

Randolph, Peyton, made President of Continental Congress, i. 110; called back to Virginia, i. 132.

Rawdon, Lord, ii. 176; at Camden, ii. 188–192; leaves Camden, ii. 264; aids Ninety-Six, ii. 265; goes to England, ii. 265.

Reed, General Joseph, charges against Arnold at Philadelphia, ii. 210, 211; mutiny of troops, ii. 241.

Regulating Act, i. 95; set at defiance, i. 105, 106.

"Regulators," i. 75.

Revere, Paul, his picture of the Boston Massacre, i. 72; carries news of the Tea Party to Philadelphia, i. 90.

Sons of Liberty opposed to Stamp Act, i. 23.
South Carolina, helps Boston, i. 103; slaves in, ii. 164; Scotchmen in, ii. 165; wrath at advice of Congress to arm negroes, ii. 171; Clinton's proclamation, ii. 180; disorders in, ii. 181; Greene's campaign, ii. 262.
Spain, relations to France and England, ii. 131; treaty with France, ii. 134; attempts invasion of England, ii. 136; and neutrals, ii. 139.
Stamp Act, i. 16; the colonies protest, i. 17; Franklin's views after its passage, i. 18; its reception in New York and Boston, i. 18; Patrick Henry in Virginia, i. 18; congress at New York, i. 21; resistance in Boston, i. 23; Stamp Act repealed, i. 27.
Stanhope, Lord, on André's sentence, ii. 232.
Stark, John, i. 126; arrives at Bunker Hill, i. 139; on Cambridge Common, i. 149; pledges his private fortune to pay the army, i. 244; at Bennington, i. 281.
Stedman, British historian, on Anthony Wayne, ii. 113.
Stephen's brigade at Germantown, i. 322, 323.
Steuben, Baron von, character of, ii. 50; comes to America, ii. 51; presented with a farm, ii. 53; drills soldiers, ii. 54; at Monmouth, ii. 65; on André, ii. 229; on the sentence of André, ii. 233; in Virginia, ii. 251.
Stevens, General, joins General Gates at battle of Camden, ii. 189, 191.
Stirling, Lord, i. 207; informs Washington of the duplicity of Gates, ii. 40; at Saratoga, ii. 277.
Stone, W. L., his version of Jenny McCrea's death, i. 278.
Stony Point, stormed, ii. 55; captured by Clinton, ii. 111; stormed by Anthony Wayne, ii. 112; evacuated, ii. 113.
Stormont, Lord, ii. 147.
Strachey, Sir Henry, possesses documents showing Charles Lee's treason, i. 302.
Stuart, Colonel, ii. 265; at Eutaw Springs, ii. 266.
Suffolk County Resolves, i. 108.
Sullivan, John, i. 149; retreats from Canada, i. 168; at battle of Long Island, i. 208; sent by Howe to Congress, i. 212; at Trenton, i. 229; at Morristown, i. 310; at the Brandywine, i. 313, 315; at Germantown, i. 320; seizes Butts Hill, ii. 76; vexed at Estaing, ii. 77; volunteers leave him, ii. 78; expedition against Iro-

quois, ii. 91; returns to New Jersey, ii. 93.
Sullivan's Island, defended by Moultrie, i. 199.
Sumner, Charles, assault by Brooks, compared to that upon Otis, i. 65.
Sumter, Thomas, ii. 184; defeated by Tarleton, ii. 195; defeats Tarleton at Blackstock Hill, ii. 249.
Sunbury, captured by General Prevost, ii. 167.

Tallmadge, Major Benjamin, and André, ii. 224, 228.
Tarleton, Colonel Banastre, ii. 177; defeats Buford, ii. 178; at Camden, ii. 192; defeats Sumter, ii. 195; at Blackstock Hill, ii. 249; at battle of the Cowpens, ii. 254; attempts to capture Thomas Jefferson, ii. 271.
Tarrytown, capture of André, ii. 222.
Tea, the tax on, i. 82, 83; tea-ship arrives in Boston, i. 85; meeting in the Old South Church, i. 86; ships under guard, i. 87; final plans, i. 89; Boston Tea Party, i. 90; action at Charleston, i. 91; at Philadelphia, i. 91; John Adams on the Tea Party, i. 91; Lecky and Green, i. 91; Gordon, i. 92; Lord North, i. 93; General Gage, i. 94.
Tennessee, settlement of, ii. 102.
Ternay, Admiral, ii. 200; arrives at Newport, ii. 203.
Thirty Years' War, ii. 19.
Thomson, Charles, his opinion of the Stamp Act, i. 18.
Throg's Neck, Howe moves upon, i. 217.
Thurlow, Lord, in North ministry, i. 73; on the Quebec Act, i. 97.
Ticonderoga, and Crown Point, i. 129; capture of, i. 131; garrisoning, i. 133; taken by General Phillips, i. 269.
Tories, support George III., i. 41; receive news from Saratoga, ii. 8; go to New York, ii. 58; indicted for treason, ii. 59; flee to Canada, ii. 85; savage deeds of, ii. 86; intend to assassinate Schuyler, ii. 94; opposed to Congress making an alliance with France, ii. 208.
Town meetings, in the Regulating Act, i. 96.
Townshend, Charles, his knowledge of American affairs, i. 14, 28; joins Grafton ministry, i. 28; plans to tax America, i. 29; compared with Beaconsfield, i. 36; death, i. 38.
Townshend Acts, i. 29, 30; their purpose, i. 31; how regarded in England, i. 32, 33; Dickinson on, i. 47; opposition to, i. 49; Pownall moves their repeal, i. 61, 71.
Trenton, attack upon, i. 229.

Trumbull, Governor, on Lord Howe's circular letter, i. 204.
Trumbull, Colonel Joseph, made commissariat, ii. 28.
Tryon, Governor, defeats the Regulators, i. 75; his plot discovered, i. 190; at Danbury and Ridgefield, i. 259; raids coast of Connecticut, ii. 110.
Turgot and Franklin, i. 240.

Union of colonies, planned, i. 5; weakness of sentiment for, in 1755, i. 6; and Albany Congress, i. 7; Franklin's plan in 1754, i. 10.

Valcour Island, battle of, i. 251.
Valley Forge, i. 324; sufferings at, ii. 29.
Vattel and Bynkershoek, on maritime law, ii. 140.
Vaughan, General, at St. Eustatius, ii. 159.
Venango, Washington's mission to, i. 134.
Venn, on the Boston Tea Party, i. 93.
Vergennes, on the battle of Bunker Hill, i. 146; desire to aid America, i. 239; and Steuben, ii. 51, 80; and Spain, ii. 131, 133.
Vermont, i. 254, 274.
Vincennes, captured by Hamilton, and recaptured by Clark, ii. 106.
"Vindex," letters of, i. 60.
Viomenil, Baron de, at Yorktown, ii. 282.
Virginia, liberties in, i. 4; and the Stamp Act, i. 18; not represented at the congress in New York, i. 21; resolutions of, 1769, i. 64; committees of correspondence, i. 80; Lord Dunmore's proclamation, i. 178; declares for independence, i. 180; Cornwallis in, ii. 269.
Voltaire and Franklin, i. 240.
Vulture, sloop-of-war, ii. 218.

Walpole, Horace, on the king's joy at the fall of Ticonderoga, i. 271; thinks America at the feet of England, ii. 178.
Walpole, Sir Robert, laughs at plan for taxing the colonies, i. 4; a wise prime minister, i. 39.
Ward, Artemas, i. 136; and Bunker Hill, i. 142.
Warner, Colonel Seth, takes Crown Point, i. 131; at Hubbardton, i. 270, 282; at Bennington, i. 284.
Warren, Joseph, i. 107; his Suffolk County resolves, i. 108; 5th of March oration, i. 118, 131; president of Provincial Congress, i. 136; reply to Elbridge Gerry, i. 139; his death, i. 143.
Washington, George, i. 55; and relief

of Boston, i. 103; chosen commander-in-chief, i. 133; Patrick Henry on, i. 135; comes to Cambridge, i. 147; reorganizes the army, i. 155; seizes Dorchester Heights, i. 170; at New York, i. 189; and Lord Howe, i. 202; outwits General Howe at Brooklyn Heights, i. 211; at White Plains, i. 217; abandons Forts Washington and Lee, i. 218; the retreat, i. 224; attack upon Trenton, i. 229; defeats Cornwallis's reinforcements from Princeton, i. 233; proclamation to the loyalists, i. 236; "the American Fabius," i. 237; Congress increases his authority, i. 246, 247; hostages for Lee's safety, i. 300; foils Howe in New Jersey, i. 306; on Howe and Burgoyne, i. 310; reasons for offering Howe battle, i. 312; Brandywine, i. 313; granted extraordinary powers, i. 317; detains Howe, i. 317; on Burgoyne's army, i. 339; pay for officers, ii. 27; at Valley Forge, ii. 29; letter to Gates, ii. 33; accused of Fabian policy, ii. 36; detects Gates, ii. 40; forged letters attributed to, ii. 43; increasing popularity, ii. 48; desires to cripple Sir Henry Clinton, ii. 59; at Monmouth, ii. 63; stops the retreat, ii. 64; reply to Lee's letter, ii. 66; arrests Lee, ii. 67; encamps at White Plains, ii. 72; cordon about Manhattan Island, ii. 81; sends troops to Fort Niagara, ii. 90; on arming of negroes, ii. 170, 185; letter to Huntington on the army, ii. 200; order to reprimand Arnold, ii. 214, 217; and Arnold's flight, ii. 224, 227; to Clinton concerning André, ii. 229; conference with Rochambeau, ii. 273; his plans for Yorktown, ii. 275; transfers his army to Virginia, ii. 277; the surrender of Cornwallis, ii. 282; character of, ii. 290.
Washington, William, ii. 251, 252; at the Cowpens, ii. 255; at Guilford, ii. 259.
Watson, George, appointed king's councillor, i. 106.
Watts, Major, at the battle of Oriskany, i. 288.
Wayne, Anthony, at the battle of Brandywine, i. 313, 317; at Germantown, i. 322; storms Stony Point, ii. 112; mutiny of troops, ii. 240; in Georgia, ii. 289.
Waxhaws, Tarleton's army at, ii. 178.
Webster, Colonel James, at the battle of Camden, ii. 191.
Webster, Pelatiah, on paper currency, ii. 197.

Printed in the United Kingdom by
Lightning Source UK Ltd., Milton Keynes
137742UK00001B/117/A

9 780548 093863